Study G

Management
Sixth Edition

Richard L. Daft

Owen Graduate School of Business, Vanderbilt University

Prepared by

Stephen R. Hiatt

Catawba College

THOMSON

™

SOUTH-WESTERN

Australia · Canada · Mexico · Singapore · Spain · United Kingdom · United States

Study Guide to accompany *Management*, 6e

By Richard L. Daft, prepared by Stephen R. Hiatt

Vice/President/Team Leader:
Mike Roche

Acquisitions Editor:
Joe Sabatino

Developmental Editor:
Emma Guttler

Production Editor:
Kelly Keeler

Manufacturing Coordinator:
Rhonda Utley

Printer:
Globus Printing, Minster, OH

Design Project Manager:
Michelle Kunkler

Preface

This Study Guide is designed to help you understand, remember, and apply the material from Management, Sixth Edition, by Richard L. Daft. To accomplish this purpose, several sections have been included.

The chapter summary condenses the principles and facts from the text into an abbreviated overview. The summary does not provide detail or examples, but rather gives a brief synopsis that can be used to gain a basic understanding of the chapter, as well as for subsequent review. The key terms for each chapter are in the left-hand margin with blanks appearing in the text of the chapter summary where those terms belong.

The chapter review section provides a self-test of the important concepts in each chapter. The multiple-choice, true-false, and short-answer questions will aid in discovering areas of weakness and direction for further study.

Management applications allow you to relate the principles of the text to management situations and decisions. Care has been taken to present realistic solutions understandable to the typical readers of this type of text. In this section you are asked to answer questions, rank alternatives, make decisions, or explain principles based on the concepts in each chapter.

Mini-cases are designed to provide situations for the application of the principles discussed in each chapter. By answering the questions, you will see how well you can apply those principles.

The experiential exercises are designed for in-class use under the guidance of the class instructor. Alternately, they can be used by the individual student for independent study. They will help you learn the concepts through their application to learning exercises.

The chapter solutions provide answers to the multiple-choice, true/false, and short answer questions from the chapter review. Suggested answers for the solutions to the management applications, mini-cases, and experiential exercises are also provided.

Good luck in your study and application of management.

Stephen R. Hiatt

TABLE OF CONTENTS

Chapter 1

Managing the New Workplace

Chapter Summary

After you have read the text chapter, read through the summary below. Cover the left-hand margin and fill in the blanks with the appropriate terms. After you have filled in each blank, check your responses by uncovering the answer given in the margin. If you do not understand why the given answer is the correct one, refer back to the text.

The Definition of Management

Management   _____ is the attainment of organizational goals in an effective and efficient manner through planning, organizing, leading, and controlling organizational resources. This definition identifies the four functions of management and emphasizes goal attainment. The text covers skills and activities associate with these functions while also covering the environment, global competitiveness, and ethics.

The Four Functions of Management

Planning   Each of these functions is defined and explained in turn. _____ defines goals for future organizational performance and deciding on the tasks

Organizing   and use of resources needed to attain them. _____ is concerned with assigning tasks, grouping tasks into departments, and allocating resources to

Leading   departments. _____ involves the use of influence to motivate

Controlling   employees to achieve the organization's goals. _____ involves monitoring employees' activities, keeping the organization on track toward its goals, and making corrections as needed.

Organizational Performance

Performance   _____ is the organization's ability to attain its goals, and ideally, the organizational performance should be both effective and efficient. An

effective   _____ organization achieves a stated goal and an _____ efficient

organization

organization employs the minimum needed resources in its goal attainment activities. The organization employs human, financial, and raw materials, resources. The _____ is a social entity that is goal directed and deliberately structured.

Management Types and Management Skills

Top

managers

conceptual

Human

Management types can be classified by either *vertical* or *horizontal* differences. Vertical differences focus on the hierarchical position of the managers and on their corresponding responsibilities and viewpoints. _____ _____ are at the top of the hierarchy and are responsible for entire organization. For this reason top managers need to have the greatest degree of _____ skills as well as a large amount of human skills. *Conceptual skills* involve the ability see the organization as a whole and the relationship among its parts. Knowing how the organization fits into the industry and the community are also part of these skills. _____ skill is the manager's ability to work with and through other people and to work effectively as a group member.

Technical

Middle

first

second

_____ skill is the understanding of and proficiency in performing specific tasks. *Technical skills* are not as necessary for top management. _____ managers are responsible for major departments work at the middle levels of the organization. These managers need fewer conceptual skills than top management, but need instead a greater degree of technical skills while maintaining human skills. First-line managers are at the _____ or _____ level of management. They are directly responsible for the production of goods and services. These managers need the greater amount of technical skills since they must supervise, motivate, and advise the technicians producing the products or services. Human skills are also still needed, but conceptual skills are less important to first-line managers.

functional

General

Horizontal differences indicate the differences among managers due to their responsibilities for functions and skills needed. A _____ manager is responsible for a single function task in a department such as marketing, production, or finance. _____ managers are responsible for several departments performing different functions.

project

The general manager needs to be able to communicate and motivate managers from different functional backgrounds, while a _____ manager needs to coordinate the efforts of people across several functional departments to accomplish a project. While such a manager also needs more general skills than a functional manager, they need not be as great as those of the general manager.

What Is It Like to Be a Manager?

brevity

role

Studies have indicated that managerial activity is characterized by variety, fragmentation, and _____. Managers also perform a large amount of work at an unrelenting pace. A set of expectations for one's behavior is a _____. Management roles have been categorized as interpersonal, informational, and decisional. *Interpersonal roles* include the figurehead role, which handles the ceremonial activities of the organization.

leader

information

The _____ role is also an interpersonal function of motivating, communicating with, and influencing subordinates. The third interpersonal role, the liaison role, develops _____ sources used by the manager.

monitor
disseminator
spokesperson

Informational roles include the monitor, the disseminator, and the spokesperson roles. The _____ seeks current information, the _____ transmits information, and the _____ provides official statements on behalf of the organization.

entrepreneur

disturbance

resource

negotiator

Decisional roles include the _____, the disturbance handler, the resource allocator, and the negotiator roles. The entrepreneur attempts to solve problems with improvements while the _____ handler attempts to solve organizational conflicts. The _____ allocator must decide on how organizational inputs will be shared among various organizational units. The _____ bargains with others for the benefit of the unit for which the manager is responsible.

Managing in Small Business and Not-for-Profit Organizations

Small businesses are growing in importance, being started by those leaving the corporate world and women or minorities. Even in these small businesses, spokesperson

managerial dexterity is important to cope with globalization, government regulation and customer demands. Small business managers see the _____ role as their most important role, but also feel that the entrepreneur role is very important.

social impact

The main difference between managing a not-for-profit organization is that these managers direct their efforts toward generating some kind of _____ _____ . Services are provided to non-paying clients so funding is a continuing problem. This means that costs must be kept as low as possible and that efficient use of resources must be demonstrated for donors. Effectiveness in a not-for-profit is more difficult to gauge. This is complicated by the use of volunteers. Motivation of staff members must rely more upon incentives such as mission and values, requiring more emphasis on leadership.

spokesperson

Roles for not-for-profit managers differ somewhat also. There is more emphasis on the _____ role to sell the organization and the leader role to motivate employees and volunteers.

Management and the New Workplace

information

virtual

The new workplace is concerned more with _____ than with machines and physical assets. Work is free-flowing and *flexible*. Because all organizations need speed and flexibility, *empowered employees* are expected to seize opportunities and solve problems as they emerge. The organizational structure is often _____ with employees at different locations and working flexible hours. Teams may include outside contractors, suppliers, customers, competitors, and free agents.

Forces on Organizations

technology

Internet

The most striking change now affecting organizations and management is ____-_____ . Organizations are increasingly using digital networking and wireless technology to keep employees and operations together. The way work is being done is being changed by the _____. Many companies develop their on *intranets* and *extranets* which use Internet technology. Organizations are turning to *e-business* ideas and models.

The Internet and new technologies are tied closely to *globalization* that also has significant impact on organizations. Managers must understand cross-cultural patterns and work with virtual team members from many different countries.

diversity

The workforce also exhibits more _____ than ever, having more ethnic and racial groups as well as more generations working.

change, speed

Organizations are learning to value _____ and _____ over stability and efficiency. The world is now *turbulent* and *unpredictable* changing the approach to management.

New Management Competencies

Human

_____ skills are becoming increasingly important for all managers. Leadership is dispersed throughout the organization to gain ideas and creativity. Instead of controlling workers, managers mentor, provide direction, and provide support.

connected

All managers must stay _____ *to customers and employees.* They must be flexible and adaptable and learn to share their power rather than trying to control workers. *Team-building* skills are crucial for today's managers highlighting the importance of _____ to modern managers.

relationships

learning organization

It is important to build a _____ _____ by guiding an organizational climate that values experimentation and risk-taking, applies current technology, embraces ambiguity, tolerates mistakes and failure, and rewards non-traditional thinking and the sharing of knowledge.

Chapter Review

Multiple-Choice Questions: Please indicate the correct response to the following questions by writing the letter of the correct answer in the space provided.

___ 1. The management function concerned with setting organizational goals is called
    a. organizing.
    b. leading.
    c. planning.
    d. controlling.
    e. coordinating.

___ 2. _____ roles pertain to relationships with others and are related to the human skills.
    a. Interpersonal
    b. Informational
    c. Decisional
    d. Disseminator
    e. Spokesperson

___ 3. Because of changes a revolution is taking place in management and a leader is needed who
    a. can maintain stability.
    b. can guide businesses through turbulence.
    c. can find the perfect answer.
    d. exercise more top-down control.
    e. is a little bit of a rebel.

___ 4. The figurehead role is being filled by a manager when he or she
    a. seeks current information from periodicals.
    b. handles symbolic activities for the department.
    c. transmits important information to subordinates.
    d. allocates equipment to departments.
    e. negotiates with a supplier about a late shipment.

___ 5. Who in the organization is responsible for setting the organizational climate and influencing the internal corporate culture?
    a. top management
    b. personnel management
    c. functional management
    d. first-line management
    e. the operational personnel themselves

___ 6. Conceptual skills are needed by _____ managers, but especially by _____ managers.
    a. few, first-line
    b. all, middle
    c. intellectual, personnel
    d. all, top
    e. few, middle

___ 7. The learning organization is one in which
   a. everyone is expected to have a college degree.
   b. the CEO teaches everyone else how to act.
   c. everyone in the organization participates in identifying and solving problems.
   d. formal courses are offered to all employees.
   e. employees can easily learn how to progress up the career ladder.

___ 8. Managers without human skills
   a. are really being sensitive because they always get the job done.
   b. can function effectively since we can use computers to communicate now.
   c. will not appear arrogant since they are only being realistic.
   d. make subordinates feel smart because they are not being pampered.
   e. will have trouble no matter which level of management they occupy.

___ 9. Technical skills are most needed by _____ managers.
   a. top level
   b. middle level
   c. first-line
   d. staff
   e. project

___ 10. The major difference between nonmanagers and managers is
   a. the shift from reliance on technical skills to focus on human skills.
   b. that managers are always smarter than nonmanagers.
   c. the fact that managers are taller than nonmanagers.
   d. that all nonmanagers want to become managers, but not all managers want to become nonmanagers.
   e. the fact that nonmanagers work harder than managers.

___ 11. A manager who is not a good communicator is failing to perform the _____ role well.
   a. negotiator
   b. figurehead
   c. leader
   d. monitor
   e. spokesperson

___ 12. A _____ manager needs to coordinate the efforts of people across several functional departments.
   a. staff
   b. horizontal
   c. project
   d. conceptual
   e. vertical

___ 13. A manager who is known for innovation is successfully filling the _____ role.
  a. figurehead
  b. disseminator
  c. monitor
  d. entrepreneur
  e. negotiator

___ 14. Planning, organizing, leading, and controlling are referred to as the _____ of management
  a. principles
  b. objects
  c. functions
  d. antitheses
  e. nemeses

___ 15. Good managers know that the only way they can accomplish anything at all is
  a. through the people of the organization.
  b. to do it themselves.
  c. have abundant financial resources.
  d. to insist that things be done the only correct way.
  e. by giving in to the union every time.

___ 16. In telling an employee how to correctly do a task which he formerly did incorrectly, you are engaged in the _____ function of management.
  a. planning
  b. organizing
  c. leading
  d. controlling
  e. coordinating

___ 17. If *more* constraints on employees are needed because of the situation, information technology
  a. can be used effectively.
  b. cannot be used effectively.
  c. can be used only in conjunction with financial controls.
  d. will be largely ineffective.
  e. are irrelevant.

___ 18. A social entity means to be
  a. outgoing and friendly.
  b. made up of two or more people.
  c. unfriendly, and nonsocial.
  d. recognized by society as existing.
  e. part of the upper class.

___ 19. As a first-line manager one should be most concerned about which of the following?
    a. a downturn in the economy
    b. a worker who has just broken the rule concerning the wearing of safety glasses
    c. The quality control manager and the production manager don't seem to get along with each other.
    d. The company's largest customer just decided to buy from a competitor.
    e. There is a rumor of a hostile takeover attempt by a "corporate raider."

___ 20. Whenever an employee tells the manager about a new way to improve production, the manager should
    a. ignore the idea since only managers can have good ideas.
    b. listen to the idea and encourage future ideas by giving this idea serious consideration.
    c. tell the subordinate that he is not paid to think, only to work.
    d. laugh at the idea so the subordinate will not bother the manager again.
    e. steal the idea after telling the subordinate that it won't work.

___ 21. Efficiency and effectiveness in the same organization
    a. is a practical impossibility.
    b. is not a desirable outcome.
    c. can both be high.
    d. must be achieved by different persons.
    e. none of the above are true.

___ 22. A lack of planning, or poor planning, can
    a. do no real harm since plans are often changed anyway.
    b. only mean more meetings to make decisions.
    c. hurt an organization's performance.
    d. cause legal problems since the IRS mandates planning.
    e. usually be good for companies since this makes them more flexible.

___ 23. The allocation of resources is done as part of the management function of
    a. planning.
    b. organizing.
    c. staffing.
    d. directing.
    e. controlling.

___ 24. Controlling often involves using a(n) _____ system.
    a. virtual
    b. consolidated
    c. information
    d. manual
    e. closed

25. A critical skill for top-level managers in today's world is
    a. knowing whom to terminate.
    b. knowing when it is time to look for a new job.
    c. understanding how to bust unions.
    d. inspiring confidence in and support for the organization and its leadership.
    e. understanding all the latest management theories.

26. Which of the following is a top manager?
    a. president
    b. supervisor
    c. executive recruiter
    d. executive secretary
    e. all of the above

27. Today's middle managers have to learn to
    a. build relationships.
    b. empower others.
    c. promote cooperation.
    d. manage conflict.
    e. all of the above.

28. _____ managers are in charge of departments such as finance and personnel.
    a. Line
    b. Functional
    c. Project
    d. Staff
    e. First-line

29. As managers move up the hierarchy, they must develop _____ skills.
    a. human
    b. conceptual
    c. technical
    d. functional
    e. motivational

30. Not-for-profit organizations
    a. are a major source for management talent and innovation.
    b. represent a model for poor management.
    c. do not use human skills very much.
    d. illustrate that organizations can succeed without management.
    e. ignore the community in which they exist.

True/False Questions: Please indicate whether the following questions are true or false by writing a T or an F in the blank in front of each question.

1. "If you want anything done right, you should do it yourself" is the essence of sound management.

___ 2. While good planning will help an organization, poor planning can never hurt.

___ 3. New information technology is helping managers provide needed organizational control by using strict top-down constraints.

___ 4. A good manager needs to be able to communicate his vision of the company to subordinates.

___ 5. It is impossible for an organization to be both efficient and effective at the same time since efficiency may use the resources in such a way as to preclude effectiveness.

___ 6. A manager who is presenting an award is filling an informational role.

___ 7. A first-line manager is most concerned with accomplishing day-to-day objectives.

___ 8. When a manager is resolving a conflict between two subordinates, he or she is filling the disturbance handler role.

___ 9. Today's managers recognize the importance of staying connected to customers and employees on a daily basis.

___ 10. Most managers usually find time for quiet reflection, which is why many subordinates feel that managers do not work very hard.

Short-Answer Questions

1. How would you define management to a friend who is not familiar with the term?

2.   What are the four functions of management?

3.   Should a company strive for effectiveness or efficiency?

4. Why are human skills needed to some degree by all levels of management?

5. Explain why it is important to understand that managers have different types of roles.

Management Applications

What Do You Mean By Management?

After attending one week of management class, you were talking to some of your friends about school. None of these friends were business majors. When Sarah mentioned that she was taking a course in management, a debate erupted. Frank said that he thought such a course would be interesting because he always wanted to know all the details behind the lives of management personnel. Judy told Frank that management did not refer to the people who manage, but rather to an academic field of study. That is why you have Professors of Management. After arguing about what management really is, they have both turned to you to tell them just what management is. In response to their question give them a definition of management.

MANAGEMENT is

After you have answered their question by defining management, they have now asked you to explain what you mean by these functions of management. Explain each one to them in terms that a nonbusiness major could understand.

PLANNING

ORGANIZING

LEADING

CONTROLLING

Who is a Manager?

After studying the roles of a manager in class Don became involved in a conversation about whether various persons he knew were "managers" or not. Help Don decide this by placing a yes or not in the appropriate spaces below.

ROLE	MANAGEMENT PROFESSOR	BASKETBALL COACH	FATHER OF A FAMILY
Figurehead			
Leader			
Liaison			
Monitor			
Disseminator			
Spokesperson			
Entrepreneur			
Disturbance Handler			
Resource Allocator			
Negotiator			

Mini Case

Hector, who is a Hispanic, has been working for a promotion for a long time. He works for a shipping company on the loading dock. The company is located in rural North Carolina. His job has been to drive a forklift and to occasionally load by hand boxes into large trucks. He reports to a loading supervisor who coordinates all the work of four forklift operators and makes sure the loads are accurate and ready to go on time.

Finally, Hector's hard work has paid off for him. His supervisor, Paul, has been promoted, and Hector was recommended to take his place. He has now been the supervisor for two weeks. Already he has begun to worry about whether he should have taken the job or not. He just can't seem to get the men working for him to move fast enough. Frequently, his loads are late in being finished and often they contain the wrong boxes. He cannot understand where he is going wrong. As a forklift operator he always received excellent ratings and has always been a hard worker.

1. What are some possible explanations for Hector's problems?

2. If you were Hector's boss, what would you recommend that he do?

Experiential Exercise

Janet has not been working outside the home for 10 years. She does have a degree in Business Administration, but has elected to stay at home to raise her two small children. Now that her youngest child is in school, she is ready to enter the job market. She saw an advertisement in the newspaper for a management position with a local retailer and called the telephone number listed. The man who answered the telephone asked Janet to come in for an interview and to bring with her a paper describing her experience in management and ability to manage. Janet knows that you are taking this class and has asked you to help her in preparing this paper. Describe below how a mother would be involved in each of the functions of management. Be ready to discuss your answers in class.

PLANNING

ORGANIZING

LEADING

CONTROLLING

Do you think Janet will get the job? Why? Explain your answer.

Study Guide Solutions

Chapter Review

Multiple-Choice Questions

1	2	3	4	5	6	7	8	9	10
c	a	b	b	a	d	c	e	c	a

11	12	13	14	15	16	17	18	19	20
c	c	d	c	a	d	a	b	b	b

21	22	23	24	25	26	27	28	29	30
c	c	b	c	d	a	e	d	b	a

True/False Questions

1	2	3	4	5	6	7	8	9	10
F	F	F	T	F	F	T	T	T	F

Short-Answer Questions

1. MANAGEMENT is defined as the attainment of organizational goals in an effective and efficient manner through the employment of the four management functions of planning, organizing, leading, and controlling organizational resources.

2. The four functions of management are planning, organizing, leading, and controlling.

3. A company should strive for both effectiveness and efficiency. A company should try to be effective; that is, to reach its goal and get the job done. At the same time it needs to be efficient and get that job done with the least amount of resources being used.

4. Human skills are needed by all levels of management because they involve the abilities needed to get the work done through others. This is the essence of management no matter what the level of management.

5. Once you understand the various roles of a manager you will better understand what it is that a manager does. In preparing for a career in management you will be able to prepare yourself for all of these roles.

Management Applications

What Do You Mean By Management?

MANAGEMENT is the attainment of organizational goals in an effective and efficient manner through the employment of the four management functions of planning, organizing, leading, and controlling organizational resources. It can refer to a group of managers, the discipline of academic study, or the function of management.

PLANNING simply means deciding what it is you want to do and how you will go about it.

ORGANIZING means deciding who does what.

LEADING involves motivating and communicating with subordinates.

CONTROLLING means setting standards, comparing results with those standards, and then making adjustments as needed.

Who is a Manager?

Answers to this application will vary according to perceptions of each student. A discussion of the answers in class would be interesting.

ROLE	MANAGEMENT PROFESSOR	BASKETBALL COACH	FATHER OF A FAMILY
Figurehead	YES	YES	YES
Leader	YES	YES	YES
Liaison	YES	YES	YES
Monitor	YES	YES	YES
Disseminator	YES	YES	YES
Spokesperson	YES	YES	YES
Entrepreneur	MAYBE	YES	MAYBE
Disturbance Handler	YES	YES	YES
Resource Allocator	NO	YES	YES
Negotiator	NO	YES	YES

Mini Case

1. One explanation is that Hector does not know how to lead his subordinates. He may not be a very motivating leader or know how to communicate well. He also may not be very good at follow-up because, before, the supervisor did that for him. His problem is simply that he has not been trained for management.

    Another explanation is that his ethnic background could be a problem for the subordinates. This is difficult to determine without more information about the group, however.

2. Hector's boss can try to give him some on-the-job training about how to be a manager. If the company provides a supervisory training course, Hector should enroll in that course. Otherwise, Hector should consider courses available as workshops or at a local college. He needs to be taught management skills. In addition to a basic management course, he might consider courses in operations management, logistics, communication, and organizational behavior.

Experiential Exercise

The role of a traditional mother encompasses management functions as explained below:

Planning	She must plan the meals, shopping, travel, small children's activities, social events, volunteer work, self-fulfilling activities.
Organizing	She must assign household chores to family members as well as allocate her own time.
Leading	She must use her influence to motivate children and husband to fulfill their responsibilities and reach their potentials. She must be an excellent communicator also.
Controlling	She must make sure that family members are fulfilling their assigned duties and take corrective actions when needed. She must also exercise self-control.

Will Janet get the job?

It really depends on the person doing the hiring to a large degree and his attitudes towards women and homemaking. But even more important will be Janet's ability to convince him that she has the skills necessary to do the job. She has maturity and stability as added talents to bring to the job also.

Chapter 2

Historical Foundations of Management

Chapter Summary

After you have read the text chapter, read through the summary below. Cover the left-hand margin and fill in the blanks with the appropriate terms. After you have filled in each blank, check your responses by uncovering the answer given in the margin. If you do not understand why the given answer is the correct one, refer back to the text.

Management and Organization

Social forces

X

Y

Political

Economic

Studying the history of management helps today's manager to achieve strategic thinking, see the big picture, and improve conceptual skills. _____ affect the way that businesses relate to employees and the public. It refers to the aspects of a culture that guide and influence relationships among people. Generation _____ workers are those in their 20s and 30s and Generation _____ are those born between 1980 and 1995. These younger workers are more educated, technologically adept, and globally conscious. They also change jobs and careers more often and desire a work life balance. _____ forces are the political and legal institutions which influence people and organizations.. _____ forces influence the allocation of scarce resources among competing users within society. Managers must learn to cope with these allocations.

Classical Perspective

classical
Scientific

one best way

This perspective developed out of management experiences following the industrial revolution. The _____ perspective endeavored to make organizations efficient operating machines. _____ management is the term given to one of these perspectives and emphasized scientifically determined changes in management practices as the solution to improving labor productivity. Led by Frederick W. Taylor, Henry Gantt, Frank and Lillian Gilbreth, and others, this school of thought developed in the early 1900s. It assumed that there was _____ to do a job, which should be determined by scientific investigation. Managers should then assign workers to specialized tasks according to their abilities, plan the work, train and support the workers, and motivate them by the use of financial incentives. Scientific management did improve productivity, but failed to address the social context and workers' needs, and workers often felt exploited.

bureaucratic

The _____ organization developed by Max Weber was a reaction to subjective favoritism that existed in the late 1800s. The bureaucracy as conceived by Weber was to be managed on a rational and impersonal basis instead. Even though this term has taken on a negative connotation today, practically all organizations use some elements of the bureaucracy.

principles

The administrative _____ approach to management focused on the total organization and the use of management principles. Henri Fayol taught that his 14 general principles and the five functions of management have application to all managers regardless of the type of organization. The concept of superordinate goals was introduced by Mary Parker Follett and was used by practicing managers of the day. She also addressed such ideas as ethics, power, and effective leadership. Chester Barnard introduced the concepts of informal organizations and the acceptance theory of authority. These administrative principles still have a profound effect on management today.

Humanistic Perspective

The humanistic perspective emphasized the importance of understanding human behaviors, needs, and attitudes in the workplace. Three subfields of this perceptive are *the human relations movement, the human resources perspective,* and *the behavioral sciences* approach.

human relations
Hawthorne

human resources

hierarchy

Theory Y

The _____ movement developed beginning with the famous _____ studies, which were initially interpreted as demonstrating that human relations is the best approach for increasing productivity. The _____ perspective was based on the work of Maslow and McGregor. This movement emphasized worker satisfaction and need fulfillment as the key factors to productivity. Maslow formulated a _____ of needs consisting of physiological, safety, belongingness, esteem, and self-actualization needs. McGregor classified assumptions about workers under two categories, Theory X and Theory Y. He felt that _____, which is a more humanistic approach, was a more realistic view of managing.

behavioral
sciences

The _____ _____ approach of the human resource perspective applied theories and practices from the social sciences to the management of people in organizational settings. This approach borrows heavily from economics, psychology, and sociology.

Management Science Perspective

quantitative

The use of _____ methods to solve management problems and make decisions is the essence of the management science perspective. Operations research which grew out of World War II consists of using mathematical model building and other quantitative techniques to solve problems. Operations management applies quantitative techniques to the physical production of goods and services. *Information technology (IT)*, as reflected in management information systems, help managers to obtain relevant and timely information.

Recent Historical Trends

systems theory

open
entropy
closed
Synergy
subsystems

Understanding that all parts of an organization are related and that this relationship affects how the organization functions led to the development of the _____. All systems consist of inputs which are transformed into outputs giving feedback to the organization operating in a specified environment. These systems are almost always _____ and must interact with the environment to avoid _____, which means that the system runs down and dies. A _____ system does not interact with the environment. _____ means that if all parts of a system (or the _____) work well together, the result is greater than if they each worked alone.

contingency

The _____ view emphasizes the need for managers to identify key variables such as industry, technology, the environment, and international culture. After these variables have been analyzed, then managers can determine the best approach to management for that situation.

Total Quality
Management

At the forefront in helping managers to compete globally is _____ , which focuses on managing the total organization to deliver quality to customers. The four significant elements of TQM are employee involvement, focus on the customer, benchmarking, and continuous improvement.

Two current directions in management are the shift to a learning organization and managing the technology-driven workplace.

The Learning Organization

Peter Senge's book started managers thinking about *the learning organization* which is a matter of mangers developing five disciplines: systems thinking, shared vision, challenging mental models, team learning, and personal mastery.

learning
   organization

This has lead to the concept of the _____, in which everyone is engaged in identifying and solving problems, enabling the organization to continuously experiment, improve, and increase its capability. Three important adjustments to promote continuous learning are shifting to a team-based structure, empowering employees, and sharing information.   Leaders in learning organizations think in terms of "control with" rather than "control over" others. This leader creates a shared vision that must be understood by everyone in the organization. The structure of the learning organization uses self-directed teams. Employees are _____, meaning that they are given the power, freedom, knowledge and skills to make decisions and perform effectively. Open information is provided to people in a learning organization so they know what is going on and can solve problems. Everyone helps develop and control strategy.   Strategy emerges from discussions with employees. The culture is strong and adaptive.

Empowered

Managing the Technology-Driven Workplace

E-business

Today's workers work on computers, in virtual teams, and are connected electronically to colleagues around the world. _____ refers to the work an organization does by using electronic linkages. These linkages may be via the Internet, an intranet—an internal system, or extranet—which gives access to selected parties outside the organization.

E-commerce

_____ refers to business exchanges or transactions that occur electronically. It replaces or enhances the exchange of money and products with the exchange of data and information from one computer to another. Three types of e-commerce are business-to-consumer (B2C), business-to-business (B2B), and consumer-to-consumer (C2C).

enterprise
   resource
   planning

One approach to information management is _____ _____ _____ (ERP) which unites all of a company's major business functions, giving managers the big picture and up-to-date information. *Knowledge management* refers to the efforts to systematically find, organize, and make available a company's intellectual capital and to foster a culture of continuous learning and knowledge sharing so that a company's activities build on what is already known.

Chapter Review

Multiple-Choice Questions: Please indicate the correct response to the following questions by writing the letter of the correct answer in the space provided.

___ 1. A historical perspective matters to executives because it
   a. provides patterns which may recur.
   b. provides a context in which to interpret problems.
   c. helps managers learn from the mistakes of others.
   d. helps managers learn from the success of others.
   e. all of the above

___ 2. The unwritten, common rules and perceptions about relationships among people and between people and organizations are called
   a. political contracts.
   b. social contracts.
   c. human relations perspective.
   d. systems viewpoint.
   e. Hawthorne effect.

___ 3. Basic assumptions underlying political systems include
   a. property rights.
   b. contract rights.
   c. the definition of justice.
   d. managers' rights.
   e. all of the above

___ 4. Economic resources refer to
   a. money.
   b. people.
   c. materials.
   d. natural resources.
   e. all of the above

___ 5. The classical management perspective
   a. recognized environmental influences.
   b. viewed workers as the same as managers.
   c. ignored rationality in favor of human relations.
   d. relied heavily on self-interest concepts.
   e. failed to recognize the importance of individual productivity.

___   6.   The _____ approach to management initiated the careful study of tasks and jobs.
     a.   scientific management
     b.   classical management
     c.   administrative principles
     d.   systems theory
     e.   contingency

___   7.   The general approach of scientific management includes
     a.   flexibility of standards for performing each job.
     b.   selecting workers with appropriate abilities for each job.
     c.   training workers in methods according to individual abilities.
     d.   providing autonomy to workers in planning their own work.
     c.   eliminating wage incentives since they are counterproductive.

___   8.   Which of the following is *not* one of Fayol's 14 general principles of management?
     a.   unity of command
     b.   division of work
     c.   wage incentives
     d.   unity of direction
     e.   scalar chain

___   9.   Fayol's principle of unity of command means that
     a.   top management must all be of one mind before issuing orders.
     b.   each subordinate should receive orders from one—and only one—superior.
     c.   after a command is received, subordinates have the duty of rallying behind the command even if they disagree with it.
     d.   only one person should make a decision because group decision making is less efficient.
     e.   similar activities in an organization should be grouped together under one manager.

___   10.   According to Chester Barnard's acceptance theory of authority,
     a.   workers need to learn to accept the authority of managers.
     b.   managers need to learn to accept the authority vested in them.
     c.   people have free will and can choose whether to follow management orders.
     d.   people have the tendency to accept authority regardless of their perceptions.
     e.   all of the above

___   11.   Weber designed a bureaucracy mainly because
     a.   he was a German and therefore liked paperwork.
     b.   he worked for the government and saw how rational such an organization really was.
     c.   he objected to European organizations which were managed by favoritism and subjective methods.
     d.   he had studied the writings of Frederick W. Taylor and felt Taylor's ideas could be applied to government structures also.
     e.   he objected to the way organizations were so impersonally managed in his day.

___ 12. According to the text, the bureaucratic model works just fine at
    a. Boeing Corporation.
    b. United Parcel Service (UPS).
    c. research laboratories.
    d. Apple Computer Company.
    e. times when technology is changing rapidly.

___ 13. In Weber's bureaucracy, rationality means
    a. employee selection and advancement should be based on competence.
    b. rationing of rewards is beneficial to the organization.
    c. the structure of the bureaucracy is rational.
    d. rational people will appreciate a bureaucracy.
    e. none of the above

___ 14. In a bureaucracy _____ is separate from ownership.
    a. rationality
    b. funding
    c. management
    d. authority
    e. status

___ 15. Which of the following is not a significant element of Total Quality Management (TQM)?
    a. strict control of quality by top management
    b. employee involvement
    c. focus on the customer
    d. benchmarking
    e. continuous improvement

___ 16. Most early interpretations of the Hawthorne studies
    a. agreed that money was the cause of increased output.
    b. pointed to the importance of illumination in affecting productivity.
    c. supported Frederick W. Taylor's scientific management.
    d. pointed to human relations as the best explanation for increased output.
    e. were of medical importance, which led to the founding of the Mayo Clinic in honor of Elton Mayo, one of the chief researchers.

___ 17. Although team leadership is critical in learning organizations, the traditional boss
    a. is still in charge of everything
    b. must still make the tough decisions.
    c. is practically eliminated.
    d. must be maintained.
    e. is still very important.

___ 18. According to Maslow, one must first fill _____ needs before one is concerned with _____ needs.
   a. social, safety
   b. esteem, belongingness
   c. self-actualization, belongingness
   d. safety, physiological
   e. physiological, safety

___ 19. The assumption that the average human being learns, under proper conditions, not only to accept but to seek responsibility is an assumption of
   a. Theory Y.
   b. Abraham Maslow.
   c. contingency theory.
   d. Theory X.
   e. Frederick W. Taylor.

___ 20. The behavioral sciences approach draws from
   a. anthropology.
   b. economics.
   c. psychology.
   d. sociology.
   e. all of the above

___ 21. _____ is/are the management science application which is used in the physical production of goods and services.
   a. Operations research
   b. Operations management
   c. Management information systems
   d. Queuing theory
   e. Scientific management

___ 22. If Tom digs a three-foot-deep ditch by himself, he can dig it 10 feet long. If you dig one by yourself, you can dig one 8 feet long. According to synergy,
   a. if you team up and dig together, it would end up being less than 18 feet long.
   b. if you team up and dig together, it would end up being more than 18 feet long.
   c. if you team up and dig together, it would end up being exactly 18 feet long.
   d. you should start at a center point and dig away from each other in opposite directions.
   e. if you dig an 18-foot ditch together (syn), you will end up less tired (energy).

___ 23. An important contingency that management must understand is
   a. production technology.
   b. organization size.
   c. culture.
   d. all of the above
   e. a and b only

___ 24. When work is done by using electronic linkages it is called
   a. E-business.
   b. E-commerce.
   c. enterprise resource planning.
   d. knowledge management.
   e. cyber management.

___ 25. According to Theory X, the average human being has an inherent _____ work.
   a. understanding of
   b. liking for
   c. feeling, either positive or negative, towards
   d. dislike for
   e. trust in

___ 26. When a company sets up an internal communications system that uses the technology and standards of the Internet, but it is accessible only to people within the company, it is called a(n)
   a. extranet.
   b. internal Internet.
   c. intranet.
   d. cyber communications system.
   e. E-commerce system.

___ 27. When companies sell products and services to consumers over the Internet it is referred to as
   a. B2C
   b. B2B
   c. C2C
   d. C2B
   e. 2BC

___ 28. Changes in one subsystem
   a. lead to entropy.
   b. affect other subsystems.
   c. are never to be allowed by good management.
   d. are impossible in an open organization.
   e. usually result in synergy.

___ 29. In the *learning organization*
   a. everyone is expected to finish high school.
   b. everyone is expected to finish college.
   c. everyone is expected to finish graduate school.
   d. everyone is expected to complete a predetermined number of hours of continuing education each year.
   e. none of the above.

___ 30. ERP stands for
   a. Electronic Research Process.
   b. Enterprise Resource Planning.
   c. Elective Research Planning.
   d. Electronic Risk Probability.
   e. Enterprise Risk Planning.

True/False Questions: Please indicate whether the following questions are true or false by writing a T or an F in the blank in front of each question.

___ 1. Managers should not study the past, but instead concentrate on the future, since what is done is done and cannot be changed.

___ 2. The basic assumptions about justice, determination of guilt or innocence, and various rights are included in political systems.

___ 3. Frank and Lillian Gilbreth, who had 12 children, were used by Frederick W. Taylor as an example of the disadvantages of not using scientific management.

___ 4. According to Chester Barnard, people have free will and can choose whether to follow management orders.

___ 5. While popular in the academic world, the behavioral sciences approach has never really been tried by any businesses.

___ 6. Operations research consists of mathematical model building and other applications of quantitative approaches to managerial problems.

___ 7. The only problem with the systems view of organizations is that it ignores feedback.

___ 8. Entropy is a fact of nature and cannot be avoided.

___ 9. A problem with the contingency view of management is that it ignores the external environment.

___ 10. The learning organization refers to a company in which everyone is encouraged to complete a college degree.

Short-Answer Questions

1. Why were the Hawthorne studies so important to the development of management?

2.   How has scientific management contributed to management?

3.   Explain which approach, Theory X or Theory Y, you feel is most appropriate with employees today.

4. Explain how an adherent to contingency theory would react to scientific management's advocacy of "one best way."

5. What is the role of a leader in the learning organization?

Management Applications

Your Managerial Approach

Determine your own managerial approach by answering the following questions. Assume that you are the manager of a work group and answer the following questions accordingly. Put a Y for "yes" and an N for "no" in the blank preceding the question to indicate your response.

___   1.   I would try to discover the best way to get the job done.

___   2.   I would train the group to do the job the correct way.

___   3.   I would offer an incentive pay for more work done.

___   4.   I would assess workers' abilities and then assign them accordingly.

___   5.   I would take the responsibility of planning who does what.

___   6.   I would group activities of similar nature under one supervisor.

___   7.   I would allow group members to communicate directly with each other when swift action is needed.

___   8.   I would allow subordinates to use their own initiative in planning and organizing the work.

___   9.   I would try to foster a team spirit within the group.

___   10.   I would assign a place for everything and everyone.

___   11.   I would not use very much control over the group since it would tend to control itself.

___   12.   I would point out how fulfilling the job is when we reach our goals.

___   13.   I would give responsibilities to members of the group.

___   14.   I would listen to all the good ideas that group members come up with.

___   15.   I would try to think of ways in addition to the job to encourage the intellectual development of the group.

Scoring

A "yes" answer to the first five questions indicates a preference for the scientific management approach.

A "yes" answer to the second five questions indicates a preference for the administrative principles method of the classical perspective.

A "yes" answer to the third five questions indicates a preference for the human relations approach.

1. For which approach did your answers indicate a preference?

2. Did you answer "yes" to questions indicating a preference for more than one approach? If so, how do you explain it? Does the contingency approach help you to explain it?

A Case for History

This chapter points out the historical development of management thought. It makes the case that managers can learn both successful and unsuccessful practices from the past. For each of the approaches listed below identify one successful practice derived from that approach which you still see in practice today. For example, from scientific management we have the surgical techniques still used by surgeons today to eliminate wasted motion.

Scientific Management

Administrative Principles

Bureaucratic Organizations

The Human Relations Movement

Behavioral Sciences Approach

Systems Theory

Mini Case

Ivan has just been promoted to be the manager of McDonald's second restaurant in Moscow. Ivan has been working for the company for the past two years as an assistant manager. He is one of four persons sent to first Canada and then to the United States to Hamburger University for training prior to the opening of the first McDonald's in Moscow. Although it has been difficult to change the way restaurants are perceived in the Soviet Union, McDonald's has been a success and it is ready to open its second store.

Ivan has been working very hard for McDonald's. At the same time he has been reading about management in Western countries and has been very impressed with many of the theories. Since he has been promoted to open and train the personnel for the new store, he is wondering what approach he should use.

1. Pick an approach to management that Ivan should *not* use and explain why not.

2.   Pick the approach you feel would be most appropriate for Ivan to use and explain the reasons for your choice.

Experiential Exercise

Sam Slick

You are the manager of a used car lot. The policy of the company is that your sales force never sell a car for below the established base price. Each sale results in a 5% commission for the salesperson. You have recently had some complaints from some of your employees regarding the actions of one of your best salespersons, Sam Slick. It seems that Sam has been selling cars for below the established base price. When you confront him about this practice, he points out that while the established base price gives the company a nice profit, no profit is realized if a car just sits on the lot forever. Consequently, he has been selling some of these slower-selling cars. A little profit is better than no profit at all he reasons.

Your instructor will divide the class into groups of four persons. Each group will be designated as a Taylor group, a Mayo group, a Deming group, or a Referee group. Depending on your group type, answer the question below. After five minutes your instructor will have each group present its solution. The Referee group will then pick the best solution and explain its choice.

Taylor Group

You are a believer in scientific management. How would you handle this situation? Elect a spokesperson for the group to explain how and why you will handle it this way. This spokesperson will explain your rationale to the rest of the class.

Mayo Group

You follow the human relations approach to management. How might you handle this situation? Elect a spokesperson for the group to explain how and why you will handle it this way. This spokesperson will explain your rationale to the rest of the class.

Deming Group

You follow the management science approach to management. How might you handle this situation? Elect a spokesperson for the group to explain how and why you will handle it this way. This spokesperson will explain your rationale to the rest of the class.

Referee Group

You will listen to the groups present their approaches to solving this problem. Decide on the criteria for judging their solutions while they are working out their solutions.

Criteria

Which approach do you think would be best in this situation? Take a simple vote from all the referees to determine the best solution. Elect a spokesperson for the group to explain your choice to the rest of the class.

Study Guide Solutions

Chapter Review

Multiple-Choice Questions

1	2	3	4	5	6	7	8	9	10
e	b	e	e	d	a	b	c	b	c

11	12	13	14	15	16	17	18	19	20
c	b	a	c	a	d	c	e	a	e

21	22	23	24	25	26	27	28	29	30
b	b	d	a	d	c	a	b	e	b

True/False Questions

1	2	3	4	5	6	7	8	9	10
F	T	F	T	F	T	F	F	F	F

Short-Answer Questions

1. The Hawthorne studies were one of the first attempts to scientifically study human behavior on the job. They were an impetus to the human relations movement as they demonstrated that social factors were an important factor in determining behavior on the job. The belief that good human relations can improve productivity still exists today from these studies.

2. Scientific management demonstrated the importance of payment for job performance. It was also an early attempt to systematically study the tasks of work and various jobs. It explained the importance of personnel selection and training.

3. Most persons will answer that Theory Y is more appropriate for managers today since most employees meet Theory Y assumptions. Besides, it seems more decent and democratic to be more concerned for people. However, there are many situations in which Theory X is still appropriate. The contingency theory approach addresses this issue more fully.

4. An adherent of the contingency theory would reject the notion of one best way to do a job. According to contingency theory, the best way is dependent on several factors including the manager, the subordinates, and the situation. The one best way is the way that is appropriate for the set of contingencies present.

5. The leader in the learning organization creates a shared vision that includes what the organization will look like, performance outcomes and underlying values. This vision may be created with employee participation and must be widely understood and imprinted in people's minds.

Management Applications

Your Managerial Approach

1. The answer to this question depends on the scores to the questionnaire you received.

2. Most persons would probably answer "yes" to questions indicating a preference for more than one approach. The contingency approach helps to explain this because the answer one gives probably depends on the situation. Therefore, one could answer "yes" to some of the questions assuming a certain situation and "yes" to questions from a different approach assuming a different situation.

A Case for History

You are asked to give examples of practices that still exist today based on the following approaches:

Scientific Management

Bricklaying still uses the economy of motion techniques and the idea of "one best way" that were developed by scientific management.

Administrative Principles

The principle of unity of command is still used by almost all organizations today. In the military one knows exactly to whom he must report. Almost all organizations tell you who your direct supervisor is, adhering to this principle.

Bureaucratic Organizations

Several elements of a bureaucracy are identifiable in almost all organizations today. The government of almost all countries adheres to the bureaucratic model. For example, positions are organized in a hierarchy of authority in governments.

The Human Relations Movement

The assumptions of McGregor are seen in many organizations. One example that most people are familiar with occurred during the Reagan administration in the United States. President Reagan used Theory Y assumptions about his cabinet and administrative staff, and he therefore delegated to them liberally.

Behavioral Sciences Approach

Many organizations use information and techniques from the social sciences today. Personality tests such as the Myers-Briggs Type Indicator are frequently used by organizations to help them better understand employees.

Systems Theory

The concept of synergy is still used today. Almost all athletic teams understand the importance of teamwork and that by working together the team can be more successful than it can with the players working as individuals.

Mini Case

1. An approach that Ivan should *not* use is the bureaucratic approach. Of course, elements of the bureaucratic model will still be evident in the organization, but life in Russia has been dominated by bureaucracy too long. Adherence to unbending rules and emphasis on procedures rather than on results are not what McDonald's needs to be successful at this time. This is especially true, given the turbulent and uncertain environment in Russia.

2. The approach that McDonald's uses successfully worldwide is the scientific management approach. McDonald's teaches its employees that there is one best way to fry burgers and french fries, for example. It trains employees in that method. McDonald's needs uniformity in all its locations and should probably stick to this approach.

Experiential Exercise

Sam Slick

Taylor Group

As a believer in scientific management, you would try to convince Sam that there is one best way to sell used cars. You would try to train Sam in the company's prescribed way, including sticking to the established base price. You would also try to explain to Sam that by selling at a lower price he is reducing the amount of his commission. Since you believe that money is a prime motivator, this should convince him. You would also explain to him that it is management's job, not the employees', to establish procedures.

Mayo Group

You would explain to Sam that his actions were causing the other employees to complain and would not make him very popular with them. You would also emphasize the importance of teamwork. You would ask him if he had any ideas to solve this problem himself.

Deming Group

Since you subscribe to the management science approach, you would probably explain to Sam the quantitative rationale behind the present procedure. You would use logic to convince him that it is in his best interest to follow the procedure.

Referee Group

Some of the criteria you might consider using include practicality of the proposed solution, how well Sam will accept the solution, and the effect of the solution on the rest of the company.

Chapter 3

The Environment and Corporate Culture

Chapter Summary

After you have read the text chapter, read through the summary below. Cover the left-hand margin and fill in the blanks with the appropriate terms. After you have filled in each blank, check your responses by uncovering the answer given in the margin. If you do not understand why the given answer is the correct one, refer back to the text.

The External Environment

organizational

The _____ environment includes all elements outside the organization that could affect it. The organization must adapt to the organizational environment which includes competitors, resources, technology, and economic conditions. This environment is divided into two layers: the task and general environments.

general
international

The _____ environment has indirect impact on the organization. The _____ dimension is that portion of the environment that represents events originating in foreign countries as well as opportunities for American companies in other countries. It provides a context that influences all other aspects of the external environment. This means that American managers must learn to cope with goods, services, and ideas circulating around the world.

Technological
Sociocultural

_____ advancements in the industry and society at large must be integrated into the organization to remain competitive. _____ dimensions such as norms, values, customs, population age, distribution of population, and educational levels influence the demand for the organization's offerings and its relationships with its own employees and other groups.

Economic

_____ forces such as consumer purchasing power, the unemployment rate, interest rates, and mergers and acquisitions affect demand for the product

legal-political

also. The _____ factors such as governmental laws, court decisions, and regulations as well as political activities affect what the organization can

pressure groups

and cannot do. Managers need to recognize that _____ work within the legal-political framework to influence companies to behave in socially responsible ways.

task

The _____ environment includes those sectors that have a direct effect

internal
customers

Competitors

Suppliers

labor market

on the organization and the _____ environment which is within organizational boundaries. This includes _____ who determine the success of the organization through their demand for the products produced. The Internet has given customers more power and given them a way to search more effectively and to air complaints. _____ directly affect the organization also by making entry into the industry difficult and by engaging in competitive activities. However, many competitors are learning to cooperate to achieve common objectives. _____, who provide raw materials the organization uses to produce its output, also can have a direct impact on the organization. The _____ is an essential input into the productivity of the organization since an adequate, well-trained, and qualified supply of workers is needed. There is the need for continuous investment in human resources education and training.

The Organization-Environment Relationship

The relationship between the organization and its environment is influenced by the degree of uncertainty in the environment. When the external environment changes rapidly, the organization experiences very high uncertainty. Two strategies, adapting to the environment and influencing the environment, have been used to cope with this uncertainty.

boundary-
spanning

merger
joint venture

Adapting to the environment can be facilitated by several activities. The organization can create _____ roles which link organizational members with the environment to gather information and to represent the organization. A big part of bounding spanning today is gathering *competitive intelligence*. One way to adapt is to share the risk with other organizations by means of interorganizational partnerships. Some of the partnerships have been fromed by using digital network connections and the Internet. A step beyond strategic partnerships is the forming of a merger or joint venture. A _____ is the combining of two or more organizations into one, while a _____ is a strategic alliance of organizations.

The Internal Environment: Corporate Culture

Culture

symbol

_____ is the set of key values, beliefs, understandings, and norms that members of an organization share. There may be visible artifacts such as dress, stories, symbols, or ceremonies which express culture. The values and norms are evident through stories, language, and symbols. Managers need to know how to use these techniques to create the appropriate culture. A _____ of culture is an object, act, or event that conveys meaning to others such as values.

Stories
Heroes

_____ are narratives based on true events repeated frequently to keep values alive. _____ provide role models for employees by

Slogans
Ceremonies

exemplifying the deeds, characters, and attributes of the corporate culture. _____ express a key corporate value concisely. _____ are special events which provide dramatic examples of company values and is conducted for the benefit of an audience.

Environment and Culture

adaptability

achievement

clan

bureaucratic

Adaptive cultures are ones in which managers are concerned about customers and those internal people and processes that bring about useful change. Cultures can be categorized by two dimensions: the extent to which the external environment requires flexibility or stability and the extent to which a company's strategic focus is internal or external. The _____ culture focuses on the external environment and requires flexibility. The _____ culture is for organizations that serve specific customers in the external environment, but without the intense need for flexibility and rapid change. The _____ culture has an internal focus on the involvement and participation of employees to rapidly meet changing needs from the environment. The _____ culture has an internal focus and a consistency orientation for a stable environment.

Shaping Corporate Culture for the New Workplace

In today's increasingly global and virtual organizations, shared cultural values are what hold people and operations together. One way of creating and maintaining a strong culture is by emphasizing the *selection* and *socialization* of new employees. Companies also put values into writing and distributing them in newsletters, videos, intranets, and in training classes.

cultural

Cultural Leadership
A _____ leader is a manager who uses signals and symbols to influence corporate culture. This manager must articulate his vision and take care of the day-to-day activities that reinforce the vision and eventually lead to a change in corporate culture. The culture must be reinforced by words and actions.

Chapter Review

Multiple-Choice Questions: Please indicate the correct response to the following questions by writing the letter of the correct answer in the space provided.

___ 1. The task environment usually includes all of the following except
   a. employees.
   b. competitors.
   c. suppliers.
   d. customers.
   e. It consists of all of the above.

___ 2. The _____ environment refers to the external environment that affects the organization indirectly.
   a. task
   b. general
   c. internal
   d. corporate
   e. outlying

___ 3. _____ can cause the organization trouble by engaging in foreign production, making the price of entering the market high, or starting a price war.
   a. Customers
   b. Suppliers
   c. Governments
   d. Competitors
   e. Joint ventures

___ 4. A current trend affecting the labor supply is
   a. fewer expectations for democracy in the workplace by realistic, high-achieving workers.
   b. the growing need for computer-literate information technology workers.
   c. an increasing percentage of unionized workers.
   d. a pledge by large unions, especially the AFL-CIO, to unionize more companies.
   e. a decreasing number of college graduates as more workers are anxious to enter the job market.

___ 5. The sociocultural dimension includes
   a. norms and values.
   b. demographics.
   c. geographic population distribution.
   d. educational levels in the community.
   e. all of the above

___ 6. If a person in an organization is given a(n) _____, he is to link and coordinate the organization with key elements in the external environment.
   a. position as ethics advocate
   b. boundary-spanning role
   c. constituency position
   d. ethical dilemma
   e. linking-pin assignment

___ 7. When operating globally, managers have to consider
   a. legal factors
   b. political factors
   c. sociocultural factors
   d. economic factors
   e. all of the above

___ 8. Technological advancements that make the Internet accessible to nearly everyone have
   a. not affected management.
   b. changed the nature of competition.
   c. not affected organizations' relationships to customers.
   d. led to excessive regulation of the Internet.
   e. made the Internet more complex to use.

___ 9. An example of a visible organizational activity that illustrates corporate culture is
   a. a symbol.
   b. a slogan.
   c. a hero.
   d. a story.
   e. all of the above

___ 10. A special occasion that reinforces valued accomplishments is called a
   a. symbolic meeting.
   b. ceremony.
   c. story event.
   d. slogan maker.
   e. hero-izer.

___ 11. Which of the following is true in the United States?
   a. People are less interested in spirituality than ever.
   b. Most people do not feel a need to experience spiritual growth.
   c. Sales of books related to religion are booming.
   d. Some companies are openly bringing spiritual values and ideas into the workplace.
   e. The anti-cholesterol and low-fat fervor continues to increase.

___ 12. Recently pressure groups have been concerned about
   a. biotechnology.
   b. the cost of bird feed.
   c. the cost of theater tickets.
   d. too much government intervention in environmental affairs.
   e. counterfeiting.

___ 13. The _____ manager defines and uses signals and symbols to influence corporate culture.
   a. cultural
   b. pseudo-
   c. ineffective
   d. MBO
   e. Theory Z

___ 14. The internal environment includes
   a. current employees.
   b. production technology.
   c. organization structure.
   d. physical facilities.
   e. all of the above

___ 15. Which of the following would be a customer of a hospital?
   a. doctors
   b. nurses
   c. suppliers
   d. patients
   e. florists

___ 16. A sociocultural trend in recent years has been
   a. a groundswell of interest in spirituality in the U.S.
   b. the movement toward the work ethic.
   c. greater savings by families.
   d. increased homogeneity among consumers.
   e. a return to the family farm.

___ 17. Which of the following was listed in the text as a strategy for adapting to changes?
   a. buying everyone a personal computer
   b. boundary-spanning roles
   c. watching more television
   d. hiring more lobbyists
   e. traveling more

___ 18. The website united.com is a site that
  a. promotes United Airlines
  b. United Airlines employees and disgruntled fliers air their complaints.
  c. promotes unity among America's workers.
  d. promotes business in the United States.
  e. stands for patriotism in the country.

___ 19. Which of the following represents a *partnership orientation*?
  a. long-term contracts
  b. limit information and feedback
  c. contracts limit the relationship
  d. price, efficiency, own profits
  e. lawsuits to resolve conflict

___ 20. In the adaptability culture employees
  a. have the autonomy to make decisions.
  b. are expected to adapt or conform to management's will.
  c. feel demeaned.
  d. must all be male.
  e. are discouraged from engaging in teamwork.

___ 21. Most e-commerce companies, as well as companies in the electronics, cosmetics, and fashion industries use the _____ culture.
  a. adaptability
  b. achievement
  c. clan
  d. bureaucratic
  e. cybernetic

___ 22. Culture must fit the needs of the external environment and
  a. company strategy.
  b. government legislators.
  c. lobbyists.
  d. stockholders.
  e. competitors.

___ 23. One of the elements of the corporate culture at the surface level is
  a. a story.
  b. language.
  c. a ceremony.
  d. a value.
  e. a norm.

___ 24. Underlying values such as "people here care about one another like a family" or "The H-P Way" are said to be
   a. unimportant to corporate profits.
   b. highly visible.
   c. invisible.
   d. at the surface level.
   e. not very pervasive.

___ 25. A narrative based on true events that are repeated frequently and shared among organizational employees is called a
   a. story.
   b. legend.
   c. symbol.
   d. myth.
   e. ceremony.

___ 26. "Eagles don't flock. You have to find them one at a time." is an example of a
   a. story.
   b. legend.
   c. myth.
   d. slogan.
   e. misinformation release.

___ 27. Which of the following cultures is a results-oriented culture that values competitiveness, personal initiative, and willingness to work long and hard?
   a. Adaptability
   b. Achievement
   c. Clan
   d. Bureaucratic
   e. cybernetic

___ 28. Which culture places high value on meeting the needs of employees and the organization may be characterized by a caring family-like atmosphere?
   a. adaptability
   b. achievement
   c. clan
   d. bureaucratic
   e. cybernetic

___ 29. Which culture values following the rules and being thrifty while supporting and rewarding a methodical, rational, and orderly way of doing things?
   a. adaptability
   b. achievement
   c. clan
   d. bureaucratic
   e. cybernetic

___ 30. Managers can create and maintain s strong culture in a workplace by,
   a. careful selection of new employees.
   b. good socialization of new employees.
   c. putting the company's values into writing and distributing them.
   d. all of the above.
   e. none of the above.

True/False Questions: Please indicate whether the following questions are true or false by writing a T or an F in the blank in front of each question.

___ 1. It is the customers who determine a firm's success.

___ 2. Oddly enough, the technological dimension does not refer to scientific advancements.

___ 3. The organization need not be concerned with local values since it must be true to its own values.

___ 4. The lack of information about the environment leads to uncertainty.

___ 5. By 2050, non-Hispanic whites will make up only about half of the population.

___ 6. Handgun manufacturers are struggling as public acceptance and support of guns in the home has fallen.

___ 7. Stories are told to new employees to keep them in the dark as long as possible as a practical joke.

___ 8. The economies of countries are more closely tied together than ever before.

___ 9. Cultural leadership works because managers are watched by their employees.

___ 10. Through words and actions cultural leaders let everyone in the organization know what really counts.

Short-Answer Questions

1. What is the difference between the task environment and the general environment?

2.   Is culture visible or invisible? Explain the justification for your answer.

4.   Give an example of how a symbol and a ceremony you are familiar with support a corporate or
     organizational culture.

5. Explain how you might go about trying to change a corporate culture?

Management Applications

The Customer Is <u>Always</u> Right?

Jack is a buyer for Associated Grocers (AG) of Phoenix, Arizona. He buys health and beauty aids for this wholesale cooperative. Technically, its members own the company, but it survives by competing with other wholesalers for the business of its members. The members may buy from other sources if they get a better deal or product. The members are retail grocers. Some of these grocers are quite small, but several of the members are chains and buy large amounts from AG. One of the more important customers is Smitty's. Smitty's owns about 20 stores that do a tremendous volume of business. Smitty's purchases from AG account for approximately 25% of AG's business.

Jack has been buying acne medications from Helmsley Laboratories for the last few years. Its brands are well recognized and sell well. Practically all of the members buy these products. Smitty's head buyer recently called Jack and asked him to switch to Foxie, Ltd. brands instead. The buyer said that he felt that this brand would sell well in Smitty's.

1.   What would you recommend that Jack do?

2. Jack is not sure whether he has enough warehouse space allocated to him to carry both brands. If that turns out to be the case, what should he do?

3. Are there other external factors Jack should consider before making this decision?

Graduation

You hope you will soon be graduating from college. Many students elect not to go through graduation service while others do put on the robes, the funny flat hats, and listen to the long speeches.

1. How do graduation exercises help to maintain the organizational culture of a college or university?

2. What are some of the symbols evident during graduation?

3. What type of hero would you expect to find in the culture of a college or university?

Mini Case

WordPerfect Corporation was sold to Novell in March of 1994. It was thought by Novell that this would be a perfect acquisition. Novell could use its strength in networking coupled with WordPerfect's software and reputation for excellence in customer service to expand its market and compete more effectively with Microsoft. Things turned sour very quickly, however.

One of the problems with the acquisition as reported in the press was the conflict of cultures of the two companies. WordPerfect was described as a *corporate Camelot* where employees loved to work and were well-taken care of. Novell was less humanistic, but still treated its employees well. Eventually, Novell decided it needed to concentrate again on networking and sold WordPerfect again.

On January 31. 1996 Corel Corporation announced that it, together with its Irish and U.S. subsidiaries, had entered into an agreement to acquire the WordPerfect family of software programs and other related
technologies. Dr. Michael Cowpland, CEO of Corel, was very enthusiastic about prospects for the software and the impact on Corel's existing product offerings. Incorporated in 1985, Corel Corporation is recognized internationally as an award-winning developer and marketer of PC graphics and multimedia software. CorelDRAW(TM), Corel's industry-leading graphics software, is available in over 17 languages and has won over 230 international awards from major trade publications. (Source: Canada News Wire, January 31, 1996)

1. What advice would you give to the CEO of Corel as it prepares to integrate WordPerfect into its organization?

2.   Does the fact that WordPerfect is located in Utah, while Corel is a Canadian company, pose any problems?

Experiential Exercise

Every organization has a culture. The college you are now attending has its own culture also. Your instructor will divide the class into groups of four persons. In your group answer the following questions:

1.   How would you describe the culture of your college to a prospective student?

2. Based on your answer to the first question list below some of the artifacts that demonstrate and perpetuate this culture:

Stories

Dress

Symbols

Ceremonies

3. Elect a spokesperson to report to the class your conclusions. The more similar the reports of the group, the more tightly knit is the culture. This would also indicate that the culture is being communicated well. Discuss as a group the reasons for any differences in the reports.

Study Guide Solutions

Chapter Review

Multiple-Choice Questions

1	2	3	4	5	6	7	8	9	10
a	b	d	b	e	b	e	b	e	b
11	**12**	**13**	**14**	**15**	**16**	**17**	**18**	**19**	**20**
c	a	a	e	d	a	b	b	a	a
21	**22**	**23**	**24**	**25**	**26**	**27**	**28**	**29**	**30**
a	a	c	c	a	d	b	c	d	d

True/False Questions

1	2	3	4	5	6	7	8	9	10
T	F	F	T	T	T	F	T	T	T

Short-Answer Questions

1. The task environment includes all elements that have a *direct* impact on the organization, while the general environment has an *indirect* impact only.

2. Culture has both visible and invisible elements. Many artifacts such as symbols, slogans, and ceremonies are highly visible. Underlying values are invisible.

3. One example most students would be familiar with exists within churches. A priest in a Roman Catholic Church wears a robe and other artifacts to symbolize his position and authority. Communion is a ceremony that supports the position and authority of the priest and the church.

4. You would have to use the tools of the symbolic manager to change the corporate culture. For example, you would want to make sure that you can verbally speak about your vision for the company in a way that will help employees become excited about it and believe in it. You would also want to consider using new symbols and slogans to communicate that the culture has changed.

Management Applications

The Customer Is <u>Always</u> Right?

1. The ideal thing for Jack to do is to start buying Foxie, Ltd. products in addition to the current brands. This way Jack will be reacting to the needs of this important customer while at the same time not ignoring the needs of the other customers.

2. If there is not enough room allocated to carry both products, Jack's problem is more complex. One option would be to simply request that more space be allocated to carry both lines, explaining the reason for the request. Another option would be to poll the buyers of the other important customers to determine if they too are planning to switch brands. If that fails to result in a workable solution, Jack might consider arranging for Foxie, Ltd. and Smitty's to work closely with AG in forecasting the expected sales. This will reduce the amount of inventory required by AG. Hopefully, the amount of inventory for the existing products could also be reduced to make room for this new product.

3. Other factors to consider are mainly the needs of the other customers of AG. Also worthy of consideration are the anticipated reactions of competitors of Foxie, Ltd. and of AG's competitors.

Graduation

1. Graduation is a ceremony for the benefit of those graduating and their families. It is to convince them that the results of their efforts are worth it all in a serious and academic way.

2. The robes, hats, diplomas, podiums, flags, and many other artifacts, depending on the institution, are all symbols one sees at graduation exercises.

3. Most colleges and universities are in a process culture characterized by low-risk decisions and little or no feedback. Outcomes are hard to measure. Technical perfection and following procedures are characteristics of the heroes.

Mini Case

1. The CEO of Corel should probably learn as much as he can about the corporate culture of WordPerfect before trying to integrate the two cultures. He should learn to use the tools of the symbolic leader to influence the WordPerfect culture.

2. The locations of the two companies will make a difference. Often the corporate culture is influenced by the general and task environments in which it exists. Corel must be careful to study these differences to successfully merge the two cultures.

Experiential Exercise

1. The answer to the first question depends on the perceived culture of the college by the students. It may be described as a "party school," a rigorous academic school, or a cheap school, for example.
2. The answers will again vary by the perceived culture. A "party school" perception may result in some of the following:

    Stories   The stories that are told about "party schools" are usually about how wild some of the past parties have been.

    Dress   Either relaxed, informal dress or sexy dress practices will be emphasized at a "party school."

    Symbols   An important symbol at a "party school" might be a beer keg, illuminated beer signs hanging in windows, or fast, hot cars.

    Ceremonies   Important ceremonies at a "party school" would include fraternity or sorority initiations or events that are really wild.

Chapter 4

Managing in a Global Environment

Chapter Summary

After you have read the text chapter, read through the summary below. Cover the left-hand margin and fill in the blanks with the appropriate terms. After you have filled in each blank, check your responses by uncovering the answer given in the margin. If you do not understand why the given answer is the correct one, refer back to the text.

A Borderless World

domestic
international
multinational

global

Globalization of corporations generally passes through four stages. The first stage is the _____ *stage* which focuses on the domestic market. Next comes the _____ *stage* when exports increase and the company adopts an international division. The _____ *stage* finds the company with marketing and production facilities located in many countries. The _____ *(or stateless) stage* exists when companies operate in a true global manner. This means that the best opportunities, including management staffing and ownership, will come from whatever country is best.

International Business Environment

International
management

_____ is concerned with the management of business operations in more than one country. The same basic management functions are performed, but may have to be modified for the differences faced in various countries.

The Economic Environment

infrastructure

The economic development of a country affects how people behave in that country. The _____, which is a country's physical facilities that support economic activities, varies by country also. In doing business in other countries managers must also consider the resources and product markets available to them. The value of one currency in terms of another currency, or *exchange rate*, can have an impact on profits.

The Legal-Political Environment

Political risk

_____, which is a company's risk of loss of assets, earning power, or managerial control due to politically motivated events or actions by host governments, is also faced when doing business in other countries. Government takeovers occur from time to time. Laws and regulations about products and business practices vary as does the political stability of various countries. The rapid changes in the former Soviet republics illustrate this *political instability*. Countries with political, ethnic, or religious upheaval are a strong threat to global companies.

most favored
nation

Continual changes in *laws and regulations* challenge international firms. This is especially true with the emergence of international trade alliances. The General Agreement on Tariffs and Trade (GATT) has evolved into an international organization for settling trade disputes with more than 100 member countries. Members agree to the _____, that calls for members to grant each other the most favorable treatment they accord any country concerning imports and exports. The European Union (EU) has already begun integration in many areas, but the creation of a single market still faces some opposition which will take time to overcome. Eleven members of the EU adopted the _____ that will become the national currency of all 15 members eventually.

euro

NAFTA

The North American Free Trade Agreement (_____) by Canada, Mexico, and the U.S., went into effect in 1994 and provides for reductions in tariffs and a freer flow of goods among member nations over a 15 year period. The effect of these types of trade alliances is potentially great on global corporations and international managers.

The Sociocultural Environment

Culture

The sociocultural differences are more difficult to understand and cope with. _____ includes the shared knowledge, beliefs, values, behaviors, and ways of thinking among members of a society. This includes various social values, language, religion, attitudes, social organization, and educational influences. One difference is in _____, which is the degree to which people accept inequality in power among institutions, organizations, and people. _____ is a value characterized by people's intolerance for uncertainty and ambiguity and resulting support for beliefs that promise certainty and conformity. Other differences exist in views of individualism and collectivism. _____ is a preference for a loosely knit social framework in which individuals are expected to take care of themselves. _____, on the other hand, is a preference for a tightly knit social framework in which individuals look after one another and organizations protect their members' interests. The preference for masculinity or femininity will vary by culture also.

power distance
Uncertainty
avoidance

Individualism

Collectivism

Masculinity	_____ is a cultural preference for achievement, heroism, assertiveness,
Femininity	and material success. _____ is a cultural preference for modesty,
	tending to the weak, and quality of life. Some cultures have a _____
long-term	orientation while others have a _____ orientation. Almost all
short-term	cultures have an attitude called _____, which is a cultural attitude
ethnocentrism	marked by the tendency to regard one's own culture as superior to others.

Getting Started Internationally

market entry	Several different strategies are available for entry into a foreign market. A
strategy	_____ is an organizational strategy for entering a foreign market. One
global outsourcing	choice is _____, which means engaging in the international division of
	labor to obtain the cheapest sources of labor and supplies regardless of country.
exporting	Another way is _____, an entry strategy in which the organization
	maintains its production facilities within its home country and transfers its
	products for sale in foreign markets. This strategy lowers the risk and investment
	costs, but also lowers the control over the marketing of the product in that
countertrade	country. One variation of exporting is _____, in which the barter of
	products for other products, rather than their sale for currency, takes place.
	Licensing and franchising allow the product to be made and marketed in the
	foreign country by another company. This method provides income and more
	control over operations, but it does not give the home company as much profit as
Licensing	could be available. _____ is an entry strategy in which an organization
	in one country makes certain resources available to companies in another country
Franchising	in order to participate in the production and sale of its products abroad.
	_____ is a form of licensing in which an organization provides its
	foreign franchisees with a complete assortment of materials and services.

Direct investing	_____ is an entry strategy in which the organization is involved in
joint venture	managing its production facilities in a foreign country. A _____ is
	sharing of the costs and risks with another firm to build a manufacturing
	facility, develop new products, or set up a sales and distribution network. This
wholly owned	spreads the risk, but also the profits. A _____ is a foreign subsidiary
foreign affiliate	over which an organization has complete control, but is the riskiest entry
greenfield venture	strategy. Most risk is the _____, whereby a company builds a
	subsidiary from scratch in a foreign country.

Multinational Corporations

multinational	A _____ receives more than 25 percent of its revenues from
corporation	operations outside the parent company's home country. Its foreign affiliates
	cooperate closely with each other, and it is controlled by a single management
	authority. It is presumed to have a geocentric, or global orientation. Some
	MNCs have a home-country, or ethnocentric, orientation, while others have a

host-country, or polycentric, perspective.

Managing in a Global Environment

For managers to be successful in foreign assignments they must be culturally flexible and adapt easily to new situations. They must not be ethnocentric and learn to overcome loneliness and _____, which is the frustration and anxiety that result from being constantly subjected to strange and unfamiliar cues about what to do and how to do it. The way in which a manager in a foreign country leads, makes decisions, motivates, and controls varies from one country to another. Organizations must be continually learning across borders to be successful globally.

culture shock

Chapter Review

Multiple-Choice Questions: Please indicate the correct response to the following questions by writing the letter of the correct answer in the space provided.

___ 1. The criterion for being classified a less developed country is
   a. per capita income.
   b. lower moral standards.
   c. having more jungles.
   d. having less foreigners.
   e. having less agriculture.

___ 2. Infrastructure refers to a country's
   a. climate.
   b. economic physical support facilities.
   c. form of government.
   d. organizational preferences.
   e. societal structure and classes.

___ 3. Exchange rates in the text refer to
   a. the quantity of students who study in other countries.
   b. the number of students who visit a respective country.
   c. the arrangements between airlines to have reciprocal landing rights across national boundaries.
   d. the rate at which one country's currency is exchanged for another country's.
   e. the number of foreign businesses allowed to operate within a given country.

___ 4. Political risk may involve
   a. violent acts against a firm's property.
   b. outright seizure of a company's facilities.
   c. gradual government encroachment into management of the firm.
   d. a timetable for shift of ownership to local interests.
   e. all of the above

___ 5. A country that has low power distance is
   a. Malaysia.
   b. the Philippines.
   c. Israel.
   d. Panama.
   e. all of the above

___ 6. Having a feminine cultural preference means that
   a. a country has many male homosexuals.
   b. women are chosen as political leaders.
   c. there is a tendency to emphasize the quality of life.
   d. heroism is emphasized.
   e. mothers are honored more than fathers.

___ 7. The entry strategy of _____ provides the least amount of risk and resource costs, but also the least control.
   a. exporting
   b. licensing
   c. franchising
   d. a joint venture
   e. a wholly owned subsidiary

___ 8. An MNC is characterized by
   a. having foreign affiliates who do not cooperate with each other but rather act autonomously.
   b. decentralization of management.
   c. a global perspective.
   d. earning less than 25 percent of profits in foreign markets.
   e. all of the above

___ 9. A greenfield venture is
   a. building a subsidiary in a foreign country from scratch.
   b. illegal in most countries.
   c. bribing foreign officials with money (greenbacks).
   d. taking advantage of legislation introduced by Senator Greenfield.
   e. entering a market where no competition exists.

___ 10. Global outsourcing means that a company decides to
   a. attempting to influence foreign governments to allow you to do business..
   b. engaging in the international division of labor.
   c. hire managers from other countries to manage operations in its home country.
   d. seek a growth strategy by aggressively entering foreign markets.
   e. delete a product line by allowing existing supplies to run out.

___ 11. Which of the following is a characteristic of a multinational corporation?
   a. managed as an integrated worldwide business system
   b. controlled by a single management authority
   c. has a global perspective
   d. receives more than 25 percent of its total revenues from outside its home country
   e. all of the above

___ 12. Successful managers in foreign assignments are
   a. ethnocentric.
   b. set in their ways of doing things and not bothered by the new culture.
   c. culturally flexible.
   d. those who come to understand the local country like a native.
   e. all of the above.

___ 13. Culture shock refers to
   a. realizing that one's own culture is inferior.
   b. having to learn about the arts of a new country quickly.
   c. frustration and anxiety from being in a strange culture.
   d. being sleepy when you arrive in a foreign country due to *jet lag*.
   e. suddenly realizing that you cannot speak the local language.

___ 14. In Asia, the Arab world, and Latin America, managers should use a _____ management approach.
   a. task-oriented
   b. macho
   c. impersonal
   d. critical
   e. warm, relationship-oriented

___ 15. German managers expect the boss to
   a. give general guidelines and allow freedom of action by subordinates.
   b. discuss problems with subordinates.
   c. give specific instructions.
   d. be given recommendations by the subordinates.
   e. be a Nazi.

___ 16. Which of the following is/are (an) example(s) of political instability?
   a. riots
   b. revolutions
   c. civil disorders
   d. frequent changes in government
   e. all of the above

___ 17. The creation of a truly free internal market for the European Union (EU) has been dubbed
   a. ludicrous by historians and social scientists.
   b. Project Unity.
   c. Europe '92.
   d. Free Trade.
   e. the European Project.

___ 18. The term "Fortress Europe" refers to
   a. the possible trade barrier around the EU after integration.
   b. the European Defense Alliance.
   c. NATO.
   d. anti-American sentiment within Europe.
   e. the economic strength of a united Europe.

___ 19. If members of a society feel uncomfortable with uncertainty, it is called
   a. cognitive dissonance.
   b. high uncertainty avoidance.
   c. collective insecurity.
   d. cultural paranoia.
   e. security backlash.

___ 20. Finding a cheaper source of supply offshore is called
   a. foreign cost minimization.
   b. maximum materials management.
   c. a joint venture.
   d. direct investment.
   e. outsourcing.

___ 21. Global souring refers to
   a. the same thing as outsourcing.
   b. finding customers to buy your exports.
   c. conserving the environment worldwide.
   d. using international financing.
   e. joint ventures in a third country.

___ 22. An arrangement in which one company provides a foreign company with a complete package of materials and services including advice and standardized operating procedures is called
   a. outsourcing.
   b. licensing.
   c. direct investment.
   d. franchising.
   e. exporting.

___ 23. A joint venture is a type of
   a. exporting.
   b. licensing.
   c. franchising.
   d. direct investment.
   e. international division.

___ 24. Which of the following is a characteristic of an MNC?
   a. At least 15 percent of its total sales revenues comes from operations outside the parent's home country.
   b. It is managed as an integrated worldwide business system.
   c. It is highly decentralized.
   d. Top management regards the world as a series of distinct markets.
   e. Only capital and technology, but never people, are transferred among affiliates.

___ 25. An MNC that is host-country oriented is called
   a. ethnocentric.
   b. polycentric.
   c. geocentric.
   d. localcentric.
   e. forensic.

___ 26. Direct acquisition of an affiliate
   a. will result in cost increases as compared to exporting.
   b. may reduce the distribution channel.
   c. will reduce the local perspective.
   d. will likely increase storage costs.
   e. will increase transportation costs.

___ 27. One reason Japanese companies have been so successful internationally is that their culture
   a. encourages learning and adaptability.
   b. can withstand challenges from other cultures.
   c. tends to dominant other cultures.
   d. is practically nonexistent.
   e. is so complex that it encompasses all other cultures.

___ 28. A manager in Japan should realize that Japanese are motivated
   a. by time off.
   b. by individual rewards.
   c. in groups.
   d. by money only.
   e. by public praise only.

___ 29. An entry strategy in which the company maintains its production facilities at home and transfers its products for sale in foreign markets is called
   a. contertrade.
   b. licensing.
   c. franchising.
   d. exporting.
   e. direct investing.

___ 30. NAFTA is an agreement among
   a. Canada, Mexico, and the U.S.
   b. Newly Aligned Free Trade Areas.
   c. North African Free Trade Areas.
   d. Norway and Afghanistan Free Trade Areas.
   e. None of the above.

True/False Questions: Please indicate whether the following questions are true or false by writing a T or an F in the blank in front of each question.

___ 1. The basic management function of organizing becomes irrelevant when dealing with international management.

___ 2. McDonald's tires to contract with local suppliers when possible.

___ 3. If a U.S. dollar had been worth 2 German marks in 1987 and 4 German marks in 1988, then American goods would have been more expensive in Germany in 1988 than in 1987.

___ 4. In a wholly owned foreign affiliate arrangement, the local company maintains some autonomy.

___ 5. Low uncertainty avoidance means that people have a low tolerance for the unstructured, the unclear, and the unpredictable.

___ 6. The greenfield venture is the most risky type of direct investment.

___ 7. A wholly owned affiliate is under the complete control of the parent company.

___ 8. An MNC receives more than 25 percent of its total sales revenue from foreign operations.

___ 9. MNC top managers are presumed to have an ethnocentric orientation.

___ 10. The European Union has become a single market.

Short-Answer Questions

1. Is there any difference between international management and domestic management?

2. How might a difference in religion affect international business operations?

3. What are the advantages and disadvantages of using exporting as a market entry strategy internationally?

4.   Why has European industry changed from opposing to embracing the *Europe '92* initiative?

5.   Explain why anyone would oppose NAFTA.

Management Applications

Ramadan and Business

In Moslem countries Ramadan, the Moslem holy month, is celebrated each year. During Ramadan Moslems are forbidden from partaking of food, drink, tobacco, and sexual intercourse during daylight hours. As a result many of them do eat, drink, and have fun all through the night. The results are that often the next day workers are tired and sleepy. They have little energy and cannot eat or drink to revitalize themselves. Absenteeism is usually high during this period. This period of fasting lasts from dawn until sunset. Most workers expect bonuses to support their all-night hospitality. Food consumption soars as much as 50 percent above normal during this month. Traffic accidents and crimes of passion increase during this period of time also.

1. Assume that you have just been assigned by the MNC for which you work to manage a subsidiary in a strict Moslem country. What problems might you encounter as a result of Ramadan?

2. What actions, if any, would you take to deal with this situation?

Those Strange Americans

American business culture is thought to be strange in some respects to foreigners. Below is a short summary of some of the differences.

a.   Americans interrupt conversations, Japanese do not.

b.   American managers expect more autonomy than do Swiss managers.

c.   American managers expect explanations for substandard performance, Japanese managers expect repeated apologies.

d.   In Puerto Rico businesspeople begin meetings with relaxed chitchat, while Americans abruptly plunge right into the matter at hand.

e.   Americans appear more informal than Europeans by using first names. Such informality with Europeans deceives them into believing that a matter is not important.

f.   American management style is perceived to be a macho, cowboy, I'm-in-charge style, as opposed to the European collegial approach.

1.   What types of problems might an American manager who is transferred to Europe have?

2.   What types of problems might a European manager who is transferred to North America have?

3.   What types of problems might a Japanese manager who is transferred to North America have?

Mini Case

International Medical Joint Ventures

On March 24, 1999, Gambro AB, a leading international medical technology and health-care company, and Baxter Healthcare Corporation, a leading global medical products and services company, announced that they have established a U.S.-based manufacturing joint venture for dialyzers.

Dialyzers are used to purify the blood of patients suffering from kidney disease and receiving hemodialysis. With this joint venture, combined manufacturing volumes of both Baxter and Gambro will be leveraged with significant cost benefits for both companies. The manufactured dialyzers will continue to be marketed and sold independently to health-care providers by both Baxter and Gambro.

Eric Beard, corporate vice president and president of Baxter's Renal Dialysis business, said, "This agreement underlines Baxter's commitment to the continual improvement of hemodialysis therapy and will help service the growing dialysis requirements worldwide. I am pleased that the joint venture can build on Baxter's manufacturing quality and production expertise to service a large portion of both companies' dialyzer requirements."

Mats Wahlström, executive vice president of Gambro and responsible for Renal Care Services, stated, "This deal will allow Gambro to quickly establish manufacturing of dialyzers in the U.S. and to supply the demand for single-use dialyzers of Gambro dialysis clinics. The single-use strategy is an important part of our total-system approach whereby we are reengineering the entire process in our dialysis clinics to improve the long-term efficiency. We hope to generate annual savings of more than SEK 50 M (U.S. $6.1 million) in our dialysis clinics when the new dialyzers have been fully implemented. Currently single-use dialyzers are used in about one-quarter of Gambro's own clinics. We have a very deliberate strategy to increase single use, which will strengthen the position of Gambro in the U.S. as a provider of high-quality renal care."

The joint venture will source its dialyzers from an existing Baxter production facility in Mountain Home, Ark. Baxter will manage the day-to-day operations on behalf of the joint venture.

Gambro is a global medical technology and health-care company with leading positions in renal care – services and products – and blood component technology (BCT). Gambro is the second largest provider of kidney dialysis services in the world. Gambro treats about 40,000 patients in 460 clinics worldwide. Renal care products comprise dialyzers, dialysis machines, blood lines and dialysis fluid. BCT includes products for the separation and handling of blood components. The Group, with revenue of approximately SEK 19 billion (U.S. $2.3 billion) has approximately 18,000 employees in some 40 countries.

Baxter International Inc. (NYSE:BAX) is a global medical products and services company that focuses on critical therapies for life-threatening conditions. Baxter's products and services in blood therapies (biopharmaceuticals and blood collection, separation and storage devices), cardiovascular medicine, medication delivery and renal therapy are used by health-care providers and their critically ill patients in 112 countries. **Source:** http://www.baxter.com/utilities/news/index.html

1. Why do you think these two companies made this move?

2. What are the advantages to Gambro of this move?

3. Do you think alliances across national boundaries such as this will continue to occur? Explain your answer.

Experiential Exercise

Playing the Exchange Rates

You are the manager for Ford Motor Company of Europe. Currently, you are selling a Ford car in Germany for $8,000. The foreign exchange rate of 3 Euros for $1 means that the local price for the car is 24,000 Euros. You recently visited a new kind of expert, the Foreign Exchange Gypsy, who has told you that next Thursday the foreign exchange rate will be 2.4 Euros = $1.

1. Assuming the Foreign Exchange Gypsy (FEG) to be accurate, what would the price of the Ford be in local currency after next Thursday?

2. What action, if any, would you want to take? Why?

3. If the FEG is wrong and the foreign exchange rate goes to 3.5 Euros = $1, what effect would this have on the decision you made in response to the previous question?

4. Be prepared to discuss your answers in class if so directed.

Study Guide Solutions

Chapter Review

Multiple-Choice Questions

1	2	3	4	5	6	7	8	9	10
a	b	d	e	c	c	a	c	a	b

11	12	13	14	15	16	17	18	19	20
e	c	c	e	c	e	c	a	b	e

21	22	23	24	25	26	27	28	29	30
a	d	d	b	b	b	a	c	d	a

True/False Questions

1	2	3	4	5	6	7	8	9	10
F	T	T	F	F	T	T	T	F	F

Short-Answer Questions

1. The basic tasks of management are the same for international and domestic management. However, the implementation of these functions will vary because of differences in political and legal system, economy, business practices, and the sociocultural environment.

2. One must consider religious taboos for products and advertising in the host country. The ethics described by the religion will also have an impact.

3. Exporting involves the lowest cost and risk of all the strategies. It is a neat way to get your products into other markets. However, the long distances, government regulations, and differences in currencies and cultures can often cause problems. Also, the profit is not as great as it could be with more direct involvement.

4. European industry has come to embrace the *Europe '92* initiatives because it has lead to increased competition and economies of scale within Europe, which will enable companies to grow and become more competitive worldwide.

5. NAFTA is opposed by some who fear a job loss to Mexico and the potential for industrial "ghost towns." Others feel that it can also endanger the environment.

Management Applications

Ramadan and Business

1. A manager assigned to such a situation would run into many problems. Tired and unmotivated employees would obviously be a problem. The same type of behavior could also be expected from suppliers and customers. Temper flare-ups could also be expected.

2. A manager who would have to manage employees during Ramadan in a Moslem country would have to make adjustments. One approach would be to assume that nothing much was going to be accomplished and to plan the work accordingly. Shifting the hours of operation to night might also be helpful. Offering incentives such as bonuses might also be tried.

Those Strange Americans

1. An American manager would have to realize that he could not operate as autonomously or with as much of a take-charge style as he might be used to. Instead, he would have to consider other managers more as colleagues. He would also have to get used to more formal methods of interacting with others.

2. A European manager would have to realize that more autonomy is provided in North America. He would also have to be willing to take charge more often and to be more informal in communicating with others.

3. A Japanese manager who is transferred to North America would have to learn not to offer apologies for failures, nor to expect them. He would also have to learn to be more assertive including interrupting conversations when needed.

Mini Case

The International Aircraft Business

1. These companies made this move because both companies gain significant benefits from the move. They can both better serve their markets own markets and can now expand into new markets jointly. They also will generate cost savings.

2. Gambro can quickly establish manufacturing of dialyzers in the U.S. and also can better supply the demand for single-use dialyzers of Gambro dialysis clinics. Thye also hope to generate annual savings in their dialysis clinics when the new dialyzers have been fully implemented.

3. With the development of a borderless world, one could safely predict that these types of alliances would continue across national borders. The trend toward such alliances seems to be picking not only continuing, but increasing.

Experiential Exercise

Playing the Exchange Rates

1. The new local price would be 19,200 Euros if no adjustments were made.

2. You may want to keep the local price at 24,000 Euros and enjoy the increased profit. You may want to let it just drop to 19,200 Euros so that your price is lower to local consumers and therefore you should sell more.

3. If the exchange rate is 3.5 Euros = $1, the local price would be 28,000 Euros if left alone. This would make it more expensive than earlier and would probably mean lower sales. In this case you may want to keep the price at 24,000 Euros and just suffer the loss to remain competitive.

Chapter 5

Managerial Ethics and Corporate Social Responsibility

Chapter Summary

After you have read the text chapter, read through the summary below. Cover the left-hand margin and fill in the blanks with the appropriate terms. After you have filled in each blank, check your responses by uncovering the answer given in the margin. If you do not understand why the given answer is the correct one, refer back to the text.

What Is Managerial Ethics?

Ethics

_____ is the code of moral principles and values that govern the behaviors of a person or group with respect to what is right or wrong. It is the middle ground between codified law and free choice where no specific laws govern behavior and yet conduct is based on shared principles and values. An

ethical dilemma

_____ arises when all alternative choices are undesirable due to negative ethical consequences. The person who must make an ethical choice in an organization is the *moral agent*.

Criteria for Ethical Decision Making

utilitarian

One of the four normative approaches to decision making can be helpful in solving ethical dilemmas. The _____ approach holds that moral behaviors produce the greatest good for the greatest number and that the decision maker should consider the effects and choose the alternative that will

Individualism

benefit the majority. _____ contends that acts are moral when they promote the individual's best long-term interests. In the long run individualism is believed to benefit the entire society and lead to honesty and integrity. The

moral-rights

_____ approach asserts that people have fundamental rights that cannot be taken away by an individual's decision and the best decision is the

justice

one that maintains the rights of the people affected. The _____ approach holds that moral decisions must be based on standards of equity, fairness, and impartiality. There are three types of moral justice to be

Distributive

considered. _____ justice specifies that different treatment of people should not be based on arbitrary characteristics. _____ justice requires

Procedural
compensatory

that rules be administered fairly and consistently, while _____ justice says that individuals should be compensated for the cost of their injuries and that people should not be held responsible for matters over which they have no control.

Factors Affecting Ethical Choices

preconventional
conventional
principled

Both the manager and the organization affect ethical decision making. The manager has his own personality and behavioral traits that influence the decision. The manager's stage of moral development will affect behavior. At the _____ *level*, a manager is concerned with external rewards and punishment. At the _____ *level*, a manager conforms to the expectations of others. On the _____ *level*, a manager develops an internal set of standards and values. The principled level is important when considering international issues such as foreign bribery. The corporate culture also influences ethical decision making. It provides socialization and ethical signals to communicate expected behavior. Organizational culture, rules, policies, rewards, standards, and leadership also affect ethical choices.

What Is Social Responsibility?

responsibility

Social _____ is the obligation to make choices and take actions that will contribute to the welfare and interests of society as well as to the organization.

Organizational Stakeholders

Stakeholder

A _____ is any group within or outside the organization that has a stake in the organization's performance. Each stakeholder makes demands on the organization that may be conflicting with each other. These stakeholders include employees, customers, owners, creditors, suppliers, investors, the government, the community, and special-interest groups.

The Natural Environment

legal

market

stakeholder
activist

One model uses the phrase "shades of green" to evaluate a company's commitment to environmental responsibility. Under the _____ approach, an organization does just what is necessary to satisfy legal requirements. The _____ approach represents a growing awareness of and sensitivity to environmental concerns, primarily to satisfy customers. The _____ approach means that companies attempt to answer the environmental concerns of various stakeholder groups. An _____ *approach* searches for ways to conserve the earth's resources. The proportion of the population supporting environmental issues is increasing.

Evaluating Corporate Social Performance

maximize
Legal

Ethical
Discretionary

Milton Friedman has argued that a corporation has a responsibility to _____ profits, and that by so doing, market forces will direct companies to be socially responsible. _____ responsibility refers to doing what society considers appropriate behavior, as codified in laws and regulations. _____ responsibility means acting with equity, fairness, and impartiality and respecting the rights of individuals. _____ responsibility refers to actions that are strictly voluntary and go beyond societal expectations in contributing to the welfare of society.

Managing Company Ethics and Social Responsibility

code of ethics

ethics committee

chief ethics
 officer

Whistle-blowing

Management may become more responsive by employing three pillars that support an ethical organization. The first pillar is made up of managers who are ethical individuals. The second pillar is ethical leadership and the third is organizational structures and systems that support ethics. Top management provides the leadership regarding ethical behavior in any organization. A _____ is a formal statement of the organization's values regarding ethics and social issues. It may include principle-based or policy-based statements. One ethical structure is an _____, which is a group of executives appointed to over-see company ethics by ruling on questionable issues and disciplining violators. Another ethical structure is the use of ethics officers headed by a _____, who is oversees all aspects of ethics and legal compliance. Ethics training programs help employees deal with ethical questions and translate the values stated in a code of ethics into everyday behavior. _____ is the disclosure by an employee of illegal, immoral, or illegitimate practices by the organization.

Ethics and the New Workplace

Research has shown a small positive relationship between social responsibility and financial performance. Two-thirds of customers say they would switch brands to do business with a company that is ethical and socially responsible.

Chapter Review

Multiple-Choice Questions: Please indicate the correct response to the following questions by writing the letter of the correct answer in the space provided.

___   1.   The code of moral principles and values that govern the behaviors of a person or group with respect to what is right or wrong is called
     a.   codified law.
     b.   ethics.
     c.   free choice.
     d.   personal standard.
     e.   legal standard.

___   2.   Behavior for which an individual or organization enjoys complete freedom is called
     a.   ethics.
     b.   codified law.
     c.   free choice.
     d.   legal standard.
     e.   social standard.

___   3.   Which of the following is *not* a concern of ethics?
     a.   what is right
     b.   what is profitable
     c.   what is wrong
     d.   setting standards for behavior
     e.   setting standards for decision making

___   4.   According to the text, human behavior falls into the three categories of
     a.   ethical, unethical, and gray behavior.
     b.   physiological, psychological, and religious behavior.
     c.   codified law, free choice, and ethics.
     d.   social, reclusive, and ethics.
     e.   personal, social, and principle-based behavior.

___   5.   In the domain of ethical behavior is
     a.   obedience to unenforceable norms and standards.
     b.   obedience to laws.
     c.   obedience to what one personally feels is right.
     d.   obedience to regulatory agencies.
     e.   obedience to conscience.

___ 6. When the state of Oregon decided to extend Medicaid to 400,000 previously ineligible. recipients by refusing to pay for high-cost, high-risk procedures such as liver transplants and bone-marrow transplants, it used the _____ approach.
   a. utilitarian
   b. individualism
   c. moral-rights
   d. justice
   e. procedural

___ 7. Advocates of the individualism approach claim that in the long-term employing of this approach
   a. the greater good is served.
   b. people learn to accommodate each other.
   c. lying and cheating will cease.
   d. honesty and integrity will result.
   e. all of the above

___ 8. The moral right of freedom of conscience says that
   a. individuals are to be treated only as they knowingly and freely consent to be treated.
   b. individuals have a right to live without endangerment or violation of their health and safety.
   c. individuals may refrain from carrying out any order that violates their moral or religious norms.
   d. individuals have a right to an impartial hearing and fair treatment.
   e. individuals can choose to do as they please away from work.

___ 9. The argument that individuals should be compensated for the cost of their injuries by the party responsible is presented by advocates of
   a. compensatory justice.
   b. the moral-rights approach.
   c. procedural justice.
   d. the utilitarian approach.
   e. distributive justice.

___ 10. The level of moral development at which internal values are more important than expectations of significant others is the _____ stage.
   a. preconventional
   b. conventional
   c. postconventional
   d. principled
   e. self-righteous

___ 11. Social responsibility
   a. is difficult to understand.
   b. means considering the interests of society and the organization.
   c. considers only the welfare of society, not of the organization.
   d. does not mean being a good corporate citizen.
   e. does not consider managerial actions.

___ 12. Under the _____ *approach* an organization does just what is necessary to sagisfy legal requirements.
   a. *legal*
   b. *market*
   c. *stakeholder*
   d. *activist*
   e. none of the above

___ 13. The _____ *approach* attempts to answer the environmental concerns of various stakeholder groups.
   a. *legal*
   b. *market*
   c. *stakeholder*
   d. *activist*
   e. none of the above

___ 14. The ethics committee
   a. involves the disclosure by an employee to an outside authority of some company indiscretion.
   b. rules on questionable issues.
   c. directly violates a code of ethics.
   d. usually conducts social audits monthly.
   e. violates individual privacy rights.

___ 15. It has been found by research that good citizenship by companies
   a. always lowers profits.
   b. always increases financial performance.
   c. is usually ignored by everyone.
   d. usually hurts the company.
   e. has a small positive relationship with financial performance.

___ 16. _____ responsibility defines the ground rules, laws, and regulations that businesses are expected to follow.
   a. Economic
   b. Legal
   c. Ethical
   d. Discretionary
   e. Accommodative

___ 17.   _____ responsibility is purely voluntary and guided by a company's desire to make social contributions.
a.   Economic
b.   Legal
c.   Ethical
d.   Discretionary
e.   Accommodative

___ 18.   Principle-based codes of ethics include statements about
a.   treatment of employees.
b.   marketing practices.
c.   conflicts of interests.
d.   political gifts.
e.   observance of laws.

___ 19.   A chief ethics officer is responsible for
a.   developing ethics training programs.
b.   maintaining a corporate hot line.
c.   providing rulings on questionable issues.
d.   being the corporate conscience.
e.   pacifying outside groups.

___ 20.   The code of ethics at Lockheed Martin
a.   details an appropriate level of potential profits.
b.   included in the letter that accompanies a booklet sent to all employees.
c.   is determined by employee vote.
d.   violates organizational cultural norms.
e.   hurts the company's reputation.

___ 21.   Whistle-blowing refers to
a.   inflating product benefits in advertisements.
b.   telling the public about unethical practices of competitors.
c.   the reporting of questionable practices by an employee.
d.   actions by regulatory agencies in response to unethical behavior by corporations.
e.   taking time out in ethical disputes to consider the other party's point of view.

___ 22.   Recent studies have shown that when price and quality are equal, _____ of customers say they would switch brands to do business with a company that is ethical and socially responsible.
a.   one-fifth
b.   one-fourth
c.   one-third
d.   two thirds
e.   three-fourths

___   23.   When CenterBeam stuck by promises it had made that cost it money, it resulted in
      a.   the company going bankrupt.
      b.   more trust from stakeholders.
      c.   costly lawsuits from suppliers.
      d.   angry stockholders who lost money.
      e.   government intervention.

___   24.   Sears was recently hit with a lawsuit alleging that the company
      a.   charged customers for tire balancing that wasn't done.
      b.   had stolen its name from a small Wyoming store.
      c.   false advertising claims.
      d.   sexual harassment within its company.
      e.   not paying honoring its warranties.

___   25.   The domain of free choice pertains to behavior
      a.   dictated by the law that one may choose to obey or disobey.
      b.   about which the law has no say.
      c.   for which an individual does not have complete freedom.
      d.   for which standards of conduct are based on shared values about moral conduct.
      e.   of a sexual nature.

___   26.   If you have been asked to fire a marketing supervisor for cheating the company out of $500 when you know that a manufacturing supervisor allows thousands of dollars of waste due to poor work habits, you are dealing with
      a.   an ethical dilemma.
      b.   a utilitarian decision.
      c.   a stupid company.
      d.   a question of social responsibility.
      e.   an issue for an chief ethics officer.

___   27.   According to the _____ approach, the ethically correct decision is the one that best maintains the rights of those people affected by it.
      a.   utilitarian
      b.   individualism
      c.   moral-rights
      d.   justice
      e.   ethics

___   28.   _____ requires that different treatment of people not be based on arbitrary characteristics.
      a.   Ethical behavior
      b.   Distributive justice
      c.   The utilitarian approach
      d.   The ethics committee
      e.   Compensatory justice

___ 29. When a Navy pilot disobeyed orders and risked his life to save men from the *USS Indianapolis* when it sank, he was operating from the _____ level of moral development.
   a. invisible
   b. rebellious
   c. highest
   d. selfish
   e. social

___ 30. At the _____ level of moral development one follows the rules to avoid physical punishment.
   a. physiological
   b. preconventional
   c. conventional
   d. postconventional
   e. principled

True/False Questions: Please indicate whether the following questions are true or false by writing a T or an F in the blank in front of each question.

___ 1. Personal ethics may come from an individual's religious background.

___ 2. An accommodative response means being socially responsible due to external pressures.

___ 3. Social audits are used frequently by U.S. businesses.

___ 4. Whistle-blowers are guaranteed protection by the Civil Rights Act of 1964.

___ 5. If it's not illegal, it must be ethical.

___ 6. According to the right of due process, individuals have a right to an impartial hearing and fair treatment.

___ 7. Procedural justice requires that rules be administered fairly.

___ 8. Upholding values and rights regardless of majority opinion illustrates the principled stage of moral development.

___ 9. In most companies employees do not believe that if they do not go along with the ethical values expressed, their jobs will be in jeopardy or they will not fit in.

___ 10. Those who follow the *market approach* respond to customers demands.

Short-Answer Questions

1. Which choice is more difficult to make, one governed by law or ethics?

2. Explain which approach you feel is more prevalent among managers today—the utilitarian, individualism, or moral-rights approach?

3. How might a manager whose personal moral development is at the conventional level make a decision in an organization that tends to operate "on the shady side"?

4. Explain a time when you think it would be appropriate to take each one of the four corporate responses to social demands.

Management Applications

Tobacco Advertising

A court in Paris has banned an advertising campaign by Philip Morris that argues breathing secondhand tobacco smoke poses a smaller health risk than eating cookies or drinking milk or fluoridated water.

It is the first time a court has banned an issue-based ad campaign by the European unit of the maker of Marlboro cigarettes.

Meanwhile, challenges to the ads, now running many European countries, are still underway.

Source: *ASH - ACTION ON SMOKING AND HEALTH; 2013 H Street, NW / Washington, DC 20006 / (202) 659-431.* Webpage: http://ash.org/deceptive.html

1.   If you were a television station in Germany, would this court ruling in France influence your decision to continue running the Philip Morris ads?

2.   If you worked for a grocery chain in Europe that made a nice profit on the sale of Marlboro cigarettes, would you take a stand against smoking?

3. If you worked for a television station in Europe that decided to continue running the Philip Morris ads, what would you do?

A Gift or a Bribe?

Steve enjoyed his job as a wholesale buyer for Affiliated Grocers of Phoenix. He was assigned to buy health and beauty aids for the wholesaler who then resold these products to retail accounts. Steve had the opportunity to buy his products not only from national manufacturers, but also from private brand manufacturers and other intermediaries. Sometimes when he needed to buy more of a product, he had a choice among several sources of supply for the same brand name. By looking through the catalogs of these suppliers, he could often save the company money on a purchase.

One of the benefits to being a buyer was being taken out to lunch by the sales representatives who called on Steve. He enjoyed the nice restaurants and the chance to get to know his suppliers better. Often these suppliers would give Steve free samples of their products to facilitate the buying decision. When Steve asked senior management whether it was okay to keep these samples, he was told that if they were smaller than a TV set, he could keep them. If they were larger than a TV set, they belonged to the company.

One day Steve mentioned to one of his suppliers in Los Angeles over the telephone that he was coming to L.A. that weekend with his wife. The supplier asked where he was staying, and when Steve said he wasn't sure, the supplier offered to pay his hotel bill in one of the more swanky hotels in the area. Knowing that this was probably bigger than a TV, Steve again went to senior management for guidance. He was told in essence to go ahead and enjoy the trip, but not to let it influence his buying.

1.   Is this an ethical dilemma for Steve?

2.   If you were in Steve's position, what would you do? Why?

3.   Do you think that this trip, if taken, would affect his buying practices?

Mini Case

Gwen Ferguson is a Communications Management Consultant in Charlotte, North Carolina. She conducts various workshops to help persons improve communication skills. Most of the work she does is "in-house" training. She goes to the place of business of the client and conducts training sessions for the employees of the client. She is very good at what she does and stays very busy. Recently, Gwen was approached by a college executive training center to provide training for a client. She was asked to visit with the client and design a series of workshops to be provided through the executive training center.

Gwen met with the client and had a very good meeting. She and the client agreed on 12 different training sessions for Gwen to present. In the course of the discussion the client representative, Mr. Brown, said, "I wish we could just take the middleman out of this arrangement. Would it be possible for us to hire you directly rather than your going through the college's executive training center?"

1. How would you answer this question if you were in Gwen's position?

Gwen said that she felt that she had a moral obligation to work through the college since it had provided the contact in the first place. Mr. Brown said he understood. Gwen then provided the college with the outline of proposed workshops. The director of the college executive training center said to Gwen, "You know that we will only tell you how much we will pay you for providing these workshops to the client. You will not know how much the client is paying us."

Gwen felt very uncomfortable with this arrangement. She does not want the client to be taken advantage of even if she is paid what she feels is reasonable. She is considering demanding that the college tell her how much the client is paying for this service so she will feel comfortable with the arrangement. If the college will not tell her this information or provide a price to the client that she feels is fair, she is considering withdrawing from the arrangement altogether.

2.   Do you think the college has the right to withhold this information from Gwen?

3.   Do you feel that Gwen has the right to demand to know all of the financial arrangements? Why do you think she wants to know so badly?

4.   If Gwen does end up withdrawing from the arrangement and the college finds someone else to take her place, the client could end up not liking the substitute (or the price) and decide to cancel the arrangement itself. If this happens and the client then calls Gwen directly to ask her to provide the services, should she do it? If so, should she pay the college anything?

Experiential Exercise

Part One

Read the following statements and then indicate the order of priority you would give them in the space provided. For example, if you feel that statement D is the most important, put it in the number 1 blank.

A.   When making a decision, it is a good idea to consult the persons who will be affected by the decision first.

B.   The best decision is the one personally that provides you with the best long-term advantage.

C.   There are certain basic human rights that must be considered in every decision.

D.   The best choice is the one that does not interfere with the fundamental rights of others.

E.   If everybody did what was best for them, in the long run everyone would be better off.

F.   When computing various costs of alternative choices, the one that costs the least to the greatest number of people is the best choice.

G.   For a decision to be good, it should benefit the greatest number of people.

H.   The choice that provides you personally with more good than bad is the best choice.

I.   The best decision is the one that best protects the rights of the people affected by the decision.

Priority	Weight
1.	
2.	
3.	
4.	
5.	
6.	
7.	
8.	
9.	

Part Two

After filling in the priorities above, place a weight on each statement by placing a number between 1 and 10 in the second column. The more important you feel an item is the higher the number you should assign to it. This will allow you to indicate the distance between your ranking of statements from Part One.

Part Three

Add up your weights for the items on the form below and add up each column to determine your U score, I score, and M score.

Weight on A			Weight on B			Weight on C	
Weight on F			Weight on E			Weight on D	
Weight on G			Weight on H			Weight on I	
U score			**I score**			**M score**	

Part Four

Your **U score** indicates your leanings toward the utilitarian approach. Your **I score** indicates your leanings toward the individualism approach. Your **M score** indicates your leanings toward the moral-rights approach. Be ready to discuss the results of this in class if so directed by your instructor.

Study Guide Solutions

Chapter Review

Multiple-Choice Questions

1	2	3	4	5	6	7	8	9	10
b	c	b	c	a	a	e	c	a	d

11	12	13	14	15	16	17	18	19	20
b	a	c	b	e	b	d	a	a	b

21	22	23	24	25	26	27	28	29	30
c	d	b	a	b	a	c	b	c	b

True/False Questions

1	2	3	4	5	6	7	8	9	10
T	T	F	F	F	T	T	T	F	T

Short-Answer Questions

1. It would seem that a choice governed by ethics would be more difficult to make than one governed by law. If the law governs the choice, then the behavior is prescribed, or at least one knows the legal consequences of a given action. For ethics the behavior is based on shared principles and values, all of which may be subject to interpretation. Another factor making the ethical decision more difficult is variations of principles and values from one group to another. If a person is a member of two different groups having variations of principles and ethics, the ethical dilemmas result.

2. Since this question requires an opinion, answers will vary. An argument could be made for the utilitarian approach since managers should be considering the good of the organization. One would expect to see this more at upper levels of management where performance is judged based on the entire organization. One could also argue for the individualism approach, especially among lower-level managers who are anxious for career advancement. With the heightened level of morality in modern society, one could even make an argument for the moral-rights approach.

3. A manager whose level of personal development is the conventional stage will feel that good behavior is living up to what is expected by others. He will want to fulfill duties and obligations of the social system and uphold laws. If the most important social system to this manager is the organization for which he works, his behavior would be a reflection of the values of that

organization. Therefore, if the organization tends to operate "on the shady side" of things, so will the manager.

4.   The *obstructive* approach would seem to be appropriate when the company feels that it is being unjustly accused of wrongdoing. This also buys the company time to devise a long-range plan. The *defensive* response seems to be appropriate when it becomes obvious that the company has made a mistake and that trying to cover it up would only serve to damage the company. The *accommodative* response is appropriate when the external pressures become very severe and to further resist would be damaging. The *proactive* response is appropriate when the firm feels strongly about an issue or when it wishes to improve its public image.

Management Applications

Tobacco Advertising

1.   The answer to this question is highly personal. It depends on how strongly one feels about smoking. If it is an ethical issue to you and you feel strongly about it, you may well decided to no longer run the advertisements. If you feel that it is a matter of freedom of choice whether one smokes or not, you may decide not to follow this continue the ads. The court decision in France has no legal authority over your decision, so this is an ethical question.

2.   This question points out the ethical dilemma that many businesses face. You might say that if you do not sell the products someone else will, or that it will cause customers to shop elsewhere because these products are not available at your store. The answer will probably depend on the level of moral development of each individual.

3.   This question hints toward the difficulty one might have in distancing himself from products he feels are unethical. The answer to the question is highly personal. If you decided to continue working at the television station, you would have to come to grips with the fact that the advertisements are continuing. If you do not feel that continuing the advertisements is unethical, you would have no problem. It would take a high level of moral development to quit the job over this issue.

A Gift or a Bribe?

1.   Although Steve certainly faces a dilemma in this situation, it is not by definition an ethical dilemma. If he lets the supplier pay his hotel bill, he feels uncomfortable with the choice. He feels that this would be a negative ethical consequence. If he takes the other course of action and pays his own bill, he does not face a negative ethical consequence. The only real choice here for Steve is the question of whether accepting yet another gift is unethical.

2.   The answer to this question is personal and depends on the personal ethics of the respondent. This case is a true story, and Steve did go on the trip and enjoyed himself. Later, it bothered him that he allowed his hotel bill to be paid by the supplier, however.

3. The response to this question is once more a matter of opinion. Since this is a case based on fact, it can be said that Steve felt that it did indeed affect his buying behavior. This bothered him greatly and was one of the influencing factors in Steve's decision to seek another career.

Mini Case

1. Your answer will depend on your own value system. The standard practice in this type of situation is not to delete the middleman since he was the one who made this contact possible in the first place. He has provided both the client and Gwen with something of value and deserves to be compensated for it.

2. Certainly, the college has the right to withhold this information from Gwen. It has no legal obligation to tell her how much it is charging the client.

3. Legally, Gwen probably does not have the right to demand to know all of this information. She probably wants to know so that she can be sure that the client is not being overcharged for the service she provides. The argument could be made that if the client is willing to pay and Gwen is receiving a fee she feels good about, it is none of her business what the client pays.

4. This last question is very tough. The argument might be made that since the college provided the initial contact that resulted in Gwen's ultimately being asked to do the job, that it still deserves to receive remuneration. Gwen might argue that since the college was not willing to meet her terms, her contract with the college is null and void and that she then has the right to do business with whomever she wishes.

Experiential Exercise

The results of this exercise will vary for each person. The discussion will depend on the results. The questions are based on the material in the text.

Chapter 6

Small-Business and Internet Start-Ups

Chapter Summary

After you have read the text chapter, read through the summary below. Cover the left-hand margin and fill in the blanks with the appropriate terms. After you have filled in each blank, check your responses by uncovering the answer given in the margin. If you do not understand why the given answer is the correct one, refer back to the text.

What Is Entrepreneurship?

Entrepreneurship

entrepreneur

idealist

optimizer
sustainer
hard worker
juggler

The American dream is to own one's own business, to be an entrepreneur. _____ is the process of initiating a business venture, organizing the necessary resources, and assuming the associated risks and rewards. A person who engages in entrepreneurship is called an _____, someone who recognizes a viable idea for a business product or service and carries it out. With American corporations downsizing and frustration with corporate lifestyles, many persons are electing to become entrepreneurs. Small business owners have been classified into six different categories. The _____ is the person who likes to create something new and be creative or personally meaningful. _____ are rewarded by the personal satisfaction of being a business owner. A _____ likes the chance to balance work and personal life, while the _____ _____ enjoys putting in the long hours to build the business. The _____ likes to handle everything personally.

Entrepreneurship and the Environment

globalization

Most new businesses start small and in the U.S. economy have a chance to grow. The _____ of business with increased competitive pressures has increased small businesses. Technological advances, such as computers and the Internet, have made it possible for small businesses to thrive. Many entrepreneurs find new opportunities to meet changing needs. Most people think of a small business as having fewer than 500 employees. New businesses create jobs, create new products and services, and provide opportunities for persons who may have careers blocked in established corporations.

Who Are Entrepreneurs?

internal locus
of control
external locus
of control
need to achieve

tolerance for
ambiguity

Entrepreneurs start with vision, have knowledge of their market and industry, and are hardworking and practical. They have an _____, which is the belief that their future is within their control and that other external forces will have little influence. This is the opposite of an _____, which is the belief by individuals that their future is not within their control but rather is influenced by external forces. Entrepreneurs also have a high energy level and a _____, a human quality in which people are motivated to excel and pick situations in which success is likely. The self-confidence of entrepreneurs is high as is their _____, the psychological characteristic that allows a person to be untroubled by disorder and uncertainty. They also tend to be impatient, tend to be the first born, and have parents who were entrepreneurs.

Starting an Entrepreneurial Firm

business plan

proprietorship
partnership
corporation

Debt financing
Equity

venture capital
firm

To start a new business the entrepreneur must have a new business idea and then develop a _____, which is a document specifying the business details. Next, the legal form of the business must be determined. It may be a _____, an unincorporated business that is owned by an individual for profit. A _____ is an unincorporated business owned by two or more people, and a _____ is an artificial entity created by the state and existing apart from its owners. There are advantages and disadvantages to each form as far as liability, profits, decision making, and other issues are concerned. Raising the funds needed is another concern of the entrepreneur. The primary source of money is one's own resources. _____ may also be used by borrowing money that has to be repaid to start a business. _____ financing consists of funds that are invested in exchange for ownership in the company. The entrepreneur may also use a _____, which is a group of companies or individuals that invest money in new or expanding businesses for ownership and potential profits.

Franchising

business incubator

There are several ways of becoming a business owner. One way is to simply start a new business from scratch. Another way is to buy an existing business. _____ is an arrangement by which the owner of a product or service allows others to purchase the right to distribute the product or service with help from the owner. Entrepreneurs may also join a _____, which is an innovation that provides shared office space, management support services, and management advice to entrepreneurs.

angel

Internet start-ups continue to be a popular way to start a new business. However, this requires more money to build the technology infrastructure and requires the entrepreneur to grow quickly, while providing little time for trial and error. The business plan for an Internet start-up must be very convincing and more condensed while providing for flexibility as the Internet world changes. Often the first funding for this type of business comes through *angel financing*. An _____ is a wealthy individual with business experience and contacts

launch

partnership

initial public

takeoff

who believes in the idea for the startup and is willing to invest personally to get it started. Next the entrepreneur must build and test the product or service. This requires legal and financial advice as well as expert technological personnel. The next phase is to _____ the product and services over the Internet. A catchy logo and visually appealing Web site are important, as is the name. Additional financing is usually needed to pay salaries, maintain infrastructure and marketing, and for expansion. A board of directors helps the company stay focused and can facilitate the development of partnerships.   One type of _____ is with a larger, well-established company that can help the smaller firm gain rapid market awareness. A second type is with a company that assists in actual operations. The final step in the startup process is often the _____ _____ offering (IPO), in which the stock is sold to the public.

Managing a Growing Business

Entrepreneurial companies generally move through several stages of growth. The stages are *start-up, survival, success,* _____, and *resource maturity*. In the early stages formal planning is lacking, but a strategic plan needs to eventually be developed. Initially, the organization structure is very informal, but must become more formal as the company grows. The leader's vision drives the company initially, and the entrepreneur must learn how to motivate employees. Control is important to the firm in every stage and usually becomes more sophisticated as the firm grows. Smaller companies sometimes can weather the chaos better due to their flexibility and speed in acting.

Chapter Review

Multiple-Choice Questions: Please indicate the correct response to the following questions by writing the letter of the correct answer in the space provided.

___ 1. An entrepreneur must
    a. assemble the resources for the new venture.
    b. take the risks of the new business.
    c. have a viable idea for a business.
    d. carry out an idea for a new business.
    e. all of the above

___ 2. Most people think of a business as small if it
    a. has fewer than 500 employees.
    b. is located in a small town.
    c. has assets of less than one million dollars.
    d. does business within one state only.
    e. is run by one powerful individual.

___ 3. Technological change often _____ small businesses.
    a. hurts
    b. helps
    c. eats up
    d. equals the size of
    e. compares with

___ 4. A(n) _____ is a small business owner who likes the idea of working on something that is new, creative, or personally meaningful.
    a. idealist
    b. optimizer
    c. hard worker
    d. juggler
    e. sustainer

___ 5. A _____ is a small business owner who enjoys putting in the long hours and dedication to build a larger, more profitable business.
    a. idealist
    b. optimizer
    c. hard worker
    d. juggler
    e. sustainer

___ 6. Most entrepreneurs have a(n) _____ locus of control.
    a. unquenchable
    b. external
    c. internal
    d. variable
    e. power-driven

___ 7. A survey of new business owners shows that half worked _____ hours or more per week.
    a. 40
    b. 50
    c. 60
    d. 70
    e. 80

___ 8. A high tolerance for ambiguity means a person
    a. cannot stand picky people.
    b. is untroubled by disorder and uncertainty.
    c. can postpone tangible rewards for years.
    d. has a high degree of self-confidence.
    e. can work long hours with ease.

___ 9. The demographic characteristics of entrepreneurs include which of the following?
    a. more likely to be the last born in the family
    b. parents who work for a major corporation
    c. starting their new business between the ages of 40 and 55
    d. children of immigrants
    e. children for whom the father was always present during childhood

___ 10. When coming up with an idea for a new business, it is important to
    a. pick an area in which one already has some experience.
    b. pick an idea for which there is a need in the marketplace.
    c. come up with a better way to do something, and then the demand for the product will naturally follow.
    d. do something different than what you are used to doing.
    e. both a and b

___ 11. A business plan will contain
    a. a tentative work schedule for employees.
    b. a blueprint of the physical facilities.
    c. a certification of a CPA.
    d. information about the industry and market.
    e. a certified check for starting the business.

___ 12. In the proprietorship the owner has _____ liability for the business.
   a. limited
   b. unlimited
   c. shared
   d. no
   e. corporate

___ 13. A corporation will usually live
   a. until the owners die.
   b. until the major stockholders die.
   c. until the stock is sold.
   d. regardless of whether the owners live or die.
   e. forever, regardless of financial status.

___ 14. Equity financing refers to
   a. borrowing money from the bank.
   b. money invested by owners.
   c. money obtained from potential customers.
   d. loans from the SBA.
   e. money borrowed from family or friends.

___ 15. When you buy an existing business,
   a. you may have to pay for goodwill the owner believes exists.
   b. you are guaranteed success.
   c. it takes longer to get started.
   d. you will have to establish procedures from scratch.
   e. you will not have to worry about bad habits within the business.

___ 16. The franchisee typically pays _____ for a franchise.
   a. a flat fee
   b. a percentage of gross sales
   c. a flat fee plus a percentage of gross sales
   d. a percentage of net profit
   e. a flat fee plus a percentage of net profit

___ 17. A business incubator provides
   a. baby-sitting services for mothers wanting to start a business.
   b. free financial aid to new businesses.
   c. shared office space for new businesses.
   d. ideas for starting up new businesses.
   e. ideas for circumventing government regulations.

___ 18. For which of the following needs will the government provide financial assistance?
    a. loans for disadvantaged small businesses
    b. loans for physical disasters
    c. small-business energy loans
    d. small-business pollution-control loans
    e. all of the above

___ 19. During the survival stage of an entrepreneurial business
    a. the main problem is producing the product or service.
    b. the main problem is obtaining customers.
    c. the key problem is how to grow rapidly.
    d. the major issue is to maintain flexibility and the entrepreneurial spirit.
    e. the major concern is generating sufficient cash flow to run the business.

___ 20. An entrepreneurial company that uses a low-cost strategy builds a competitive advantage by
    a. offering products below cost.
    b. producing products at the lowest possible cost.
    c. finding a narrow market segment.
    d. doing things differently than other firms.
    e. paying its employees less than other firms.

___ 21. Financial control is important during the _____ stage of the entrepreneurial firm's growth.
    a. startup
    b. survival
    c. success
    d. takeoff
    e. all of the above

___ 22. The business plan for an Internet startup
    a. covers different areas than a traditional plan.
    b. should show how the company will remain stable.
    c. must be convincing, yet have flexibility built in.
    d. is impossible to write.
    e. is not needed.

___ 23. Initial financing for an Internet startup
    a. usually comes through an IPO.
    b. often involves an *angel.*
    c. does not need to be as much money as for a traditional business.
    d. is not very vital, since you only need a PC and internet connection.
    e. all of the above.

___ 24. The environment for entrepreneurs in the United States is
   a. negative
   b. positive
   c. guarded
   d. pessimistic
   e. overregulated

___ 25. When an Internet startup is building and testing the product or service
   a. no legal advice is needed.
   b. financial assistance and advice is important.
   c. the hiring of a system architect can be postponed.
   d. a software engineer generally gets in the way.
   e. reliability need not yet be considered.

___ 26. When a Internet startup officially makes its products available to the public over the Internet it is in the _____ phase.
   a. idea
   b. business plan
   c. initial financing
   d. building and testing
   e. launch

___ 27. Once an Internet startup product has been launched additional financing
   a. is rarely needed.
   b. should not be sought for salaries.
   c. never involves venture capitalists.
   d. may be needed for growth and expansion.
   e. should never be sought from larger companies.

___ 28. The confidence level of entrepreneurs
   a. must be high.
   b. must not be too high to avoid discouragement.
   c. has nothing to do with their success.
   d. should be low so they will learn to delegate.
   e. is ambiguous.

___ 29. Information about the number and types of personnel needed in a new firm
   a. should be included in the business plan.
   b. is anybody's guess.
   c. should not be included in the business plan; that is too specific.
   d. need not be made until financing is obtained.
   e. ought to be planned for, but not written down.

___ 30. When an Internet company decides to "go public", it is
    a. launching its product on the Internet.
    b. beginning its advertising campaign.
    c. revealing information about its founders.
    d. offering stock for sell to the public.
    e. moving its headquarters to an open location.

True/False Questions: Please indicate whether the following questions are true or false by writing a T or an F in the blank in front of each question.

___ 1. Women and minorities are discovering the promise of entrepreneurship.

___ 2. An external locus of control is the belief that one's future is within one's own control.

___ 3. People with high achievement needs select goals that are very difficult to meet.

___ 4. Entrepreneurs tend to be very patient so their new business can thrive.

___ 5. Partnerships often dissolve within five years.

___ 6. Venture capital firms want new businesses with an extremely high rate of return.

___ 7. In some cases entrepreneurs start a new business because they disagree with former employers.

___ 8. The key problem during the *takeoff* phase is how to grow rapidly and finance that growth.

___ 9. During the success stage the company is solidly based and profitable.

___ 10. During the latter stages of entrepreneurial growth, the manager must learn to centralize authority.

Short-Answer Questions

1. What role does entrepreneurship play in the creation of jobs?

2. Why does the energy level of an entrepreneur have to be high?

3. Why is it important for an entrepreneur to write a business plan?

4. Which stage of growth is the "pivotal period in an entrepreneurial company's life?"

Management Applications

Why Do I Need a Business Plan?

Kay Payne is the director for the Nebraska Business Development Center at a medium-sized college in Nebraska. She has many people drop in to ask her for help. Many of them have ideas for new products or new businesses. The first thing she asks them to do after listening to their ideas is to write out a business plan.

1.   Why do you think that Kay asks these would-be entrepreneurs to write out a business plan?

2.   Many of these people have no idea of what a business plan is. What should Kay do about this?

3. Kay reports that many persons give up on their plans to become entrepreneurs after attempting to come up with a business plan. Do you think that this is good or bad?

Battery Cable Clamps

The management class listened intently as Donald Barker described his business. He had become tired of loosening the nuts that held on the battery cable clamps on the batteries of his vehicles whenever he wanted to change the battery. He had several farm vehicles and frequently had to change batteries or get them in out of the cold. So he had developed clamps that worked on the principle of levers without the use of bolts and nuts. The battery cables could be disconnected or connected in about one third of the time with his product.

1.   What do you think of Donald's product? Is there a market for it?

Donald had been so excited about his product that he had built a machine to produce it and had produced several thousand of the clamps. He had a package designed for the product and had put 12 packages in a shipping box. He and his wife had used their savings to buy a vacant store building for production and storage. In the evenings they would work producing the devices. He had sold several dozen of them through publicity and word of mouth. However, the inventory was now stacking up, and he wanted advice from the class on how to market this product.

2. What has Donald forgotten to do?

3. What advice would you give him?

Mini Case

The Porcelain Turtle

The student consulting team finally located the business it had been assigned to visit *The Porcelain Turtle*. It was located in a strip mall about one-half mile from a regional mall. The students and their faculty advisor had driven to make an initial visit to discover what they could do to help this business. The business had requested help from the Business Development Center of a local college. The students were to act as consultants for the business under the leadership of the faculty advisor. The visit yielded the following facts:

- The business had been in existence for three years and had not yet returned a profit.

- The business sold porcelain items, mainly for gifts, and other giftware.

- The business was located in a strip mall to avoid the high cost of rent in the regional mall. The population of the city, Grand Island, Nebraska, was about 30,000.

- The business was owned by Mr. and Mrs. Green. Mr. Green was a retired postal worker, and Mrs. Green had retired from teaching school prior to opening this business.

- The idea for the business came from the Greens' daughter who had a similar business in a major mall in Denver, Colorado.

- Mr. and Mrs. Green spent most of their time running the business, but Mr. Green said he would rather be traveling in his RV.

1. Do Mr. and Mrs. Green meet the personal characteristics of successful entrepreneurs?

2. Do you think the business has the potential for success?

3. If you were a member of this student team, what do you think your general recommendation would be?

Experiential Exercise

Gary's Cleaning Service

Gary Haycock decided to start a cleaning service while attending college in Boston. He figured that since there were many professionals in the area, his services would be in demand. He could clean offices and residences. He thought that he could hire college students for his work force. Not much money would be needed to start with. Most offices and homes have their own cleaning supplies.

Your instructor will assign you to small groups for this assignment. In your groups break up the work into segments for each person to perform. Afterwards, share with each other what you have done to make sure that it all fits together. Share your results with the class as directed by the instructor.

The task is to write a brief outline of a business plan for Gary's Cleaning Service. In spots you may have to identify what information is needed. In other places you may be able to recommend the actual plan. Use the outline in the text as your guide.

Study Guide Solutions

Chapter Review

Multiple-Choice Questions

1	2	3	4	5	6	7	8	9	10
e	a	b	a	c	c	c	b	d	e
11	**12**	**13**	**14**	**15**	**16**	**17**	**18**	**19**	**20**
d	b	d	b	a	c	c	e	e	b
21	**22**	**23**	**24**	**25**	**26**	**27**	**28**	**29**	**30**
e	c	b	b	b	e	d	a	a	d

True/False Questions

1	2	3	4	5	6	7	8	9	10
T	F	F	F	T	T	T	T	T	F

Short-Answer Questions

1. Estimates are that from 40 to 80 percent of all new jobs in the United States are created by small entrepreneurial firms. Approximately 5 million jobs a year are created from new businesses.

2. The energy level of an entrepreneur must be high to overcome obstacles as they occur. Entrepreneurs also work longer than those who work for others.

3. The preparation of a business plan forces the entrepreneur to carefully think through the proposed business. It also gives potential lenders and investors something to look at when the entrepreneur tries to secure funding.

4. The takeoff stage is the pivotal period because the entrepreneur must learn how to manage growth. The owner must learn how to delegate and find capital for growth.

Management Applications

Why Do I Need a Business Plan?

1. Kay probably makes these people come up with business plans so they will have to think through their ideas more thoroughly. It will also be an aid to them when they seek financing.

2. Kay should give the persons who do not know what a business plan is some sort of guide to help them. The SBA provides an excellent publication for this.

3. It is probably good that some drop their ideas at this point. The business plan seems to be serving as a screening device for poorly thought-out ideas or for persons without the needed skills or self-discipline to succeed as entrepreneurs.

Battery Cable Clamps

1. The product seems very clever. One cannot help but wonder if there is a large market for this product. How often do large numbers of people change the batteries on their cars?

2. Donald has forgotten to discover if there is a need for this product before producing it. It would appear that he also has not developed a marketing plan for the business.

3. I would advise him to immediately write a business plan. I would also tell him to suspend further production until it can be determined if a market exists and how it might be reached. This is a true case, and the class suggested that Donald consider the marine market. Owners of boats frequently remove their batteries.

Mini Case

The Porcelain Turtle

1. No, the Greens do not have the personal characteristics of successful entrepreneurs. They are older than one would expect, seem to have little enthusiasm for the business, and probably do not have high energy levels.

2. The business probably has little chance for success. The answers to the first question indicate this. The location is also poor. Avoiding high rent is good, but this type of store probably needs to be in a high traffic area. It may be that a city of this size is too small for this type of business also.

3. The student team (with the consent of the advisor) recommended that the Greens sell the business and enjoy their retirement in some other way.

Experiential Exercise

Gary's Cleaning Service

The amount of detail provided by each team will vary. Make sure that all segments from the text are covered in your plan.

Chapter 7

Organizational Planning and Goal Setting

Chapter Summary

After you have read the text chapter, read through the summary below. Cover the left-hand margin and fill in the blanks with the appropriate terms. After you have filled in each blank, check your responses by uncovering the answer given in the margin. If you do not understand why the given answer is the correct one, refer back to the text.

Overview of Goals and Plans

mission   The _____ of the organization describes what it stands for and its reason for existence. It provides legitimacy to outsiders and helps employees identify with the organization and become committed to it. Goals are important to organizations so that they can realize that purpose. The desired future state

goal   the organization attempts to realize is a _____. Based on the goals,

plan   plans are developed. A _____ is a blueprint for goal achievement and specifies the necessary resource allocations, schedules, tasks, and other actions.

Planning   _____ means determining the organization's goals and defining the means for achieving them. Goals are important for several reasons. They serve to indicate legitimacy, as a source of motivation and commitment, guide actions and decision making, and provide standards of performance.

Goals in Organizations

mission statement   The formal _____ is a broadly stated definition of basic business scope and operations that distinguishes the organization from others of a similar

strategic   type. A _____ goal is a broad statement of where the organization wants to be in the future. The difficult step of translating goals into plans

Strategic   involves several types of plans. _____ plans, the action steps by which an organization intends to attain its strategic goals, are usually long term and provide the design for organizational activities and resource distribution. A

tactical goal   _____ defines the results that major divisions and departments must

Tactical   achieve. _____ plans are designed to help execute major strategic plans and to accomplish a specific part of the organization's strategy. Tactical plans specify what the major units will do to activate the overall strategic plan. They involve a shorter time period and only a part of the strategic plan. An operational

Operational

_____ goal is the specific results expected from departments, work groups, or individuals. _____ plans indicate the action steps of lower-level managers towards achieving operational goals. They include the exact periods of time for completion of the objectives and must be correlated with the budget.

Criteria for Effective Goals

key result areas

For goals to be effective they should be specific and measurable and cover _____ of the organization. They must be challenging, but also realistic. The time period in which they are to be accomplished must also be defined, and they should be linked to rewards.

Planning Types and Performance

Management by
 Objectives

action plan

Planning and goal setting is to help the organization achieve high performance. One approach to planning is _____ which is a method whereby managers and employees define objectives for each department, project, and employee and use those objectives to control subsequent performance. The manager and subordinate jointly set goals, devise action plans to meet those objectives, review progress periodically, take corrective action if needed, and appraise overall performance. An _____ _____ defines the course of action needed to achieve stated objectives. MBO can be beneficial for maintaining focus on goals, improving performance, increasing motivation, and keeping objectives aligned. Problems with MBO include the fact that constant change prevents it from taking hold, poor human relations reduces its effectiveness, discouraging participation can harm it, and excessive paperwork saps its energy.

Single-use

Standing
policies

contingency plan
crisis

prevention

preparation
Containment

_____ plans are developed for one-time organizational goals. A *program* is a complex set of objectives and plans for achieving an important, one-time organizational goal, whereas a *project* is less complex, but still designed to achieve a major, one-time organizational goal. _____ plans are ongoing plans to guide the organization in repeated tasks. Standing plans include _____, which are general statements based on the organization's overall goals and strategic plans designed to provide direction. *Rules* describe how a specific action is to be performed and *procedures* specifically tell how a job is to be performed. A plan that defines company responses to be taken in the case of emergencies or setbacks is called a _____ _____. A special type of contingency planning is _____ management planning in response to a sudden and devastating event that requires an immediate response. Crisis management has three stages. The _____ stage involves activities managers undertake to prevent crises from occurring and to detect warning signs of potential crises. The _____ stage includes all the detailed planning to handle a crisis when it occurs. _____ focuses on the organization's response to an actual crisis and any follow-up concerns.

Planning in the New Workplace

central

In today's workplace, everyone becomes involved in strategy and planning. Three different approaches have been used to structure the organization for planning. The first of these approaches is the _____ planning department. This consists of a group of planning experts who develop plans for the entire organization and its major divisions and departments, reporting directly to the president or CEO. The second approach is to have planning experts assigned to major departments to help managers formulate their own plans. This approach is called the _____ planning staff. In the new workplace planning starts with a strong mission. Next you must set _____ goals which are highly ambitious goals that are so clear, compelling, and imaginative that they fire up employees and fuel progress. In the new workplace, managers create an environment that celebrates diversity, supports risk-taking, and encourages constant experimentation and learning. Another approach is the planning _____ method in which a temporary group of line managers is responsible for formulating strategic plans.

decentralized

stretch

task force

Chapter Review

Multiple-Choice Questions: Please indicate the correct response to the following questions by writing the letter of the correct answer in the space provided.

___ 1. What does a plan specify?
   a. resource allocations
   b. schedules
   c. future ends
   d. actions
   e. all of the above

___ 2. Which of the management functions is considered the most important?
   a. planning
   b. organizing
   c. leading
   d. controlling
   e. coordinating

___ 3. Which of the following indicates the correct chronological sequence of plans and goals?
   a. Plans must precede goals so that goals remain practical and realistic.
   b. Goals must precede plans so that we know what to plan for.
   c. They must occur simultaneously and influence each other.
   d. They must occur simultaneously, but be independent of each other to be objective.
   e. Goals must precede plans, but remain independent of the planning process.

___ 4. The _____ set(s) the planning premises for the organization.
   a. mission
   b. strategic goals
   c. strategic plans
   d. strategic objectives
   e. tactical plans

___ 5. Goals are the guide by which lower-level personnel _____ and _____.
   a. hire employees, fire employees
   b. set objectives, make plans
   c. impose sanctions, offer rewards
   d. conduct performance appraisals, give pay raises
   e. All of the above must be in accordance with goals.

___ 6. The _____ describes the organization's values and aspirations.
   a. strategic goal
   b. planning premise
   c. corporate plan
   d. mission statement
   e. strategic plan

___ 7. Broad statements of where the organization is going as a whole are called
   a. mission statements.
   b. strategic goals.
   c. strategic plans.
   d. organizational objectives.
   e. strategic objectives.

___ 8. Relationship building is an important part of the _____ stage of crisis management
   a. prevention
   b. preparation
   c. containment
   d. recovery
   e. exit

___ 9. A marketing vice-president has said that he is committed to introducing two new product lines this year. This is an example of
   a. a mission statement.
   b. a strategic goal.
   c. a tactical goal.
   d. an operational goal.
   e. a strategic plan.

___ 10. The _____ level of management is responsible for strategic goals.
   a. lowest
   b. middle
   c. top
   d. lowest and middle
   e. middle and top

___ 11. Effective goals should
   a. be left somewhat vague to allow flexibility.
   b. not specify key areas of responsibility to permit innovation in new areas.
   c. "reach for the stars" regardless of abilities so employees will always be required to do better.
   d. have defined time limits on their accomplishment so their achievement cannot be put off.
   e. not be linked to rewards because so many things outside the control of the individual can cause goals not to be met.

___   12.   Which of the following goals is stated best?
     a.   Be the best convenience market in town.
     b.   Trim the work force by 50 persons by December 31.
     c.   Become the best teacher in the school.
     d.   Find a job where I will be a success.
     e.   Achieve job satisfaction by the end of five years.

___   13.   Which of the following is/are included in an operational plan?
     a.   quantitative description of meeting goals
     b.   schedules
     c.   a coordination with the budget
     d.   specific action steps for achieving goals
     e.   All of the above are included in an operational plan.

___   14.   A _____ defines the boundaries within which to make decisions and is a general guide to action.
     a.   rule
     b.   policy
     c.   procedure
     d.   program
     e.   project

___   15.   Decentralized planning
     a.   usually causes conflicts between planners and staff.
     b.   decreases the ability of line managers to make strategic plans.
     c.   gives back to line managers planning responsibility.
     d.   robs the organization of the expertise of planning specialists.
     e.   makes the coordination of plans and different levels more difficult.

___   16.   At which of the following levels may an organization's goals and plans exist?
     a.   strategic
     b.   tactical
     c.   department
     d.   operational
     e.   all of the above

___   17.   Which of the following is *not* provided by a goal or a plan?
     a.   the "why" of an organization's existence
     b.   the "how" to achieve the goal
     c.   facilitation of employees' identification with the organization
     d.   the "do's and the don't's" of the operation
     e.   reduction of uncertainty

___ 18. Some mission statements describe corporate
   a. values.
   b. profits.
   c. directors.
   d. logos.
   e. headquarters.

___ 19. A detailed crisis management plan is developed during the _____ phase of crisis management.
   a. prevention
   b. preparation
   c. containment
   d. recovery
   e. exit

___ 20. The mission statement of Mail Boxes Etc.
   a. is very lengthy, but very good.
   b. was developed by outside consultants.
   c. ignores to good business practices.
   d. expresses a commitment to ethical considerations.
   e. all of the above.

___ 21. Operational objectives lead to the achievement of
   a. profits.
   b. rules.
   c. procedures.
   d. tactical goals.
   e. high morale.

___ 22. In the MBO process individual objectives are
   a. mutually derived by the supervisor and the subordinate.
   b. developed by the subordinate.
   c. assigned by the supervisor.
   d. independent of departmental objectives.
   e. not translated into action plans.

___ 23. During the _____ phase of crisis management, the company must "get the awful truth out."
   a. prevention
   b. preparation
   c. containment
   d. recovery
   e. exit

___ 24. _____ define precise time frames for the completion of each objective required for goals.
   a. Schedules
   b. Strategic plans
   c. Tactical plans
   d. Mission statements
   e. all of the above

___ 25. Rules usually pertain to
   a. a series of steps.
   b. a series of activities.
   c. one specific action.
   d. the long-term view.
   e. profitability.

___ 26. Many well-managed companies resist
   a. planning altogether.
   b. making long-term plans.
   c. setting objectives.
   d. short-term pressures.
   e. evil.

___ 27. The central planning department
   a. is a well-accepted idea.
   b. is implemented in almost every company.
   c. has run into trouble in some companies.
   d. never has problems with line managers.
   e. is used only in countries with a dictator.

___ 28. The planning task force is a group of
   a. consultants brought in for a short time.
   b. tactical planners.
   c. nonmanagers who assist managers in developing plans.
   d. permanently assigned managers.
   e. line managers who have a temporary assignment.

___ 29. When little top management support for planning exists,
   a. planning occurs more smoothly.
   b. the time for planning is allocated by middle management.
   c. things go more smoothly.
   d. poor planning usually results.
   e. a planning department is needed.

___ 30. Today's companies are highly focused on satisfying the needs and interests of all stakeholder groups, so they
    a. listen to focus groups from these stakeholders when planning.
    b. bring these stakeholders into the planning and goal setting process.
    c. ask consultants to tell them what the stakeholders want.
    d. design different sets of goals to present to different stakeholders.
    e. none of the above.

True/False Questions: Please indicate whether the following questions are true or false by writing a T or an F in the blank in front of each question.

___ 1. In MBO employees are motivated because they know what is expected and yet are free to choose how to meet objectives.

___ 2. Goals can be the source of motivation and commitment.

___ 3. The mission statement often focuses on the market and customers.

___ 4. Strategic goals are not the same as official goals.

___ 5. Tactical objectives define the outcomes for major divisions and departments.

___ 6. The "means-ends chain" refers to the hierarchy of objectives.

___ 7. At lower levels of the organization innovation goals are inappropriate.

___ 8. During crisis management, the crisis team gathers as much information as possible and the designated spokesperson presents the facts as they are known.

___ 9. A project is an example of a single-use plan.

___ 10. A central planning department sometimes makes mistakes.

Short-Answer Questions

1. What is a mission statement and why is it important?

2.   Why must a goal be specific and measurable?

3.   Why is it important to use participation in setting goals?

4.   Why is the decentralized planning staff idea a good one?

5.   Why is it important to have top management support to organizational planning?

Management Applications

A Strategic Plan for the IRS

The stated mission of the Internal Revenue Service is given below:

> The purpose of the IRS is to collect the proper amount of tax revenues at the least cost to the public, and in a manner that warrants the highest degree of public confidence in our integrity, efficiency and fairness.
>
> **Source:** *Internal Revenue Strategic Plan*, Document 6941 (5-84).

With this mission statement in mind evaluate whether the following objectives fit with the organizational mission or not and give your rationale for the answer.

1. Encourage and achieve the highest possible degree of voluntary compliance in accordance with the tax law and regulations.

2. Avoid publicity regarding rights of the public or its responsibilities.

3. Continually search for and implement new, more efficient and effective ways of accomplishing our goals.

The Purpose of a Community College

Read the following "statement of purpose" of Rowan-Cabarrus Community College (RCCC) and then answer the questions that follow:

RCCC is an open-door, comprehensive, community-based institution of higher learning serving the citizens of Rowan and Cabarrus counties. The college, a member of the North Carolina Community College System, offers occupational education programs leading to an Associate in Applied Science Degree. Diplomas and certificates are awarded for other occupational, adult, and continuing-education programs. The focus of the college's offerings is to meet the educational needs of the individual as well as meet the changing training requirements of business, industrial firms, and other employers in the service area.

The college strives to inspire adults in the service area to increase their knowledge, develop occupational proficiencies, respond to lifelong learning opportunities, and participate as responsible citizens in a democratic society.

1. Is this a mission statement or a broad goal?

2. Do you feel that this statement is appropriate for a community college?

3.   How do you think this statement is different from a mission statement of a major university?

Mini Case

When Honda Motor Company first introduced its cars into the United States in 1970, it had a distinctive corporate culture that helped it succeed. It was fast to react to changes in the marketplace, could make decisions quickly, refused alliances with other manufacturers, and even required a dress code.

Honda has been successful in the U.S. market. In 1979 Honda decided to begin building cars in the United States and targeted 1982 for completion of its new U.S. plant. This goal was met. By 1988 Honda had built its one-millionth car in the United States. In 1989 Honda planned to begin production at its second U.S. plant.

1. What type of goal is the decision to build Honda autos in the United States?

2. Based on the decisions of Honda, what strategic plan does the company seem to have?

Experiential Exercise

Bethlehem Mission's Mission

The management of Bethlehem Mission to help it determine its mission, policies, strategic goals, and strategic plans has contacted you. It has been working on this project already and has given you the statements below. This effort on its part has greatly simplified your job. All you need to do is decide whether each statement is a mission, policy, strategic goal, or strategic plan. Read the statements and then indicate below which type they are.

Statements

1. Bethlehem uses the normalization principle in all its activities.

2. To allow the highest degree of freedom for clients as possible.

3. Train personnel in the use of normalization techniques.

4. Bethlehem strives to address the needs of all people who are affected by a developmental disability in Christ-centered treatment facilities.

5. Bethlehem serves each individual in the least restrictive environment possible.

6. To help all clients to become as "normal" as possible.

7. Bethlehem employs only positive behavior management techniques.

8. Analyze procedures periodically to insure that undue restrictions are not being employed.

9. Bethlehem respects human and civil rights in delivering its services.

10. To help clients develop a positive self-image.

Indicate below whether the above statements are a mission, policy, strategic goal, or strategic plan. Discuss this with the rest of the class.

Statement	Mission	Policy	Strategic Goal	Strategic Plan
1	____	____	____	____
2	____	____	____	____
3	____	____	____	____
4	____	____	____	____
5	____	____	____	____
6	____	____	____	____
7	____	____	____	____
8	____	____	____	____
9	____	____	____	____
10	____	____	____	____

Study Guide Solutions

Chapter Review

Multiple-Choice Questions

1	2	3	4	5	6	7	8	9	10
e	a	c	a	e	d	b	a	c	c

11	12	13	14	15	16	17	18	19	20
d	b	e	b	c	e	d	a	b	d

21	22	23	24	25	26	27	28	29	30
d	a	c	a	c	d	c	e	d	b

True/False Questions

1	2	3	4	5	6	7	8	9	10
T	T	T	T	T	T	F	T	T	T

Short-Answer Questions

1. A mission statement is a broadly stated definition of the organization's scope of operations that distinguishes it from similar organizations. It is important because it defines what the entire organization is all about and leads to the development of goals and plans.

2. A goal must be specific and measurable to be motivating for employees. Otherwise, it is too vague and one cannot tell when enough is enough and the goal has been met.

3. Participation should be used in goal setting so that all employees adopt the goals as their own. They will then be more motivated to reach those goals.

4. The decentralized planning staff uses more participation in the goal setting and planning functions. This helps to reduce conflicts and takes advantage of improved levels of knowledge of modern managers.

5. Top-level managers are needed to provide the direction, scope, and statement of purpose for the strategic plan. If they are not involved, the message received at lower levels is that it is not very important and need not be done.

Management Applications

A Strategic Plan for the IRS

1. This statement fits with the mission statement of the IRS since part of the mission is to collect taxes with the least cost to the public. Voluntary compliance costs less than using the coercion of law enforcement agencies. Voluntary compliance will also enhance the image of efficiency and fairness.

2. This statement does not seem to fit with the mission statement because it would not spark confidence in the integrity and fairness of the IRS. It would seem that the IRS were trying to hide something from the public. The IRS in reality tries to advise the public of its rights and responsibilities in line with its mission statement.

3. This statement fits nicely with the emphasis in the mission of being efficient and collecting tax revenues at the least cost to the public.

The Purpose of a Community College

1. This appears to be a mission statement.

2. This mission statement appears to be appropriate for a community college. It tells what businesses the college is in and specifies the scope quite well.

3. A major university would probably say more about research and increasing the bounds of human knowledge. It would also say less about occupational courses, training, and meeting the needs of industry.

Mini Case

1. The goal set by Honda to build autos in the United States seems to be a physical and financial resources goal. It pertains to the use and acquisition of a physical resource. It could also be viewed as a profitability goal since the decision has led to greater profits.

2. Based on the decisions of Honda, the strategic plan seems to be to build a stronger market presence in the United States to use as a base to increase market share in Japan.

Experiential Exercise

Bethlehem Mission's Mission

Statement	Type
1	policy
2	strategic goal
3	strategic plan
4	mission
5	policy
6	strategic goal
7	policy
8	strategic plan
9	policy
10	strategic goal

Chapter 8

Strategy Formulation and Implementation

Chapter Summary

After you have read the text chapter, read through the summary below. Cover the left-hand margin and fill in the blanks with the appropriate terms. After you have filled in each blank, check your responses by uncovering the answer given in the margin. If you do not understand why the given answer is the correct one, refer back to the text.

Thinking Strategically

Strategic
management

_____ is the set of decisions and actions used to formulate and implement strategies that will provide a competitively superior fit between the organization and its environment to achieve organizational goals. There are several aspects of strategic management.

grand

stability

globalization

multidomestic
transnational

The _____ strategy of the organization is the general plan by which long-term objectives will be achieved. One type of grand strategy is *growth*, which may be realized by growth of current products in present or new markets or by diversification. Another grand strategy is _____, which involves remaining the same size or growing in a controlled manner. *Retrenchment* is a grand strategy meaning forced decline by liquidation or divestiture of business units. In the international arena a company may follow a strategy of _____, which means the standardization of product design and advertising strategies throughout the world. The multinational company may choose to modify the product design and advertising strategies to suit the specific needs of individual countries, which is a _____ strategy. A _____ strategy combines global coordination to attain efficiency with flexibility to meet specific needs in various countries

strategy

core competence

synergy

A _____ is a plan of action that prescribes resource allocation and other activities for dealing with the environment and helping the organization attain its goals. Through strategy management attempts to develop a _____, which is something the organization does especially well in comparison to its competitors. The increased benefit an organization obtains by the interaction of its parts as compared to the benefits of the parts acting independently is _____. Through core competencies and synergy a firm can create *value*, which is the combination of benefits received and costs paid.

Corporate
Business

Functional

Another aspect of strategy is the organizational level to which strategic issues apply. _____-level strategy pertains to the entire organization and relates to the nature of the business. _____-level strategy is associated with each business unit or product line and relates to how the organization competes. _____-level strategy is concerned with how to support the business-level strategy and pertains to the major departments of the organization.

formulation
implementation

Strategy _____ involves the planning and decision making needed to develop the organization's strategic plan. Strategy _____ refers to how the strategic plan is actually set in motion to get the desired results.

Situation

The organization must analyze its situation to develop an effective strategy. _____ analysis discovers the strengths, weaknesses, opportunities, and threats (SWOT) that affect organizational performance. The SWOT analysis serves this purpose. First, a company looks internally to assess its strengths and weaknesses. Then, an external scan reveals its opportunities and threats. This analysis helps the organization to redefine its mission, goals, and strategies.

Formulating Corporate-Level Strategy

SBU

portfolio strategy

Corporate-level strategy must determine the mix and utilization of strategic business units (SBUs). An _____ is a division of the organization that has a unique business mission, product line, competitors, and markets. The _____ pertains to the mix of business units and product lines that fit together in a logical way to provide synergy and competitive advantage.

BCG matrix

The _____ classifies strategic business units by their business growth rate and market share. The *star* has a large market share in a rapidly growing industry. The *cash cow* has a large market share in a mature, slow-growth industry. The *question mark* is in a new, rapidly growing industry but has only a small market share. The *dog* has a small market share in a slow-growth market. The categorization then tells a manager what strategic action should be taken with these units.

Formulating Business-Level Strategy

new entrants

substitute

Michael E. Porter identifies five competitive force which help determine a company's competitive position. The first factor is the *potential of _____*. Barriers exist to entry of any industry. The second and third factors, *the bargaining power of buyers and of suppliers* also have impact. The fourth factor is the *threat of _____ products* and the fifth is *competitor's rivalry*. These factors will influence the determination of a strategy.

Differentiation
Cost leadership

Focus

Porter's competitive strategies include differentiation, cost leadership, and focus. _____ is a competitive strategy with which the organization seeks to distinguish its products or services from those of its competitors. _____ involves aggressively seeking efficient facilities, cutting costs, and employing tight cost controls to be more efficient than competitors. _____ emphasizes concentration on a specific regional market or buyer group. These three strategies indicate the required skills and resources along with the organizational requirements for each strategy.

An alternative to competition is collaboration with other companies. Partnership strategies include preferred supplier appointments, partnering, joint ventures, mergers, acquisitions. Often companies compete and cooperate at the same time

Formulating Functional-Level Strategy

action plans

Functional-level strategies are the _____ adopted by major functional departments of the organization to execute business-level strategy. These strategies are coordinated with business-level strategies to achieve corporate goals.

Putting Strategy into Action

Strategy implementation is a difficult task for managers. Strategy can be implemented through *leadership, structural design, information and control systems,* and *human resources.* Implementing global strategy is more difficult. It requires flexibility, superb communication, an alignment of structure with culture, and handling of human resources issues.

Chapter Review

Multiple-Choice Questions: Please indicate the correct response to the following questions by writing the letter of the correct answer in the space provided.

____ 1. Taking the long-term view and seeing the big picture are part of
    a. tactical planning.
    b. strategic management.
    c. the mission statement.
    d. operational planning.
    e. tactical implementation.

____ 2. Stability is sometimes called a(n) _____ strategy.
    a. pause
    b. aggressive
    c. diversification
    d. obtuse
    e. synergistic

____ 3. United Airlines achieved _____ by acquiring Westin Hotels and Hertz Rent-A-Car and creating more business for the whole corporation than the individual units alone.
    a. a corporate-level strategy
    b. a business-level strategy
    c. a functional-level strategy
    d. synergy
    e. a coalition

____ 4. To discover the strengths and weaknesses in a SWOT analysis the organization must
    a. scan the external environment.
    b. look at internal characteristics.
    c. spy on competitors.
    d. look for unfilled needs in the market.
    e. survey government documents.

____ 5. Diversification refers to
    a. getting rid of poorly performing SBUs.
    b. acquiring unrelated product lines.
    c. spreading the risk to overseas SBUs.
    d. changing top management to implement a new strategy.
    e. the acquisition of related product lines.

___ 6. The most profitable business units or products will be classified as _____ in the BCG matrix.
   a. stars
   b. dogs
   c. question marks
   d. cash cows
   e. problem children

___ 7. If you were the manager of a consumer products company and received a report that a certain product had been classified as a dog by the BCG matrix, the appropriate strategy to pursue would be to
   a. invest in this product more.
   b. encourage market development.
   c. divest of this product.
   d. encourage product development.
   e. seek rapid growth and expansion.

___ 8. The international strategy in which the product design and advertising may be modified to meet the needs of the country is called a _____ strategy.
   a. multidomestic
   b. globalization
   c. worldwide
   d. ethnocentric
   e. specialized

___ 9. In Porter's competitive strategies scheme, the _____ strategy is exemplified by strong coordination among functions in R&D, product development, and marketing.
   a. focus
   b. differentiation
   c. overall cost leadership
   d. core competency
   e. cash cow

___ 10. The business activity that an organization does particularly well in comparison to competitors is called its
   a. synergistic point.
   b. cash cow.
   c. walk away feature.
   d. core competency.
   e. mature stage product.

___ 11. Which of the following has the highest degree of collaboration?
   a. preferred supplier arrangement
   b. strategic business partnering
   c. join venture
   d. merger
   e. acquisition

___ 12. The scrambling and jockeying for position is called _____ by Porter.
   a. synergism
   b. bargaining
   c. competitor's rivalry
   d. illegal in most cases
   e. cannibalism

___ 13. Leadership includes
   a. appraising employee performance.
   b. motivation of employees.
   c. controlling employees.
   d. evaluating organizational structure.
   e. none of the above

___ 14. The responsibilities of managers, their authority, and the consolidation of jobs into departments are part of
   a. leadership.
   b. organizational structure.
   c. the information system.
   d. the control system.
   e. the technological environment.

___ 15. The human resource function _____ employees.
   a. subordinates
   b. leads
   c. selects
   d. organizes
   e. all of the above

___ 16. A differentiation strategy
   a. can reduce rivalry.
   b. reduces the bargaining power of large buyers.
   c. erects entry barriers.
   d. increases customer loyalty if successful.
   e. all of the above.

___ 17. Corporate-level strategy asks the question
   a. "How do we compete?"
   b. "What business are we in?"
   c. "How do we support the mission?"
   d. "What is the competition doing?"
   e. "What will happen in five years?"

___ 18. A transnational strategy combines
   a. Americans with Europeans.
   b. cultural norms to achieve synergy.
   c. management styles of different cultures.
   d. culture and business.
   e. global coordination and flexibility to meet specific needs.

___ 19. The opening up of Eastern Europe represents a(n) _____ to some Western businesses.
   a. strength
   b. weakness
   c. opportunity
   d. threat
   e. either c or d

___ 20. Which of the following could be a *marketing* strength?
   a. product quality
   b. management quality
   c. worker satisfaction
   d. laboratory capabilities
   e. return on investment

___ 21. An SBU has
   a. a unique product line.
   b. the same business mission as other SBUs.
   c. a grand strategy.
   d. no personnel since it is a "paper entity."
   e. a short life span.

___ 22. _____ pertains to the mix of business units and product lines that fit together in a logical way.
   a. SBU
   b. Grand strategy
   c. Portfolio strategy
   d. SWOT
   e. Retrenchment

___ 23. Which of the following is a "grand strategy"?
   a. a portfolio strategy
   b. retrenchment
   c. SWOT
   d. milking the cash cow
   e. having a party

___ 24. Motel 6 follows a _____ strategy.
   a. differentiation
   b. retrenchment
   c. focus
   d. cost leadership
   e. portfolio

___ 25. Which of the following requires the lowest amount of collaboration?
   a. preferred supplier arrangement
   b. strategic business partnering
   c. join venture
   d. merger
   e. acquisition

___ 26. When companies in the sugar industry suffered form the growth of sugar substitutes, it was an example of
   a. maturity.
   b. competitor's rivalry.
   c. threat of substitute products.
   d. divestiture.
   e. diversification.

___ 27. If leaders let other managers participate during strategy formulation,
   a. implementation will be easier.
   b. implementation will be harder.
   c. commitment to strategy will be weakened because it did not come from top management.
   d. motivation to accomplish goals will be more difficult to obtain.
   e. they are exhibiting poor and weak leadership tendencies.

___ 28. The organization's human resources are its
   a. customers.
   b. employees.
   c. personnel department.
   d. psychologists.
   e. social security account balance.

___ 29. Which of the following is *not* a human resource function?
    a. recruiting new employees
    b. selecting new employees
    c. training employees
    d. laying off employees
    e. All of the above *are* human resource functions.

___ 30. Managers _____ strategy through the tools of leadership, information and control systems, and human resources.
    a. implement
    b. derive
    c. control
    d. develop
    e. formulate

True/False Questions: Please indicate whether the following questions are true or false by writing a T or an F in the blank in front of each question.

___ 1. Every organization should be concerned with strategy.

___ 2. Although strategic management includes goal setting, it does not include devising plans to meet the goals.

___ 3. *Value creation* refers to adding more features to a product or service so consumers feel they are getting more for their money.

___ 4. Strategy formulation may include assessment of both the external and the internal environments.

___ 5. A strategy of stability is sometimes called a pause strategy.

___ 6. When Warner Communications and American Express got together to form MTV networks, a joint venture was being used.

___ 7. Some products are more suited toward global standardization than others.

___ 8. Using Porter's model, the overall cost leadership strategy means that efforts are directed at a strategic target.

___ 9. Functional-level strategies are the action plans adopted by major functional departments.

___ 10. Some people argue that strategy implementation is the most difficult and important part of strategic management.

Short-Answer Questions

1. What is meant by corporate-level strategy?

2. Explain what SWOT stands for and whether each part is internal or external.

3. What skills and resources are needed to successfully employ the overall cost leadership strategy?

4. What are some activities leaders can use to implement strategy?

5. Why is the consideration of human resources important in the implementation of strategy?

Management Applications

The Lion Is Attacked

Food Lion is a very strong grocery store chain operating primarily in the Southeast. Food Lion has used the focus strategy as it has aimed its strategy at customers of smaller towns in this one geographic region. It has combined this effectively with a cost leadership strategy. As Food Lion developed, it has built in efficiencies of operation that make it a very low-cost operation. These savings can then be passed on to customers, making it very competitive in all its markets. So far, it has been able to compete successfully with larger chains.

In a television report alleged that Food Lion was re-wrapping outdated meat and engaging in other practices which were unsanitary.

1.   Should Food Lion continue its cost leadership strategy? Why or why not?

2.   How will its information and control system need to operate to combat this new external threat?

3.   Will this event have an effect on the growth rate of Food Lion?

Sports Season for Four Seasons?

Four Seasons, Inc., has been a very successful recreation vehicle sales and repair facility over the last four years. In fact, three years ago demand for RVs was so strong that Four Seasons could hardly keep enough inventory on hand. As sales started to slow down, management decided to add RV accessories to its product offering. All sorts of accessories ranging from mud flaps to seats to battery-powered television sets were sold from its showroom floor. However, as the demand for RVs dropped off, so too did the demand for RV accessories.

The president of Four Seasons spends much of his time scanning the environment for opportunities. He has recently been reading some trade literature about the increased popularity of sporting goods spurred on by the fitness craze sweeping the country. He has even sent off for and received information about a franchise type of buying organization called Sportabout. For what he considers a reasonable franchise cost he receives guidance on store layout, merchandising, advertising, pricing guidelines, and also access to the buying power of the purchasing group. This buying power will allow him to buy sporting goods at a low enough price to undercut most of the sporting goods stores in the town of 35,000 where he is located.

If he buys this sporting goods franchise, he still intends on continuing his RV sales and service business along with the accessories business. He would allow the sporting goods to take up one half of his retail showroom.

1. Which grand strategy (growth, stability, retrenchment, globalization, or multidomestic) does the president seem to be following? Justify your choice.

2. Would you recommend that the president buy the franchise? Explain the rationale behind your recommendation.

3. What additional information would you want to know before buying the franchise, and why?

Mini Case

The Americana Stamp Company

The Americana Stamp Company is a family-owned small business. The Jones family purchased 25 used stamp vending machines from a cousin. So far, 9 of these machines have been placed in convenience markets and 1 has been placed in a motel. The other 15 have not been placed. The company pays the retail outlet 10 percent of net profit, but emphasizes providing a service to customers in convincing stores to allow the machines to be placed.

The Jones family purchases 25¢ and 15¢ stamps from the post office. The family places the stamps in small cardboard holders to be placed in the vending machines. The machines must be serviced only once a month. The 25¢ stamps are sold from the stamp vending machine for 35¢, and the 15¢ stamps are sold for 25¢. Each sale results in 10¢ net profit, 1¢ of which is paid to the retail outlet.

The business is not going the way the Jones family had hoped. Some of the locations are very good, yielding $10-$12 net profit per month. The motel is the worst, providing only $2-$3 per month. The Jones family has contacted you and asked you for advice.

1.   Apply a SWOT analysis to the Americana Stamp Company.

   Strengths

   Weaknesses

Opportunities

Threats

2.   Which of Porter's strategies would you recommend to the family?

Experiential Exercise

Based on the descriptions that follow, indicate whether a preferred supplier arrangement, strategic business partnering, joint venture, merger, or acquisition is described.

Description	Classification
U.S. Airways and American Airlines decide to become one airline.	_____
J.C. Penney agrees to buy all the shirts produced by Mesa Textile Company if Mesa will produce the styles its buyers request.	_____
America Online purchases Compuserve.	_____
The Rowan County Health Department and Rowan Regional Medical Center open a free an urgent care center for low-income families.	_____
Mountain University agrees to supply faculty for online courses sponsored by textbook publisher Dryden Press.	_____

Study Guide Solutions

Chapter Review

Multiple-Choice Questions

1	2	3	4	5	6	7	8	9	10
b	a	d	b	e	d	c	a	b	d

11	12	13	14	15	16	17	18	19	20
e	c	b	b	c	e	b	e	e	a

21	22	23	24	25	26	27	28	29	30
a	c	b	d	a	c	a	b	e	a

True/False Questions

1	2	3	4	5	6	7	8	9	10
T	F	F	T	T	T	T	F	T	T

Short-Answer Questions

1. Corporate-level strategy is concerned with the question: What business are we in? It pertains to the entire organization and affects all lower levels of the organization.

2. SWOT stands for strengths, weaknesses, opportunities and threats. Strengths and weaknesses are internal to the organization and opportunities and threats are external.

3. The skills and resources needed for an overall cost leadership strategy are process engineering skills, intense supervision of labor, and products designed for ease in manufacture.

4. Leaders can persuade and communicate to implement new strategy by making speeches, building coalitions, and convincing middle managers to go along with their vision for the corporation.

5. Human resources are important in implementing strategy because it is people that are needed to make things happen. It is necessary to have the right number of people with the right skills, motivation, and understanding of strategy for the strategy to be successfully implemented.

Management Applications

The Lion Is Attacked

1. No, it should probably not continue its cost leadership strategy, at least not with the same degree of emphasis. It must now convince the public that its quality is good and its products are safe. This sounds closer to a differentiation strategy.

2. Its information and control system must operate extremely well to be a success given this new environment. It cannot allow quality to slip at this point.

3. Yes, the growth rate will probably be affected by this event. A stability or pause strategy seems to be appropriate in the short term.

Sports Season for Four Seasons?

1. It is difficult to exactly tell which strategy is being followed. One could easily make a case for the growth strategy since the president is trying to find a new market. One could also make the argument that he is merely reacting to a slump in sales and is striving for stability.

2. I would probably not recommend that he buy the franchise. In the first place he needs additional information before making the decision (see the answer to question 3 below). He also needs to define better his corporate strategy and answer the question, "What business am I in?" It seems that he will only confuse the public as to what type of business he is in by opening a sporting goods store. His old market of RV customers will feel that he is forsaking them, and his new target market of sports enthusiasts will feel he is only an RV place trying to make a few extra bucks on the side.

3. I would want to know more about the market in which he will be operating. He needs to know how strong the competition is and whether potential customers are satisfied with the offerings of the competition at present. He is also assuming that customers want low prices more than anything else. He needs to determine if this is indeed true. He also needs to know more about the franchise operation and how it has worked in other similar locations.

Mini Case

1. **Strengths** include a "natural" management structure of the family, a product that is needed and is relatively inexpensive, and low investment in equipment or inventory.

    Weaknesses include an unprofessional management team and work force, probable loose record keeping and controls, and small amount of financial resources.

    Opportunities exist to place the other 15 machines or to place machines from poor locations to better locations. Other types of locations such as restaurants and malls might also be considered.

Threats include the impending boosting of postage rates by the Postal Service, stamps sold by the Post Office, stamps sold by retailers over the counter, and the possibility of government regulations outlawing the reselling of postage stamps.

2.   A focus strategy seems to be called for in this case. The company needs to establish itself in the local market and grow to be successful and be worth the effort. Since the machines have already been purchased, the risk is low. The other 15 machines need to be placed and new locations need to be considered.

Experiential Exercise

Description	Classification
U.S. Airways and American Airlines decide to become one airline.	<u>Merger</u>
J.C. Penney agrees to buy all the shirts produced by Mesa Textile Company if Mesa will produce the styles its buyers request.	<u>Preferred Supplier Arrangement</u>
America Online purchases Compuserve.	<u>Acquisition</u>
The Rowan County Health Department and Rowan Regional Medical Center open a free an urgent care center for low-income families.	<u>Joint Venture</u>
Mountain University agrees to supply faculty for online courses sponsored by textbook publisher Dryden Press.	<u>Strategic Business Partnering</u>

Chapter 9

Managerial Decision Making

Chapter Summary

After you have read the text chapter, read through the summary below. Cover the left-hand margin and fill in the blanks with the appropriate terms. After you have filled in each blank, check your responses by uncovering the answer given in the margin. If you do not understand why the given answer is the correct one, refer back to the text.

Types of Decisions and Problems

decision

Decision making

Programmed
Nonprogrammed

A _____ is a choice made from the available alternatives. _____ is the process of identifying problems and opportunities and then resolving them. Decisions may be viewed as either programmed or nonprogrammed. _____ decisions involve problems that are recurring and for which decision rules can be made. _____ decisions are unique, are poorly defined and largely unstructured, and have important consequences for the organization.

certainty

risk
Uncertainty

Ambiguity

Four situations exist under which managers must make decisions. The easiest condition is that of _____, in which all the outcomes are known and the manager has all the information needed to make a decision. Under a condition of _____ the outcomes are known, but the outcomes associated with each alternative are subject to chance. _____ is a situation in which objectives are known, but information about alternatives and future events is incomplete. _____ exists when not only are the outcomes not known, but the objectives to be reached and the available alternatives are also not known. Managers must be concerned with all these types of situations from time to time.

Decision-Making Models

normative

classical

Two models of decision making are used by managers. The classical model is called _____ because it describes how managers ought to make decisions and provides guidelines for reaching an ideal outcome. The _____ model is based on rationality and economic assumptions. This is often unrealistic for the practicing manager.

administrative
descriptive
Bounded
Satisficing

Intuition
coalition

The _____ model of decision making is considered _____ because it tells how managers actually do make decisions, not how they should make decisions. _____ rationality assumes that managers do not have the time or other resources to make the optimal decision. _____ is often used, which means the decision will be satisfied with the first alternative which meets the minimal criteria. Intuition is often used in this model to make decisions. _____ is not irrational or arbitrary, but rather is based on past experience, but without conscious thought. A _____ is an informal alliance among mangers who support a specific goal. Forming these alliances is called *coalition building*. Building coalitions is a tool of the *political model* of decision making and is useful for uncertain or ambiguous conditions where conflicting goals exists. It uses bargaining and discussion among coalition members to gain support.

Decision-Making Steps

problem
opportunity

Diagnosis

Risk propensity

Implementation

The first step in the decision-making process is the recognition of a decision requirement. The manager must identify and define the problem or opportunity requiring a decision. A _____ happens when organizational success is less than established objectives. An _____ exists when managers see potential accomplishment that exceeds specified current objectives. Next, managers must diagnose and analyze the problem or opportunity. _____ means analyzing underlying causal factors associated with the decision situation. Based on this analysis managers can then develop alternatives to solve the problem or take advantage of the opportunity. Based on an evaluation and the manager's propensity for risk, an alternative is selected. _____ is the willingness to undertake risk with the opportunity of gaining an increased payoff. _____ consists of the use of managerial, administrative, and persuasive abilities to insure that the chosen alternative is carried out. Success of the selected alternative requires communication, motivation, and leadership. After implementation, managers should evaluate and follow up to make sure the decision helped reach the desired goal. *Evaluation* involves gathering information that tells how well the decision was implemented and whether it was effective. Feedback is important because decision making is a continuous, never-ending process.

Personal Decision Framework

decision style

directive
analytical

conceptual

Personal _____ _____ refers to difference s between people with respect to how they perceive problems and make decisions. Research has identified four major decision styles. The _____ *style* is used by people who prefer simple, clear-cut solutions. Managers with an _____ *style* like to consider complex solutions based on as much data as they can gather. Those who prefer the _____ *style* like to consider

behavioral

a broad amount of information and like to talk to others about the problem and possible solutions before making a decision. The _____ *style* is characterized by have a deep concern for others and wanting to determine how the decision may affect them. Although managers may have a dominant style, most will use several styles depending on the situation.

Increasing Participation in Decision Making

Vroom-Jago

The _____ model helps the manager decide on the amount of participation for subordinates. This model consists of leader participation styles, a set of diagnostic questions with which to analyze a decision situation, and a series of decision rules to select a decision style.

groupthink

There are both advantages and disadvantages to group decision making that must be considered. Groups provide a broader perspective, more expertise, and produce more decision alternatives. They are more satisfying for participants and facilitate commitment to the decision reached. A major disadvantage is _____, a mode of thinking that people engage in when they are deeply involved in a cohesive in-group and when the members' strivings for unanimity override their motivation to realistically appraise alternatives.

New Decision Approaches for the New Workplace

decision learning

five whys

Collective

Devil's advocate

point-counterpoint

Effective decision making in today's organization relies on new guidelines. Managers should learn from their mistakes, not be punished if decisions do not turn out as planned. By making mistakes, people go through the process of _____. People should not get so attached to their own ideas that they are unwilling to recognize when to move on. To help people to think more broadly and deeply about problems, some companies have used the _____ . This means asking *why* five times for every problem and its explanation to improve how people think about problems and generate alternatives for solving them. _____ intuition comes from the combined knowledge, experience, and understanding of the group and can improve decision making. Decision making can also be improved by encouraging constructive conflict. This can be done by assigning a _____ _____. Encouraging as many ideas as quickly as possible, without debate can stimulate creative alternatives. Assigning groups to provide different sides of arguments is the technique called _____.

Chapter Review

Multiple-Choice Questions: Please indicate the correct response to the following questions by writing the letter of the correct answer in the space provided.

___ 1. Which of the following is an example of a nonprogrammed decision?
   a. reordering office supplies
   b. developing a new product
   c. deciding which motor oil to put in the company car
   d. responding to a customer request for a sales demonstration
   e. deciding when to hold the office Christmas party

___ 2. When R.J. Reynolds Company decided to move its corporate headquarters from Winston-Salem, North Carolina, to Atlanta, Georgia, it was making a(n) _____ decision.
   a. nonprogrammed
   b. ambiguous
   c. programmed
   d. group
   e. delphi

___ 3. If you knew in advance that a horse race had been fixed so that "Whirlaway" was going to win, you would be operating under a condition of
   a. risk.
   b. uncertainty.
   c. ambiguity.
   d. certainty.
   e. intuitiveness.

___ 4. A decision in an ambiguous situation
   a. is easy to make since no one knows what to expect.
   b. is sometimes called a "wicked" decision.
   c. is difficult to make since we know too much.
   d. involves knowing the probabilities of the outcomes associated with the alternatives.
   e. makes defining alternatives easy.

___ 5. According to the classical model of decision making
   a. objectives are not known or agreed upon.
   b. the decision maker operates under conditions of risk.
   c. criteria for evaluating alternatives are known.
   d. the decision maker is often irrational.
   e. we often make decisions which do not maximize our payoff.

___ 6. When a manager chooses the first alternative to meet the minimal decision criteria, he is said to be
    a. using the classical model of decision making.
    b. using bounded rationality.
    c. maximizing his payoff.
    d. minimizing his risk.
    e. satisficing.

___ 7. If you are satisficing, when you graduate from college you will
    a. hunt until you find the ultimate job meeting all your expectations.
    b. take the first job offer that meets your minimal criteria.
    c. ask for a raise within the first six months of taking a job.
    d. look for a job that gives you the most personal satisfaction.
    e. give up on some of your criteria for a good job to have other criteria met.

___ 8. When you use intuition to make a decision, you are
    a. basing your decision on past experience.
    b. being arbitrary.
    c. being irrational.
    d. being foolish.
    e. All of the above except a are correct.

___ 9. Administrative decision-making procedures are most appropriate for _____ situations and problems.
    a. clear-cut
    b. rational
    c. vague
    d. stable
    e. slow-moving

___ 10. When you ask the question, "What is the state of disequilibrium affecting us?" you are trying to
    a. be vague to buy time to make a better decision later.
    b. develop effective alternatives.
    c. use intuition to make the decision.
    d. discover the underlying causes of the problem.
    e. decide how to implement the solution.

___ 11. If you were the coach of a football team that is one point behind and you chose a play which would result in a tie rather than a win, you could be said to have
    a. a low propensity for risk.
    b. a high propensity for risk.
    c. an intuitive approach to decision making.
    d. low ethical standards.
    e. a fear of making decisions.

12. Implementation of an alternative may require
    a. discussion with those affected.
    b. communication.
    c. motivation.
    d. leadership skills.
    e. all of the above

13. Generation of many ideas as rapidly as possible is used
    a. to filter out the bad ideas as soon as they are mentioned.
    b. to allow the "brains" of the group to feel important.
    c. in situations where alternatives are defined by the nature of the problem.
    d. to allow the group to work with multiple alternatives.
    e. to encourage critical considerations for alternatives suggested.

14. Nonprogrammed decisions usually
    a. involve routine situations.
    b. are well defined.
    c. are largely structured.
    d. have important consequences for the organization.
    e. have occurred several times before.

15. An assumption underlying the classical model is that
    a. problems are precisely formulated and defined.
    b. only some alternatives need to be considered.
    c. the alternative that will minimize economic return is the best.
    d. the decision maker should not order preferences.
    e. the decision maker strives for conditions of risk.

16. According to the administrative model
    a. managers are always aware of problems that exist in the organization.
    b. rational procedures are always used.
    c. managers always strive for maximizing.
    d. managers' search for alternatives is limited.
    e. decision objectives are clear-cut.

17. For nonprogrammed decisions, alternatives
    a. are easy to identify.
    b. usually are already available.
    c. must be developed.
    d. must ignore company objectives.
    e. are relatively straightforward.

___ 18.   An opportunity exists in a situation when
    a.   accomplishments have failed to meet established goals.
    b.   fear of actions of competitors is present.
    c.   nonprogrammed decisions merge with programmed decisions.
    d.   potential for organizational accomplishments that exceed current goals is present.
    e.   all of the above.

___ 19.   _____ is the most difficult decision situation.
    a.   Ambiguity
    b.   Risk
    c.   Certainty
    d.   Uncertainty
    e.   none of the above

___ 20.   The implementation stage of decision making involves the use of
    a.   persuasive abilities.
    b.   an environmental scan.
    c.   an analysis of the situation.
    d.   an evaluation of alternatives.
    e.   feedback.

___ 21.   Which of the following is considered the most highly democratic?
    a.   You make the decision yourself with the available information.
    b.   You share the problem with subordinates as a group, try not to influence the group, and are willing to go along with the decision of the group.
    c.   You obtain information from subordinates and then decide yourself.
    d.   You share the problem with subordinates as a group, get their ideas, and then you make the decision.
    e.   You share the problem with subordinates individually and then make the decision.

___ 22.   The diagnostic questions of the Vroom-Jago model
    a.   cannot be answered with a "yes" or "no" answer.
    b.   help the manager decide which leader decision style to use.
    c.   are not able to consider the type of problem.
    d.   consider the problem, but not the required level of decision quality.
    e.   ignore the importance of having subordinates accept the decision.

___ 23.   The directive style is used by managers who
    a.   like to consider complex solutions.
    b.   prefer to gather as much data as they can.
    c.   are very concerned about the impact of the decision on others.
    d.   prefer simple, clear-cut solutions.
    e.   want to understand the feelings of others before making the decision.

___ 24. The behavioral style is used by managers who
    a. like to consider complex solutions.
    b. prefer to gather as much data as they can.
    c. are very concerned about the impact of the decision on others.
    d. prefer simple, clear-cut solutions.
    e. search for the best possible decision based on the information available.

___ 25. Group decision making
    a. is faster than individual decision making.
    b. avoids compromises.
    c. provides for more knowledge, facts, and alternatives.
    d. is most appropriate for programmed decisions.
    e. provides a clear focus for decision responsibility.

___ 26. When a manager makes a decision that turns out to be a bad one
    a. he/she should immediately be punished.
    b. he/she should be fired.
    c. he/she should learn from that decision to improve the next time.
    d. he/she should be forced to clean up his/her own mess.
    e. he/she should be told to avoid risks in the future.

___ 27. A devil's advocate is supposed to
    a. challenge the assumptions and assertions made by the group.
    b. point out the evil side of the alternative being considered.
    c. try to get the group to make an immoral decision.
    d. speak on behalf of the competition.
    e. try to disrupt the decision-making process.

___ 28. If you come up with a really neat idea that does not seem to be working out, you
    a. should stick with it anyway.
    b. should know when it is time to abandon the idea.
    c. should try to transfer the credit for the idea to someone else to avoid the blame.
    d. should ask everyone for forgiveness.
    e. will have to pay for the mistake out of your own pocket.

___ 29. When using the technique called the *five whys*, you
    a. assign five different people to ask why a decision was made.
    b. ask why five times for every problem so you will think more broadly and deeply about it.
    c. ask why, and then why not, five times.
    d. are expressing your disappointment that an idea did not work out.
    e. none of the above.

___   30.   Collective intuition means
      a.   asking all the women in the organization what they think.
      b.   seeking a detailed analysis of a problem from a large group of people.
      c.   seeking for a solution that benefits the group, not an individual.
      d.   using the combined knowledge, experience, and understanding of the group.
      e.   assessing a fine on those who rely on intuition for decision making.

True/False Questions: Please indicate whether the following questions are true or false by writing a T or an F in the blank in front of each question.

___   1.   Programmed decisions involve situations that occur often.

___   2.   The value of the classical model has been its ability to help decision makers be more rational.

___   3.   The classical model represents an ideal model of decision making that is attainable by real people in real organizations.

___   4.   Awareness of a problem is the first step in the decision-making process.

___   5.   Creativity and flexibility are especially important in the diagnosis stage of decision making.

___   6.   Decision alternatives can be thought of as the tools for reducing the difference between the organization's current and desired performance.

___   7.   A manager's goal is to make the choice with the least amount of risk and uncertainty.

___   8.   Individuals always make better decisions than do groups.

___   9.   Coalitions are usually formed in the political model of decision making.

___   10.   Point-counterpoint breaks a decision making group into two subgroups and assigns them different, often competing responsibilities.

Short-Answer Questions

1. Explain whether decision making is more difficult under conditions of certainty, risk, uncertainty, or ambiguity.

2. Would you say that there is any value to the classical model of decision making since all of its underlying assumptions are rarely ever true?

3. Explain why recognition of decision requirement is the *first* step in the decision-making process.

5. How will a devil's advocate improve decision making?

Management Applications

A Percentage of the Take?

Mr. Lee Peterson, a local real estate agency manager, has just left your office. You have just started a marketing research business and Mr. Peterson wants you to do some research for him. He has invented a new product and wants you to do marketing research to determine if there is a demand for the product.

After he leaves, you make a few calculations and decide that you would normally charge about $18,000 to do this job. Your actual out-of-pocket expenses other than labor are about $500.

Your problem is that Mr. Peterson does not have the cash up front to pay you to do this job. He has all his money tied up in the product already. Instead of paying for the job upon completion, he has offered to pay you 10 percent of his product royalties for 10 years. You are trying to decide whether to take on this job with such an arrangement.

1. How would your propensity for risk enter into this decision?

2. Under which condition—certainty, uncertainty, risk, or ambiguity—is this decision being made?

3.   Use each of the following decision-making steps to make this decision:

Recognition of Decision Requirements

Diagnosis and Analysis of Causes

Development of Alternatives

Selection of Desired Alternative

Implementation of Desired Alternative

Control and Follow-up

Offer an MBA?

Catawba College is a small liberal arts college of 1,500 students located in central North Carolina. Recently, it has received several requests from individuals and local companies that it begin offering an MBA program. This would be offered by the School of Business, which currently offers no graduate degrees. Apply the Vroom-Jago model to this decision, making any needed assumptions along the way.

Turn to Exhibit 9.7 on page 287 in the text and see where you end up.

1. Do you feel that the Vroom-Jago model would be useful in making this decision? Why or why not?

2. What additional information would you need to make this decision?

Mini Case

Who Should Suzanne Choose?

Suzanne is a college senior. She makes the dean's list in her business courses, is active in several student organizations, and serves as an officer for her sorority. While studying management, she read the chapter on decision making and is trying to apply it to a real decision she is about to make. She has had two guys ask her to the sorority's important Spring Dance, and she is trying to decide which of the two to go with.

Anthony asked her first. He is good-looking, has a great personality, but he goes to a different school. He won't know many people at the dance, and Suzanne is worried that she would have to spend most of the time just with him. On their previous dates, they have had wonderful conversations, and Suzanne knows they would get along well.

Joey is also handsome, very outgoing, and knows many of the other people who will be at the dance. He would be able to entertain himself while Suzanne is attending to her duties as an officer at the dance. They have had fun together in the past, but Suzanne is concerned that Joey's feelings for her may be stronger than her feelings for him.

1. Explain which type of decision this appears to be. Is it programmed or nonprogrammed? Is the situation one of certainty, risk, uncertainty, or ambiguity?

2.   Should Suzanne use the classical or the administrative model in making this decision? Why?

3.   The problem has been defined for you and the alternatives provided. Make the selection for Suzanne, justify your recommendation, and explain how she should implement her choice.

Experiential Exercise

For this exercise your instructor will assign you to groups of 6 persons. Your instructor will provide each group member with a slip of paper. This paper will describe the role that each person is to play. The roles are shown below:

Devil's Advocate	Your job is to question the assumptions and to point out weaknesses of proposed alternatives.
Groupthinker	Your job is to go along with everything that the leader says and to criticize anyone who opposes the leader.
Group Leader	Your job is to take charge of the group and make sure that a decision is made in the time allotted.
Financial Officer	Your job is to make sure that any decision made does not have adverse financial impact and to make sure that finances are considered in the decision-making process.
Marketing Officer	Your job is to make sure that the customer is not forgotten in this decision. You are to be the customer's advocate and consider his/her reactions to proposed solutions.
Union Officer	Your job is to consider the impact of decisions made on union members.

The Situation

Your company has just received the contract to produce and sell a one-man helicopter invented by a renowned aerospace engineer. You are trying to decide how expensive to make the helicopter, what market target, how much to automate, and other related questions. You are part of a project team that is today having its first meeting. You will be allowed 10 minutes to come to a solution.

Discussion

After the group has used its allotted 10 minutes, discuss the following questions:

1. Could you tell who was assigned to each role?

2. Who helped the group most toward the goal of reaching quality decisions?

3. Would this decision have been made better as an individual?

Study Guide Solutions

Chapter Review

Multiple-Choice Questions

1	2	3	4	5	6	7	8	9	10
b	a	d	b	c	e	b	a	d	d

11	12	13	14	15	16	17	18	19	20
a	e	d	d	a	c	c	d	a	a

21	22	23	24	25	26	27	28	29	30
b	b	d	c	c	c	a	b	b	d

True/False Questions

1	2	3	4	5	6	7	8	9	10
T	T	F	T	T	T	T	F	T	T

Short-Answer Questions

1. Decision making is most difficult under conditions of ambiguity because the objectives and problem are unclear. This means that alternatives are hard to develop and information is probably not available.

2. The classical model is valuable even though the assumptions may not always be true. It helps a manager know how decisions should be made and to be more rational. It is an ideal for which managers can strive.

3. If one does not recognize that a problem exists, no search will be made for a solution. If the problem is not defined accurately, the chosen alternative may not solve the problem.

4. A devil's advocate will improve decision making by pointing out opposing viewpoints and weaknesses in the assumptions of alternatives being presented. Groupthink will then be avoided.

Management Applications

A Percentage of the Take?

1. If you have a high propensity for risk, you are more likely to take this job on and hope for a big payoff. If you have a low risk propensity, you would either demand payment before taking the job or not take the job at all.

2. This could be a condition of uncertainty only if you knew the expected payoffs, but not their probabilities. As it is described here, it seems to be a condition of ambiguity since even the amount of the payoffs is not known. After completing the marketing research project you would probably know more, but by then the decision will have already been made.

3. **Recognition of Decision Requirements**

    This decision should really be classified as an opportunity and not as a problem. There is a potential for a payoff exceeding the normal fee for this job.

    Diagnosis and Analysis of Causes

    The real cause of the dilemma is that you are unsure whether you will get a payoff or not. Another underlying cause for the reluctance to make a decision is the feeling that you might be setting a precedent that future clients will also want to claim.

    Development of Alternatives

    One alternative is to take the offer and do the job as proposed by Mr. Peterson. A second choice is to reject the offer altogether. A third choice would be to offer to do the job only if Mr. Peterson can arrange for payment to be made. A fourth choice would be to propose a compromise solution and take a proportion of the normal fee with a lower percentage of the royalties.

    Selection of Desired Alternative

    The choice here depends on your own feeling toward risk. The author of this study guide took Mr. Peterson's offer in the real-life version of this case. The product was subsequently bought by a company and a payoff will be received. How large the payoff is to be is yet to be determined.

    Implementation of Desired Alternative

    This again depends on which alternative you preferred. The author had a letter of commitment signed by Mr. Peterson and then undertook the project. Payment of out-of-pocket costs was borne by the author. Student aid for an even smaller percentage of the take was also arranged. The students are still waiting for their payoff too.

Control and Follow-up

The type of control and follow-up depends on the decision made. The author made several presentations to investment groups and wrote letters concerning the results of the study. He also keeps in close contact with Mr. Peterson to monitor the progress of the product's development.

Offer an MBA?

1. The Vroom-Jago model could be useful as a guide in making this decision. It forces the decision maker to consider all the relevant factors and implications.

2. More information is needed about the faculty of the college and the school of business, the extent of MBA offerings in the area, and the strength of demand for this degree.

Mini Case

Choosing Suzanne's Husband

1. This is definitely a nonprogrammed decision because it is unique and one for which she has not made up decision rules. The situation appears to be one of ambiguity since she doesn't really know what the outcomes of her choice will be or what their probabilities are.

2. Since this is a nonprogrammed decision in an ambiguous situation, Suzanne would be well-advised to choose the administrative model. In fact, she will probably have to rely on intuition in this situation. Trying to rely on economic rationality and maximize her choice as needed in the classical model would not work in this situation. She will have to decide what is most important to her to make the decision.

3. The choice you make will probably reveal your own values and feelings toward the factors mentioned in behalf of each man. The implementation probably consists of simply saying, "Yes," to her choice and then seeing what happens.

Experiential Exercise

The answers to the discussion questions depend on the group.

Chapter 10

Fundamentals of Organizing

Chapter Summary

After you have read the text chapter, read through the summary below. Cover the left-hand margin and fill in the blanks with the appropriate terms. After you have filled in each blank, check your responses by uncovering the answer given in the margin. If you do not understand why the given answer is the correct one, refer back to the text.

Organizing

_____ is the deployment of organizational resources to achieve strategic goals. Organizing defines how the organization will carry out its strategy.

Organizing the Vertical Structure

Organizational structure

organization chart

Work specialization

chain of command

Authority

Responsibility

Accountability

Delegation

_____ is the framework in which the organization defines how tasks are divided, resources are deployed, and departments are coordinated. This framework becomes the _____, which is the visual representation of an organization's structure. Workers specialize in tasks to promote efficiency and expertise. _____ is the degree to which organizational tasks are subdivided into individual jobs. Each worker should understand how the chain of command works. The _____ is an unbroken line of authority that links all individuals in the organization and specifies who reports to whom. _____ is the formal and legitimate right of a manager to make decisions, issue orders, and allocate resources to achieve organizationally desired outcomes. Authority is vested in the organization, is accepted by subordinates, and flows down the vertical hierarchy. _____ is the duty to perform the task or activity that an employee has been assigned. Authority equal to the responsibility should be given. Accountability balances authority and responsibility. _____ is the fact that the people with authority and responsibility are subject to reporting and justifying task outcomes to those above them in the chain of command. It must be understood by subordinates and may be built into the organizational structure. _____ is the process managers use to transfer authority and responsibility to positions below them in the hierarchy. This provides flexibility.

Line authority

A line department performs tasks related to the primary goal of the organization. _____ is a form of authority in which individuals in

staff authority

management positions have the formal power to direct and control immediate subordinates. Staff departments support line departments. They have _____, which is a form of authority granted to staff specialists in their areas of expertise.

Span of management
Tall

flat

Centralization
decentralization

_____, or *span of control*, is the number of employees who report to a supervisor. It determines how closely subordinates can be monitored by the supervisor. _____ structure is a management structure characterized by an overall narrow span of management and a relatively large number of hierarchical levels, while a _____ structure is a management structure characterized by an overall broad span of control and relatively few hierarchical levels. The recent trend has been towards flat structures. _____ is the location of decision authority near top organizational levels and _____ is the location of decision authority near lower organizational levels. While the trend has been for firms to decentralize, there are several factors which influence the best degree of decentralization.

Formalization

_____ is the written documentation used to direct and control employees. This includes rule books, policies, procedures, job descriptions, and regulations.

Departmentalization

Departmen-
talization
vertical functional

divisional

matrix

_____ is the basis on which individuals are grouped into departments and departments into the total organization. There are five basic approaches to departmentalization. The _____ structure is an organizational structure in which positions are grouped into departments based on similar skills, expertise, and use of resources. There are many advantages as well as several disadvantages of this approach, but it is the most common approach used. An organizational structure in which the departments are grouped based on similar organizational outputs is called a _____ structure. The division may be based on geographic region. The division also has both advantages and disadvantages to consider. The _____ structure is an organizational structure that uses functional and divisional chains of command simultaneously in the same part of the organization. The matrix structure is used when there is strong pressure for both a strong functional and a team-based departmentalization.

two-boss

matrix boss

The matrix structure provides both of these simultaneously in the same part of the organization. While providing these and other advantages, the matrix structure does violate unity of command, which often leads to problems if not managed correctly. This structure has a _____ employee, who is an employee that reports to two supervisors simultaneously. Such an employee must resolve conflicts from each _____, who is a product or functional boss, responsible for one side of the matrix. Disputes can ultimately be solved

top leader

by the _____, who is the overseer of both the product and the functional chains of command, responsible for the entire matrix.

The most widespread trend today is the use of teams in organizations. A

cross-functional

_____ team is a group of employees from various functional department that meets as a team to resolve mutual problems. These are

permanent

especially popular in the computer industry. A _____ team is a group of participants from several departments that meets regularly to solve ongoing

reegineering

problems of common interest. Many companies organize into teams after _____, which is the radical redesign of business process to achieve dramatic improvements in cost, quality, service, and speed. The newest

network

departmentalization approach is the _____ structure, which is an organizational structure that allows the firm to subcontract many of its major functions to separate companies that are coordinated by a small headquarters

modular

organization. In the _____ approach, a manufacturing company uses outside suppliers to provide entire chinks of a product which are then assembled into a final product by a handful of workers. This is particularly

virtual

popular among international corporations. A _____ *organization* is a continually evolving group of companies that unite temporarily to achieve an objective. Each company remains independent, but gives up some control temporarily. Data and information is hared electronically among participating companies.

Chapter Review

Multiple-Choice Questions: Please indicate the correct response to the following questions by writing the letter of the correct answer in the space provided.

___ 1. Organizational structure includes all of the following except
   a. division of labor.
   b. hierarchy of authority.
   c. hiring procedures.
   d. departmentalization.
   e. All of the above are part of the organization structure.

___ 2. Although work specialization has many advantages, _____ is a disadvantage of specialization.
   a. the development of boring jobs
   b. inherent inefficiency
   c. lack of development of expertise by workers
   d. lack of standardization
   e. not being able to select employees with proper abilities

___ 3. A larger span of control is called for when
   a. work performed by subordinates is unstable and changing.
   b. subordinates perform dissimilar tasks.
   c. subordinates are spread out geographically.
   d. little time is required in nonsupervisory activities.
   e. there are no support systems available for the manager.

___ 4. As a staff person, a personnel manager would most likely
   a. tell a line manager when to fire an employee.
   b. help a line manager develop a job description.
   c. determine which employee a line manager hires.
   d. give advice on employee grievances.
   e. both b and d

___ 5. The five approaches to departmentalization reflect differences in
   a. chain of command.
   b. departments.
   c. lateral relationships.
   d. all of the above
   e. b and c only

___   6.   Grouping employees into departments based on similar skills has what advantage?
    a.   quickness of response to environmental changes
    b.   better coordination across functions
    c.   better communication among departments
    d.   economies of scale
    e.   produces motivating employee tasks

___   7.   The divisional structure is sometimes called a _____ structure.
    a.   product
    b.   program
    c.   self-contained unit
    d.   all of the above
    e.   only a and b

___   8.   A divisional structure can be based on
    a.   geography.
    b.   functions.
    c.   teams.
    d.   staffs.
    e.   all of the above.

___   9.   The divisional structure may result in
    a.   slow responses to the environment.
    b.   poor coordination across divisions.
    c.   more top management control.
    d.   difficulty in pinpointing responsibility for product problems.
    e.   poor coordination across functional departments.

___   10.   The matrix structure _____ the vertical chain of command for functional departments.
    a.   maintains
    b.   weakens
    c.   destroys
    d.   ignores
    e.   none of the above

___   11.   The matrix structure is often
    a.   less efficient in the use of resources than the divisional structure.
    b.   inflexible to a changing environment.
    c.   a good training ground for general and functional managers.
    d.   the reason for reduction of conflict between divisional and functional interests.
    e.   the reason for reduced scope of tasks for employees.

___ 12.   The _____ structure allows efficient use of scarce resources, but it does not enable the organization to be flexible or innovative.
   a.   matrix
   b.   divisional
   c.   vertical functional
   d.   team
   e.   vertical functional with lateral relations

___ 13.   Which of the following is true of authority?
   a.   It is vested in people, not their positions.
   b.   A manager has authority only if subordinates choose to accept his or her commands.
   c.   Positions at the bottom of the hierarchy are vested with more formal authority than are those at the top.
   d.   A subordinate will obey an order outside his or her zone of acceptance.
   e.   Authority cannot be illustrated by the organizational chart.

___ 14.   _____ is the duty to perform the task or activity an employee has been assigned.
   a.   Authority
   b.   Accountability
   c.   Power
   d.   Responsibility
   e.   Span of management

___ 15.   Accountability means that the people with authority and responsibility are subject to _____ those above them in the chain of command.
   a.   reporting and justifying task outcomes to
   b.   the whims of
   c.   the mercy of
   d.   the span of management of
   e.   the decentralization of

___ 16.   The process whereby managers transfer authority and responsibility to lower positions is called
   a.   accountability.
   b.   responsibility sharing.
   c.   departmentalization.
   d.   creation of span of management.
   e.   delegation.

___ 17.   A department that performs tasks reflecting the organization's primary goal and mission is called a _____ department.
   a.   line
   b.   staff
   c.   functional
   d.   product
   e.   production

___ 18. The trend in the today is toward _____ spans of control.
 a. smaller
 b. no
 c. larger
 d. equalized
 e. managerial

___ 19. Johnson & Johnson gives almost complete authority to its 166 companies to develop and market their own products. This is an example of
 a. loss of control.
 b. spreading oneself too thinly.
 c. authoritarianism.
 d. decentralization.
 e. centralization.

___ 20. Many companies have made a religion out of
 a. Christianity.
 b. profit maximization.
 c. staying lean at the top.
 d. increasing formalization.
 e. increasing the number of top managers.

___ 21. The _____ approach creates a series of task forces to accomplish specific tasks.
 a. vertical functional
 b. divisional
 c. horizontal matrix
 d. team
 e. network

___ 22. Which approach provides poor training for general managers?
 a. vertical functional
 b. divisional
 c. horizontal matrix
 d. team
 e. network

___ 23. The most widespread trend in departmentalization has been the effort to implement the _____ approach.
 a. vertical functional
 b. divisional
 c. matrix
 d. team
 e. network

___ 24. With a cross-functional team the team members formally report up the chain of command, but they have a _____ relationship to the team.
   a. stronger
   b. direct
   c. poor
   d. dotted-line
   e. personal

___ 25. Permanent team employees are placed in
   a. a series of temporary relationships on a permanent basis.
   b. the same location.
   c. an off-site office.
   d. the organizational chart within a dotted-line box.
   e. high esteem by the rest of the organization.

___ 26. The question, "Where is the organization?" is most likely to be asked concerning the
_____ approach.
   a. vertical functional
   b. divisional
   c. horizontal matrix
   d. team
   e. network

___ 27. Which of the following is an advantage of the network structure?
   a. less hands-on control, providing autonomy
   b. less employee loyalty, meaning more motivation
   c. more administrative tasks
   d. global competitiveness
   e. easy to understand

___ 28. Turnover tends to be higher in a _____ organization.
   a. vertical functional
   b. divisional
   c. matrix
   d. team
   e. network

___ 29. The matrix organization uses _____ simultaneously.
   a. two chains of command
   b. authority and responsibility
   c. authority and delegation
   d. expectations and goals
   e. centralization and decentralization

___ 30. The best organizational structure to use is
a. vertical functional.
b. divisional.
c. matrix.
d. team.
e. dependent on the needs of the competitive situation.

True/False Questions: Please indicate whether the following questions are true or false by writing a T or an F in the blank in front of each question.

___ 1. Differences in structure have major consequences for employee goals, but do not affect employee motivation.

___ 2. The chain of command shows who reports to whom.

___ 3. Written documentation often creates more problems than it solves.

___ 4. Departmentalization by function means that employees with diverse skills are grouped together to achieve a specific product or project outcome.

___ 5. Generally, when supervisors must be closely involved with subordinates, the span of management should be large.

___ 6. A fundamental principle is that work can be performed more efficiently if employees are allowed to specialize.

___ 7. In a vertical functional organizational structure employees tend to focus on the attainment of departmental goals.

___ 8. In very large companies a divisional structure just doesn't make sense.

___ 9. If the efficient use of internal resources, top management control, and employee specialization and expertise are of primary importance, a vertical functional structure is better than a divisional structure.

___ 10. In the matrix structure one actually has dual lines of authority.

Short-Answer Questions

1.   Explain why the chain of command is important to an organization.

2.   What are the advantages and disadvantages of decentralization?

3.   Explain the reasons for the vertical functional approach to departmentalization.

4.   What are the disadvantages of the divisional structure?

5.   Why are organizations turning to the team approach of departmentalization?

Management Applications

Putting It on the Line or Staff

Someone would have to settle this dispute. It looked like the Executive Vice-President, Don King, would have to settle it. Things were just getting out of hand. Here's the problem.

The buyers for Independent Affiliated Grocers, headquartered in Kansas City, wanted to have control over setting prices for the products that they bought. Their rationale is as follows: We know both our retail clients and their customers the best. We have the responsibility of being in touch with the market in making the buying decision. When we buy a product, we expect it to sell well for the company. We base that expectation on many factors, one of which is price. We know approximately what the product must sell for in the marketplace. When the pricing department sets a price that is too high, then sales are below expectations and we get the complaints for having made a poor buying decision. If the pricing department sets the price too low, then the company not only loses money, but we run out of inventory too soon because sales are too brisk. We again get blamed, this time for buying the wrong quantity.

The pricing department also wants to control the setting of prices on items bought by the company for resale to its retail accounts. Its reasoning goes like this: We have to have uniform procedures in place to run an orderly business. We can't just let every buyer set prices as he or she sees fit. That way we have no logic or order to the systems. Some prices will look too high or low as compared to others by our customers. Such a practice also makes the job of the pricing department only clerical in nature, and that is not our function. We are the pricing department, not just people who fill out forms. Besides, we can keep the big picture in mind when it comes to pricing items and consider the pricing strategy of the entire company.

1.   What kind of departments are the buying and pricing departments in this case, line or staff?

2. Does the age of the company have any impact on this conflict?

3. Assume that you are Don King, the Vice-President who has to make the decision on who will determine the prices. How would you settle this issue?

How Does It Look to You?

Look at the following organizational structure and identify what, if anything, is wrong with it:

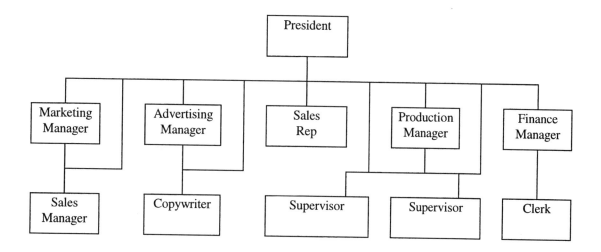

Mini Case

The Unorganized Church Office

You have been called in as a consultant for a regional office of a church. They tell you they need to come up with a better organizational structure. When you ask them for a copy of their current organization chart, you are told they have none. However, they are willing to draw a depiction of the current positions and relationships on a chalkboard for you. The finished chart looks like the following.

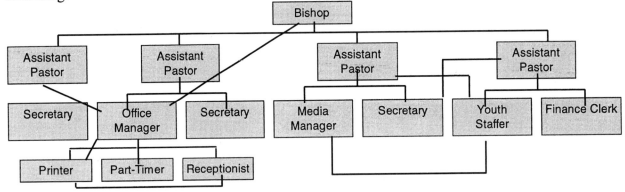

1.   What is wrong with this organization chart?

2.   What would you recommend the organization do to fix this chart?

3.   Draw an improved organization chart for this church office.

Experiential Exercise

Portable Holes

The geniuses in the Physics Department at your college have just created PORTABLE HOLES. This product comes in small to large cylinders that one places where a hole is desired. You only need to indicate the depth of the desired hole on the small LCD indicator on the top of the cylinder and then press a button. A hole is instantly created in the spot you have placed the cylinder. The cylinders come in different diameters to produce holes of various sizes. The holes can be made in any type of material. You are not sure exactly how it all works, but have been told that a tiny laser actually cuts the hole. Your class has been asked by the Student Physics Club to organize a business to produce and sell this product.

1. Your job is to draw the organization chart below and be ready to explain the rationale for the structure and defend it.

2. The instructor will then ask a number of students to draw their proposed structures on the board.

3. The class will then be allowed to ask questions and discuss the charts on the board. Then the class will vote on which structure it feels is the best.

Study Guide Solutions

Chapter Review

Multiple-Choice Questions

1	2	3	4	5	6	7	8	9	10
c	a	d	e	d	d	d	a	b	a

11	12	13	14	15	16	17	18	19	20
c	c	b	d	a	e	a	c	d	c

21	22	23	24	25	26	27	28	29	30
d	a	d	d	b	e	d	e	a	e

True/False Questions

1	2	3	4	5	6	7	8	9	10
F	T	T	F	F	T	T	F	T	T

Short-Answer Questions

1. The chain of command is important because it communicates to the persons in the organization the formal flow of communications and authority. It will tell each person to whom s/he should report and for whom s/he is responsible.

2. Decentralization provides greater use of human resources, unburdens top managers, ensures that decisions are made close to the action by well-informed people, and permits more rapid response to external changes. However, there will be less control by top management, less standardization, and the loss of economies of scale.

3. One will choose a vertical functional structure to take advantage of economies of scale, provide for more efficiency, greater specialization, and career progress by personnel. It is also useful for maintaining control by top management who can coordinate the functions well. It provides for high-quality technical problem solving.

4. The divisional structure duplicates resources across divisions and provides less technical depth and specialization. Usually, there is poor coordination across divisions and less control by top management. Often, the divisions compete with one another for corporate resources.

5.　The team approach allows companies to make decisions more quickly, pushes the responsibility to lower levels, gains commitment of workers through participation, and allows more flexibility to changes in the environment.

Management Applications

Putting It on the Line or Staff

1.　The buying department is a line department since it is performing a major function of this business, which evidently is to buy goods from manufacturers and resell them to retailers. The pricing department is a staff department since it contains specialists who are there to facilitate business.

2.　It could well be that in the younger days of the company there were not many professional staff or clerical personnel. In those days the buyers were probably free to set their own prices. As the company has become more mature and hired staff specialists, it is facing some resistance from buyers who are used to having more freedom.

3.　This is a difficult situation to be in for Don King since both sides have some valid points. One approach might be to try to use a conflict resolution technique to allow the two warring factions to settle the conflict themselves and still feel good about it. I would probably let the pricing department make the decision, but reserve some overriding authority for the buyers, as approved by some higher authority such as the vice-president.

How Does It Look to You?

There are several things wrong with this organizational structure:

1.　The President's span of management appears to be too large, which would make him ineffective.

2.　The principle of unity of command is violated for several persons. The Sales Manager reports to both the Marketing Manager and the President. The Copywriter reports to both the Advertising Manager and the President. The two Supervisors report to both the Production Manager and the President.

3.　It appears that the Sales Rep, who reports directly to the President, should report to the Sales Manager. In fact, the Advertising Manager should probably also report to the Marketing Manager.

Mini Case

The Unorganized Church Office

1. The receptionist reports to no one. Many persons have more than one boss. The reporting relationships are very confused.

2. It seems the office needs to find out just what everyone does. Job descriptions need to be developed. Then lines of authority and responsibility need to be determined.

3. The chart that each student will draw will vary. Following is a chart developed by one student.

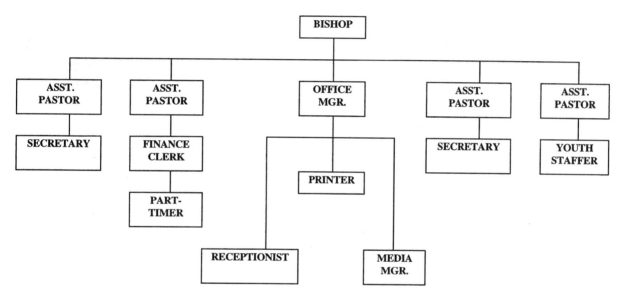

Experiential Exercise

The results of this exercise will vary by class. Most students will probably use the vertical functional approach since that is what most of us are familiar with in our own experiences.

Chapter 11

Using Structural Design to Achieve Strategic Goals

Chapter Summary

After you have read the text chapter, read through the summary below. Cover the left-hand margin and fill in the blanks with the appropriate terms. After you have filled in each blank, check your responses by uncovering the answer given in the margin. If you do not understand why the given answer is the correct one, refer back to the text.

The Horizontal Organization

In today's changing environment companies are moving toward horizontal structures based on work processes rather than departmental functions. Management needs mechanisms for horizontal coordination. _____ is the quality of collaboration across departments. A _____ _____ is a person responsible for coordinating the activities of several departments on a full-time basis for the completion of a specific project. _____ involves the radical redesign of business processes to achieve dramatic improvements in cost, quality, service, and speed. This leads to strong coordination across functional areas and greater flexibility in responding to changes in the environment. It involves identifying customer needs and then designing processes and aligning people to meet those needs. This often entails use of small, cross-functional work teams. A _____ is a temporary team or committee formed to solve a specific short-run problem involving several departments. While representing their own departments, the task force members share information which facilitates coordination. A _____ is a group of participants from several departments who meet regularly to solve ongoing problems of common interest. Business process _____ is the radical redesign of business processes to achieve dramatic improvements in cost, quality, service, and speed. It emphasizes stronger horizontal coordination and greater flexibility in responding to changes in the environment. The emphasis is on teams and providing value to customers. A _____ is an organized group of related tasks and activities that work together to transform inputs into outputs and create value.

Margin answers: Coordination / Project manager / Reengineering / task force / team / reengineering / process

Traditional versus the New Workplace

The trend is a shift away from a vertical or traditional organization toward a horizontal or learning organization. A traditional organization has little horizontal coordination, information is communicated vertically and not shared, employees are highly specialized, decision making is centralized, and the culture is rigid. The *learning organization* uses a horizontal team-based structure, opens information, decentralized decision making, empowers employees and has a strong adaptive culture. Self-directed teams are the fundamental unit in a learning organization. The culture values change, risk-taking, and improvement.

Factors Affecting Structure

The strategic goals of the organization will affect the type of organization structure it employs because structure follows strategy. Another major factor is the degree of certainty in the environment. When the external environment is certain, the organization should have a traditional vertical structure that emphasizes control. When the environment is uncertain, an new workplace horizontal structure is more appropriate.

Technology

As the manufacturing and service technological complexity of an organization increases, so does the degree of formalization. _____ is the knowledge, tools, techniques, and activities used to transform the organization's inputs into outputs. In the manufacturing sector small batch and continuous process technologies call for a new workplace horizontal structure, while the mass production type of business is better off with a traditional vertical

Small batch

structure. _____ is a type of production technology that involves the production of goods in batches of one or a few products designed to customer

Continuous

specifications. _____ process production is a type of technology involving mechanization of the entire work flow and nonstop production. The

technical complexity

difference among the three manufacturing technologies is called _____, which is the degree to which complex machinery is involved in the production process to the exclusion of people. Technology that is characterized by intangible outputs and direct contact between employees and

service

customers is called _____ technology. In the service sector, the more routine the service, the more traditional vertical it should be. If the service is nonroutine, it is better to use the new workplace horizontal structure. Organizations based on digital technology also tend to be flexible and decentralized.

interdependence

The last contingency factor affecting organizational structure is called _____ and refers to the extent to which departments depend on each other for resources or materials to accomplish their tasks. This interdependence may be pooled, sequential, or reciprocal.

Chapter Review

Multiple-Choice Questions: Please indicate the correct response to the following questions by writing the letter of the correct answer in the space provided.

___ 1. Reengineering involves
   a. radically revising business processes.
   b. organizing around key business processes.
   c. throwing out all the notions of how work *was* done.
   d. identifying customer needs and designing process to meet them.
   e. All of the above.

___ 2. Which of the following would most likely be responsible for coordinating the activities of several departments on a full-time basis for the completion of a specific project?
   a. project manager
   b. personnel manager
   c. advertising manager
   d. vice-president of finance
   e. production manager

___ 3. In a(n) _____ three things happen: differentiation, need for greater coordination, and the need to adapt to change.
   a. certain environment
   b. uncertain environment
   c. contingency environment
   d. traditional vertical organization
   e. service economy

4. Which of the following describes the learning organization?
   a. everyone is engaged in identifying and solving problems
   b. the organizations continuously experiments
   c. the organizations continuously improves
   d. the organizations increases its capacity to learn and grow
   e. all of the above.

5. The open information aspect of a learning organization means that
   a. information is widely shared.
   b. the government has access to all our books.
   c. even the competition knows what we are doing.
   d. special interest groups are given free access to everything.
   e. all of the above.

6. In a _____ production system, one finds the manufacturing of large, one-of-a-kind products.
   a. mass
   b. continuous process
   c. small batch
   d. service
   e. technically obsolete

7. In a mass production manufacturing environment
   a. an new workplace horizontal structure is best.
   b. a high degree of centralization works best.
   c. a small span of control is needed.
   d. there is a low degree of technical complexity.
   e. the amount of written (vertical) communications is low.

8. Reegineering
   a. is inexpensive to implement.
   b. is implemented in a relatively short time.
   c. is often painful.
   d. does not involve management.
   e. does not involve rank and file workers.

9. The traditional vertical organization is characterized by
   a. many teams.
   b. open information.
   c. centralized strategic decision making.
   d. strong adaptive culture.
   e. empowered employees.

10. Coordination is required in large organizations using a _____ structure.
    a. functional
    b. divisional
    c. team
    d. all of the above
    e. only a and b

11. When a project manager is used in an organization,
    a. he has authority over the people assigned to the project.
    b. he does not have authority over the project, just the people who work on it.
    c. he is responsible for coordination with assigned team members.
    d. he has line authority over functional employees.
    e. he is usually shown on the organizational chart with a solid line to indicate this authority over team members.

___ 12. An emphasis on vertical structure means
   a. less opportunity for horizontal coordination.
   b. decentralized decision making.
   c. cross-functional teams are implemented.
   d. employees are given great freedom to pursue their tasks.
   e. less control by top management.

___ 13. The _____ structure uses two chains of command, a functional hierarchy to promote efficiency and a product hierarchy to promote innovation and coordination.
   a. divisional
   b. functional
   c. team
   d. matrix
   e. traditional vertical

___ 14. Reengineering is sometimes called
   a. total quality management.
   b. business process reengineering.
   c. quality circles.
   d. insane.
   e. humanistic.

___ 15. Organizations based on digital technology tend to
   a. be flexible and decentralized.
   b. be unorganized.
   c. be tightly organized.
   d. use the traditional vertical structure.
   e. none of the above.

___ 16. A low level of interdependence means that departments
   a. do their work independently.
   b. have a high need for interaction.
   c. need to coordinate more closely.
   d. need to exchange materials.
   e. have immature employees.

___ 17. Pooled interdependence means that
   a. each department is relatively dependent.
   b. work flows between units.
   c. each department contributes to the common good.
   d. financial resources are the only resource not shared.
   e. betting on college football games is allowed.

___ 18. The type of interdependence in which the outputs of one department become the inputs to another department is called _____ interdependence.
   a. pooled
   b. sequential
   c. reciprocal
   d. synergistic
   e. new workplace horizontal

___ 19. With reciprocal interdependence the output of operation A is the input to operation _____, and the output of operation B is the input to operation _____.
   a. B, A
   b. B, C
   c. B, B
   d. A, B
   e. A, A

20. The new workplace learning organization is characterized by
   a. few teams.
   b. horizontal communication.
   c. centralized strategic decision making
   d. specialized tasks.
   e. rigid culture.

___ 21. The learning organization
   a. strives to break down boundaries with other companies
   b. will avoid virtual teams
   c. does not employ structural innovations
   d. fosters non-collaboration between organizations
   e. fosters non-collaboration within organizations

___ 22. The divisional structure promotes differentiation because
   a. each division can focus on specific products and customers.
   b. individualism is highly valued.
   c. teamwork is not needed.
   d. government regulations require nonstandardized procedures for such an organization.
   e. managers of these types of organizations are prejudiced.

___ 23. With greater environmental differences more emphasis on _____ is required to link departments together.
   a. new workplace horizontal structure
   b. informal communications
   c. lateral coordination
   d. vertical control
   e. a traditional vertical structure

___ 24. When the external environment is highly uncertain,
  a. the structure can emphasize specialization.
  b. centralized decision making works best.
  c. a wide span of control is wise.
  d. there will be little emphasis on vertical control.
  e. the organization should have a traditional vertical structure.

25. A participative strategy relies on a(n) _____ mindset.
  a. rigid
  b. strong
  c. experimental
  d. humanistic
  e. none of the above

___ 26. _____ interdependence is the most difficult.
  a. Pooled
  b. Sequential
  c. Reciprocal
  d. Synergistic
  e. New workplace horizontal

___ 27. Task force members represent
  a. management.
  b. the union.
  c. their departments.
  d. no one so they can remain objective.
  e. integrated coordination.

28. The set of key values, beliefs, understandings, and norms shared by members of the organization is what is known as
  a. corporate policies.
  b. corporate culture.
  c. norming.
  d. participative management.
  e. strategy.

___ 29. When the vertical structure is very tight, the organization is very
  a. traditional vertical.
  b. new workplace horizontal.
  c. well integrated.
  d. uptight.
  e. poorly organized.

___ 30. The divisional structure promotes _____ because each division can focus on specific products or customers.
   a. coordination
   b. a common goal
   c. inefficiencies
   d. differentiation
   e. economies of scale

True/False Questions: Please indicate whether the following questions are true or false by writing a T or an F in the blank in front of each question.

___ 1. In the new workplace learning organization, the vertical structure that created distance between the top and bottom of the organization is disbanded.

___ 2. When the vertical structure is very strong, it is said to be new workplace horizontal structure because it can adapt so well to the environment.

___ 3. When the external environment is certain, the organization should have a traditional vertical structure that emphasizes vertical control.

___ 4. There is an increasing shift toward more horizontal structures rather than vertical structures.

___ 5. Structure must be designed to fit the technology as well as to accommodate the external environment and organization size.

___ 6. The nonroutine, people-oriented services tend to use the new workplace horizontal structure.

___ 7. When managers use the wrong structure for the environment, reduced performance will result.

___ 8. Due to the increasing use of the Internet in the new workplace, organizations need to use stronger horizontal coordination.

___ 9. Reengineering refers to an event that happens only in the engineering department.

___ 10. A useful way to think about technology is as "work flow."

Short-Answer Questions

1. Why are the formal chain of command and supervision not adequate in providing coordination?

2. If an organization has the strategic objective of cost leadership, why would the functional structure be appropriate?

3. Should an organization maintain flexibility in an uncertain environment? Explain your answer.

4.   Provide an example of sequential interdependence at the school you are presently attending.

Management Applications

Top Hat Furniture Store

When the founder of Top Hat Furniture Store decided to retire, he turned the business over to his two sons; Jim and Ed. Jim had been with the company for several years and had specialized in buying appliances for the company. Ed had also worked for the company for several years, and he specialized in buying the furniture items the store sold. These two brothers ran the business jointly. They had employed by the business two service persons, eight salespersons, a secretary, two delivery persons, and five part-time employees.

When asked by a consultant who was in charge of what, Ed replied that it depended on who was around. If someone could find Jim, he would make the decision. Otherwise, Ed would make the decision. Assignments were made according to the product line that each brother specialized in. Some decisions such as personnel, running a sale, and maintenance items were made jointly by the brothers.

Both brothers felt just a little uncomfortable with this organizational structure. Even though things seemed to be running fairly well, they thought maybe things could run smoother if the structure were improved. They have called in a consultant to analyze their structure and tell them what to do. Based on an initial meeting, the organization chart that follows was developed.

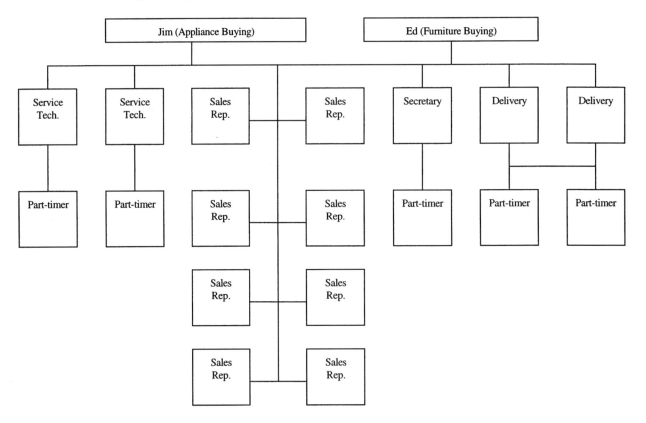

1. Is it possible to classify the existing organizational structure as functional, functional with lateral relationships, divisional, or matrix?

2. How would you suggest that the company be organized?

Good Samaritan Hospital

Good Samaritan Hospital is organized like many other hospitals. The medical staff reports to the medical staff executive council and is considered under the authority of the administrator. However, the medical staff executive council has direct communication with the board of directors. Five persons report directly to the administrator: director of community relations, vice-president of human resources, and three assistant administrators. One assistant administrator is in charge of professional services, which includes the following fifteen departments: home health, social service, medical records, pharmacy, cardiopulmonary services, rehabilitation and EEG, volunteer services, educational services, mobile intensive care unit, hospice, anesthesia, diagnostic imaging, laboratory, pastoral care, and radiation therapy.

Another assistant administrator is in charge of the following six fiscal and general services departments: accounting and data processing, patient accounts and communications, food services, housekeeping, maintenance/engineering, and materials management.

The third assistant administrator is in charge of the following fourteen nursing service units: assistant director of nursing, patient care coordinators, outpatient services, surgery/recovery, CICU, dialysis, 2 north (designated by location of nurse station), 3 north, 3 south, 4 central, pediatrics, OB, nurseries, and quality assurance and information control nurse.

1.   What approach is this to structural design?

2. Lately, the hospital has faced several changes in its environment. The nation and government have become concerned with the containment of health costs, which impacts charges the hospital can make for its services. A managed health care system integrating doctors, clinics, hospitals, and other health care providers is also being developed. Another change is the growth in the number of outpatient services. Now people are staying shorter times in the hospital or getting treatment at the hospital and going home for recovery. Good Samaritan is also experiencing competition from other hospitals in the area who are aggressively marketing themselves. Competition is also coming from the home birth movement and the number of licensed midwives delivering babies at home. In light of all these factors should Good Samaritan change its organizational structure? Justify your answer, and if you recommend a change, specify how it should change.

Mini Case

The Business Department

The University of Wahoo used to be a small state-supported teacher's college located in the middle of Nebraska. Now it has grown to a college of over 9,000 students with about 35 percent of its graduates in business. It also has an MBA program with about 200 students. The business department is now assessing its organizational structure. There is only one single business department with 22 full-time and 16 part-time instructors. The department chairman works very hard to keep this department running smoothly. It consists of professors from many different disciplines: management, marketing, accounting, finance, business law, computer information systems, and business education. Making decisions and coming to agreements on goals are always a hassle. The dean of the School of Business & Technology is considering how this department might be restructured.

1. If you were the dean, how would you restructure this department? Justify your answer.

2. Would it be better to leave the department the way it is now?

Experiential Exercise

Build the Organization from Scratch

For this exercise you should be divided into small groups of about four persons. Each group has the assignment of designing an organization from scratch. The type of business and its environment are described below. After describing the organizational structure, be ready to justify it when called on by the instructor.

The Company

Jeff Barker has decided to start a new company. This company will manufacture foam products. The foam is produced through a chemical process and comes out in giant "loaves" which are cut to various sizes for customers. Jeff has worked for such a company for over 10 years and understands the business well. He recently moved to a new state in the Midwest where no foam company is located. He has received strong financial support and has the time needed to make the company a success.

The Industry

Most of the companies in the industry are located in the Southeast. It is a very competitive business. The major customers of the product are industrial customers who are very conscious of both quality and price. Since most of the companies have mastered the technology, no one company has an advantage in quality.

Study Guide Solutions

Chapter Review

Multiple-Choice Questions

1	2	3	4	5	6	7	8	9	10
e	a	b	e	a	c	b	c	c	d

11	12	13	14	15	16	17	18	19	20
c	a	d	b	a	a	c	b	a	b

21	22	23	24	25	26	27	28	29	30
a	a	c	d	c	c	c	b	a	d

True/False Questions

1	2	3	4	5	6	7	8	9	10
T	F	T	T	T	T	T	T	F	T

Short-Answer Questions

1. The chain of command and supervision are not enough to provide coordination because the organization needs to also be concerned about the flow of information and of communications. The organizational structure defines a system for these factors.

2. The functional structure is most appropriate for achieving internal efficiency. This will result in lower operating costs, allowing the organization to pursue a cost leadership strategy.

3. Yes, an organization in an uncertain environment should maintain a high degree of flexibility. An uncertain environment often changes, which requires the organization to change also. Flexibility must be present so the organization can adapt to the change.

4. Sequential interdependence means that parts of the outputs of one department become inputs to another department. In a typical college setting this could be illustrated by the relationship between the admissions department and the registrar's office. The students admitted and their paperwork, which is the output of the admissions office, are input to the registrar's office in preparing registration materials for new students.

Management Applications

Top Hat Furniture Store

1. It is very difficult to categorize the organizational structure as described. It is probably closest to the functional with lateral relationships approach. However, the top of the organization is really not defined very well.

2. One suggestion is that the brothers each pick out a functional area to specialize in and that the company then be organized fully on a functional with lateral relationships basis. For example, one brother could be in charge of sales and plan all marketing activities and take care of deliveries as well as manage the salesforce. The other brother could be in charge of administration and take charge of the secretary, service personnel, bookkeeping, and personnel functions. A close communication between the partners as well as the departments underneath them will be necessary for this structure to work.

Good Samaritan Hospital

1. It appears to be a functional structure, although the span of management for the assistant vice-presidents seems to be rather large and broad in scope. One might also classify this as a professional bureaucracy.

2. It seems that with this changing environment, the hospital needs something to give it more flexibility. Probably a hybrid structure would be more appropriate. This would provide it with the structure needed for the routine tasks it must perform as well as the flexibility to cope with a changing environment.

Mini Case

The Business Department

1. The dean would probably advocate a professional bureaucracy and break the department into functional areas. This seems to be justified by the diverse instructional areas, each having different educational goals.

2. One could make a good argument for leaving the department in its present structure. It is not really too large for a department as many departments at large universities have departments of this size. However, in context of the diversity of the functional areas, the size of the school, and the size of other departments on the campus, most observers would probably recommend a change.

Experiential Exercise

Build the Organization from Scratch

The answers developed with the students will probably vary greatly. Most students will design a company that is organized along functional lines since that is what most of us are familiar with. Since this industry seems to be highly price conscious, keeping costs under control is very important. A functional structure is probably the most appropriate design for accomplishing this purpose. It will be interesting to see how many student teams decide to have a research and development department. Investments in R&D could result in technological breakthroughs, allowing the company to offer lower-priced products.

Chapter 12

Change and Development

Chapter Summary

After you have read the text chapter, read through the summary below. Cover the left-hand margin and fill in the blanks with the appropriate terms. After you have filled in each blank, check your responses by uncovering the answer given in the margin. If you do not understand why the given answer is the correct one, refer back to the text.

Change and the New Workplace

change
learning
organization

Organizational _____ is the adoption of a new idea or behavior by an organization. The current trend is toward development of the _____, in which everyone is engaged in identifying and solving problems, enabling the organization to continuously improve and increase its capability. Included in this type of organization are elements which influence each other. These elements include leadership, empowerment, culture, information sharing, strategy, and horizontal structure. The learning organization embraces both operational change and transformational change.

Model of Planned Organizational Change

A model for planned change consists of environmental and internal forces for change which are monitored to make managers aware of the need for change. This awareness triggers the initiation of change, which is then implemented. External forces such as customers, competitors, technology, the economy, and international events can cause changes. Internal forces for change come from internal activities and decisions. Managers need to learn to sense

performance gap

_____, which is a disparity between existing and desired performance levels by analyzing strengths and weaknesses in the organization and problems and opportunities in the environment.

Initiating Change

search

Before change can occur, ideas to solve needs must be developed. One way this can occur is through the process of searching. A _____ is the process

creativity

idea champion

new-venture team

skunkworks

new-venture fund

idea incubator

of learning about current developments inside or outside the organization that can be used to meet a perceived need for change. If none is found, then _____, which is the development of novel ideas that may meet perceived needs or offer opportunities for the organization, must be fostered. Just as creative people have certain characteristics; departments have certain qualities that encourage creativity also. They are more open, allow different behaviors, are more loosely defined, allow more autonomy, and reward creativity. For a creative idea to be adopted by the organization, an _____ has to be present. This is a person who sees the need for and champions productive change within the organization. Some organizations have a _____, which is a unit separate from the mainstream of the organization that is responsible for developing and initiating innovations. A _____ is a separate small, informal, highly autonomous, and often secretive group that focuses on breakthrough ideas for the business. Another rendition of new-venture teams is the _____, which provides resources from which individuals and groups draw to develop new ideas, products, or businesses. An _____ _____ is an in-house program that provides a save harbor where ideas from employees throughout the organization can be developed without interference from company bureaucracy or politics.

Implementing Change

force field

To implement change managers need to realize that change is often resisted. Employees may resist change because of their own self-interests, because they don't understand the purpose or distrust the stated intentions, because of uncertainty about what it means, or because they assess the outcomes of the proposed change differently. Often, a _____ analysis can help in getting a change implemented. This entails determining which forces drive and which resist a proposed change. Next, a manager has to determine imple-mentation tactics. One tactic is to use communication and education. Partici-pation, negotiation, or even coercion may also be useful tactics, depending on the situation. Regardless of the tactic used, it is essential to have the support of top management to implement a change.

Types of Planned Change

technology

product

One type of change is a _____ change, which involves a change in the production process. This type of change is most effective when the ideas are developed at lower levels of the organization (the bottom-up approach). A _____ change, which is a change in the organization's product or service output, should also use the bottom-up approach, but must also cut across functional lines to be effective. One approach to product change is the

horizontal linkage
time-based

Structural

_____ model, which emphasizes shared development of innovations among several departments. Also useful is _____ competition, which is a strategy of competition based on the ability to deliver products and services faster than competitors. _____ change, which involves the way in which the organization is designed and managed, is most successful using a top-down approach.

Culture/People Changes

culture/people

A _____ change refers to changes in employees' values, norms, attitudes, beliefs, and behavior. Training is one of the most frequently used approaches to changing the organization's mindset. Training and development programs are often aimed at changing individual behavior and interpersonal skills.

team-building

survey feedback

Large group

Organizational development (OD) involves the use of behavioral science techniques to improve an organization's health and effectiveness through its ability to cope with environmental changes, improve internal relationships, and increase problem-solving capabilities. Current problems addressed by OD include *mergers/acquisitions*, *organizational decline/revitalization*, and *conflict management*. OD often uses _____ which enhances the cohesiveness of departments by helping members to learn to function as a team. The _____ technique uses questionnaires on organizational climate and other factors collected from employees and reports back to them the results by a change agent. _____ _____ intervention is an approach that brings together participants from all parts of the organization to discuss problems or opportunities and plan for major change.

Unfreezing

Changing
Refreezing

OD uses an unfreezing of attitudes or behaviors, a changing to new attitudes or behaviors, and refreezing on these new ways by reinforcement of their use. _____ is the step in the diagnosis stage of OD in which participants are made aware of problems to increase their willingness to change their behavior. _____ is the step in the intervention stage of OD in which individuals experiment with new workplace behavior. _____ is the step in the reinforcement stage of OD in which individuals acquire a desired new skill or attitude and are rewarded for it by the organization.

Chapter Review

Multiple-Choice Questions: Please indicate the correct response to the following questions by writing the letter of the correct answer in the space provided.

___ 1. The change sequence includes
   a. internal and external forces for change.
   b. managers becoming aware of a need for change.
   c. the initiation of change.
   d. the implementation of change.
   e. all of the above

___ 2. Which of the following is/are an **internal** force for change?
   a. customers
   b. competitors
   c. A higher growth rate goal is set.
   d. a depressed economy
   e. an international political incident

___ 3. _____ typically uncovers existing knowledge that can be applied or adopted within the organization.
   a. Search
   b. Creativity
   c. Intrapreneurship
   d. A venture team
   e. A skunkworks

___ 4. A creative person is usually
   a. more authoritarian.
   b. highly disciplined.
   c. not very persistent.
   d. open-minded.
   e. less playful.

___ 5. To encourage a creative department a manager should
   a. insulate that department from outside contacts.
   b. run a tight ship to force innovation.
   c. absolve members of peripheral responsibilities.
   d. have the group avoid risk taking.
   e. do all of the above.

___ 6. An idea champion is playing the role of _____ when he is a high-level manager who approves of an idea.
   a. inventor
   b. sponsor
   c. grid manager
   d. entrepreneur
   e. informal facilitator

___ 7. Venture teams should
   a. be relatively large groups to facilitate more ideas.
   b. report through the normal organizational structure.
   c. give free reign to members' creativity.
   d. be subject to all organizational rules and procedures.
   e. develop a bureaucratic structure as rapidly as possible.

___ 8. When an employee resists change because he disagrees with the expected benefits from it, this would be classified as
   a. irrational resistance.
   b. legitimate resistance.
   c. a lack of trust.
   d. self-interest resistance.
   e. uncertainty resistance.

___ 9. To use the results of a force field analysis a manager should
   a. force the employees to accept the change.
   b. analyze the field of workers to find the resistance and then threaten these workers if they do not accept the change.
   c. selectively remove forces that restrain change.
   d. selectively remove the driving forces.
   e. do any or all of the above.

___ 10. When a group has power over the implementation or will lose out in the change, the appropriate tactic for overcoming resistance is
   a. communication or education.
   b. participation.
   c. negotiation.
   d. coercion.
   e. top management support.

___ 11. Top management support for a change
   a. symbolizes to employees that it is important.
   b. is not necessary if the change involves multiple departments.
   c. usually causes changes to get bogged down since most people naturally resist authority figures.
   d. often undercuts that very change.
   e. all of the above

___ 12.   The type of planned organizational change needing horizontal linkage is a
    a.   technological change.
    b.   product change.
    c.   structure change.
    d.   people change.
    e.   itemized change.

___ 13.   A product change
    a.   may define a new market.
    b.   does not usually involve a new technology.
    c.   need not consider customers' needs.
    d.   is successful 9 times out of 10.
    e.   must be restricted to one department.

___ 14. If a manager uses coercion to implement a change
    a.   he is using formal power to force the employees to change.
    b.   resisters are told to accept the change or lose rewards.
    c.   employees can be made to feel like victims.
    d.   anger may result on the part of the employees.
    e.   all of the above are true.

___ 15.   OD might solve which of the following types of problems?
    a.   working relationships that are poor
    b.   goals within the organization that are not agreed upon
    c.   disagreement over priorities
    d.   unclear roles
    e.   all of the above

___ 16.   During the search phase managers
    a.   talk to friends.
    b.   read professional reports.
    c.   talk to colleagues.
    d.   hire consultants.
    e.   any or all of the above

___ 17.   The role of the critic requires the idea champion to
    a.   challenge the concept.
    b.   criticize those who oppose the concept.
    c.   solicit criticism from the organization.
    d.   criticize customers who do not like the concept.
    e.   listen to criticism, but not heed it.

____ 18. The most creative companies encourage employees to
    a. always make sure they are right before proceeding.
    b. make mistakes.
    c. avoid taking risks.
    d. follow procedures for research and development.
    e. put ideas into suggestion boxes.

____ 19. A *learning organization* is one in which
    a. everyone is required to get a high school diploma or its equivalent.
    b. the same mistakes are never made twice.
    c. consultants are called in to teach workers.
    d. literacy is placed as a top priority.
    e. everyone is engaged in identifying and solving problems, enabling the organization to continuously improve and increase its capability.

____ 20. When General Stair Corporation decided to initiate a change
    a. all employees embraced the idea immediately.
    b. the company settled on a money back guarantee for late shipments.
    c. the company settled on $50 per day for late deliveries
    d. employee income went down
    e. labor costs went up.

____ 21. Delivering products and services faster than competitors is called
    a. just-in-time inventory.
    b. the marketing concept.
    c. just plain luck.
    d. time-based competition.
    e. vaporware.

____ 22. Top-down changes mean that
    a. initiation of the idea comes from below but is implemented from the top down.
    b. initiation of the idea occurs at the upper levels and is implemented downward.
    c. lower-level employees are not educated about the change.
    d. lower-level employees are not allowed to participate in the change.
    e. top management forces its ideas on lower levels without regard for the consequences.

____ 23. Changes in culture and people pertain to
    a. technology.
    b. structure.
    c. products.
    d. how employees think.
    e. how refined the employees are.

___ 24. Which of the following problems can OD help managers address?
   a.   mergers/acquisitions
   b.   organizational decline
   c.   conflict management
   d.   organizational revitalization
   e.   all of the above

___ 25. In the survey-feedback method of OD
   a.   the employees receive feedback on the results of a questionnaire regarding values, climate, participation, leadership, and group cohesion in the organization.
   b.   employees are allowed to give feedback on the questions that should be asked on a survey.
   c.   the OD specialist receives feedback on his survey to help refine and improve the questionnaire.
   d.   similar organizations are surveyed to determine problems in the current organization.
   e.   communication style is classified as parent, child, or adult.

___ 26. A technology change is related to
   a.   the organization's production process.
   b.   the way people relate to each other.
   c.   the products the company makes.
   d.   the organizational structure of the company.
   e.   none of the above.

___ 27. The first step in the change process of OD is
   a.   unfreezing, which makes the participants aware of problems and helps them become willing to change.
   b.   changing behaviors so that attitudes will follow.
   c.   refreezing on the desired attitude.
   d.   intervention in the problem at hand.
   e.   survey of the organization to discover who is willing to change.

___ 28. An example of a structural change is illustrated by the
   a.   story by Mary Kay Ash of a change in commission.
   b.   "workslate" portable computer story.
   c.   Integrated Genetics experience.
   d.   Tenneco classes in machine maintenance.
   e.   retraining programs of IBM.

___ 29. If resources are allocated to creative personnel and projects without immediate payoff, the result will be
   a.   a more creative organization.
   b.   wasting of resources.
   c.   lack of discipline needed to be creative.
   d.   lack of focus on the mission of the organization.
   e.   short-term high profits.

___ 30. When an organization is caught flat-footed, failing to anticipate or respond to new needs, _____ is at fault.
  a. no one
  b. the competition
  c. management
  d. the union
  e. the government

True/False Questions: Please indicate whether the following questions are true or false by writing a T or an F in the blank in front of each question.

___ 1. Managers should monitor events in the environment and within the organization and attempt to make changes to meet observed needs.

___ 2. Managers sense a need for change when there is a performance gap.

___ 3. Managers can directly influence whether idea champions will flourish in their organization.

___ 4. A *learning organization* learns from its mistakes the first time they are made.

___ 5. Legitimate disagreements over the proposed benefits of a change can exist.

___ 6. Communication and education are used when users or others who may resist implementation need no solid information about the change.

___ 7. The top-down approach means that ideas are developed at lower organization levels.

___ 8. When the horizontal linkage model is used, the decision to develop a new product is a joint one.

___ 9. Successful structural change is through a bottom-up approach.

___ 10. Team-building activities enhance the cohesiveness and success of organizational groups and teams.

Short-Answer Questions

1.   Explain why management should allow external forces to compel it to change.

2.   What are the four events that make up the change sequence?

3.   What are idea champions and why are they important to organizations?

4. Explain when it is appropriate to use top management support as an approach in overcoming resistance to change.

5. Exactly what is organizational development?

Management Applications

A Dream Shot

Last night John had an unusual dream. John is an excellent high school basketball player and has been highly recruited by major colleges. Last night he dreamed that he had accepted an offer to play for the Duke University. When John showed up for his first practice in this dream, Coach K. told John that while his jump shot had been okay for high school basketball, it would need to be altered for college-level play. John is only 5'10" tall and he has always shot the standard jump shot, which means releasing the ball at the height of his jump. Coach K. explains to him that if he continues to shoot that way in college ball, he will get his shot blocked. John refused the coach's offer to help learn to shoot differently since he was such a great player in high school. He just did not believe that his shot would be blocked even in college.

Coach K. then called a scrimmage session with the freshman players playing against the varsity. In the huddle before the start of the session he told the varsity players to really go after John and try to block every shot he attempted. Being the tall and great players they were, the varsity players blocked every single shot that John attempted. John left the court a very depressed man. John awoke in a cold sweat.

1.   In this dream which OD step can you recognize? Explain it.

2.   If this were a real situation and Coach K. believed in OD, what would be the next step?

3. How would you implement this step?

4. What would be the final step and how would you implement it?

Act Like Managers

When Mr. Nichols became president of Associated Grocers of Arizona, he implemented several changes. One change that was noticed by many managers was his policy of having all persons above a certain level dress appropriately. All the managers were to wear a tie. Another change was implemented regarding smoking. The only authorized place to smoke was in the lunchroom. When managers arrived each morning, they were to sign in. Each time they left the office, they were to sign out. He felt the company needed to be made more professional.

Since the company was located in Arizona, many managers started wearing the western "bolo" tie. This met with the letter of the new policy, but not the spirit. Other managers started closing their doors, which were previously left open, so they could "sneak a smoke." Managers often "forgot" to sign in or out.

1. Why did some persons resist this change?

2. How could Mr. Nichols have approached this change differently to get more acceptance?

Mini Case

Can Wilhelm Change the Workers?

Wilhelm Schmidt had been the manager of a chocolate factory in East Germany for 20 years. Now that of East and West Germany have been merged, Wilhelm is worried. His workers are not used to having to work hard, the equipment used in the factory is old, the product is packaged poorly, and foreign imports are pouring into the country. Sales are down and so is morale in the factory. Everyone, including Wilhelm, is worried about his job and the future of the company.

1.   What types of change are needed in the chocolate factory?

2.   Would you recommend a top-down or bottom-up approach?

Experiential Exercise

1. Without looking at the rest of this exercise, break up into groups of four each.

2. Answer the following questions within your group:

    a. Does your group consist mainly of people you already know well or who sit near you in the class?

    b. Why do we usually join groups of people we already know?

    c. Look around the room at various ethnic or minority groups. Are they mainly together?

    d. If your instructor were to force you to break up your group now and for brand-new groups to be formed, how would you feel about it?

    e. How do you think work groups that have often been established for years feel about reorganizations?

Study Guide Solutions

Chapter Review

Multiple-Choice Questions

1	2	3	4	5	6	7	8	9	10
e	c	a	d	c	b	c	b	c	c

11	12	13	14	15	16	17	18	19	20
a	b	a	e	e	e	a	b	e	c

21	22	23	24	25	26	27	28	29	30
d	b	d	e	a	a	a	a	a	c

True/False Questions

1	2	3	4	5	6	7	8	9	10
T	T	T	F	T	F	F	T	F	T

Short-Answer Questions

1. If management does not change in accordance with external forces, it will not be able to compete. Competition will use the latest technological improvements, offer better services, and meet the latest customer needs better.

2. The first step is the existence of internal and external forces for change which make the change necessary. The second step is the monitoring of these forces so that managers become aware of the need for change. Then this perceived need initiates change. The fourth step is the implementation of change.

3. An idea champion is a person who sees the need for and champions productive change within the organization. This person is important as an impetus to change and in overcoming resistance to change.

4. Top management support is especially important when change involves several departments or the reallocation of resources. It is also appropriate when others doubt whether the change is really legitimate or not. In reality, top management support will help change in almost any situation.

5. Organizational development is a term used to describe the application of behavioral science knowledge to improve an organization's health and effectiveness. It helps the organization to

cope with environmental changes, improve internal relationships, and increase problem-solving capabilities.

Management Applications

A Dream Shot

1. What has happened here is unfreezing. Coach K. has unfrozen John from his previous behavior (his old way of shooting a jump shot) and his former attitude (he is a great player and no one could be better). He has prepared John for a change.

2. The next step would be change.

3. Change could be implemented by coaching John in how to improve his shot during a practice session. For example, Coach K. could teach John how to use his quickness and release the ball before reaching the peak of his jump while shooting his jump shot. This would give the defensive player less time to block the shot.

4. The next step would be refreezing. This means to implement and reinforce the new attitude and behavior. Coach K. could implement this by having another practice session and telling the varsity players to just play normally against John. After John scored his 30 points during the practice (remember, this is John's dream), the new way of shooting would be reinforced.

Act Like Managers

1. Change was likely resisted by some out of self-interest. They felt they were losing something of value, i.e., the right to dress comfortably, the right to smoke, the right to not punch a time clock. Others may not have understood the reasons for the change or have felt uncertain about what changes might come next. Some probably felt that the desired outcome of being more professional would not be realized by these changes.

2. This is the type of change that needed more participation by those affected. If they could have devised their own means of meeting the goals, they would more likely have been committed to these changes.

Mini Case

Can Wilhelm Change the Workers?

1. Wilhelm needs many changes, but most pressing are technology changes and culture/people changes. He needs technology changes to acquire and start using more up-to-date equipment, including packaging equipment, to allow him to compete with foreign imports. He also needs

culture/people changes to change the attitudes towards work, job security, and to get the workers to be innovative.

2. The bottom-up approach would be the best general approach to the technology changes. The culture/people change may require more of a leaning toward the top-down approach for management to show by example the type of work culture necessary to compete.

Experiential Exercise

Most groups will consist of persons you already know or who are sitting close to you since you feel that you know them somewhat. This is because others in the room are unknown quantities to you. There is the probability that those of different ethnic or minority backgrounds will be grouped together. Chances are your current group is even the same as was formed for a previous exercise. Roles and behaviors have already been established. For this reason you would probably feel uncomfortable and resist breaking up this group and starting a new group. Work groups often resist reorganizations for the same reasons. Since their relationships have been in existence even longer, their resistance will often be even stronger.

Chapter 13

Human Resource Management

Chapter Summary

After you have read the text chapter, read through the summary below. Cover the left-hand margin and fill in the blanks with the appropriate terms. After you have filled in each blank, check your responses by uncovering the answer given in the margin. If you do not understand why the given answer is the correct one, refer back to the text.

The Strategic Role of Human Resource Management

Human resource management today has evolved to a strategic role due to the increase in corporate mergers, downsizing, government regulations, and international operations. _____ Refers to the design and application of formal systems in an organization to ensure the effective and efficient use of human talent to accomplish organizational goals. It is concerned with the activities to attract, develop, and maintain an effective work force within an organization. These three aspects are the major goals of human resource management (HRM).

Human resource management

Environmental Influences on HRM

HRM executives now participate in strategy formulation and implementation, interpret federal legislation, and strive to meet the evolving needs of the work force. Human resource management is changing in three primary ways: building human capital; developing global HR strategies, and using information technology.

Federal legislation and court rulings have a major impact on the interaction of the organization with its personnel. The Equal Employment Opportunity Commission guards against _____ , which is the hiring or promoting of applicants based on criteria that are not job relevant. A remedy for this is _____ , a policy requiring employers to take positive steps to guarantee equal employment opportunities for people within protected groups.

discrimination

affirmative action

The Changing Nature of Careers

In the old social contract, the employee could contribute ability, education, loyalty and commitment in return for wages, benefits, work, advancement, and training throughout the working life. In the new social contract people are responsible for their own careers without guarantees of employment until retirement from the organization.

telecommuting

The new workplace includes the heavy use of temporary employees, the emergence of the virtual organization, the use of contingent workers, and - _____, which is using computer and telecommunications equipment to perform work from home or another remote location. Other significant trends in careers are the advent of teams and the use of project teams.

Attracting an Effective Work Force

matching model

The _____ is the basis for the organization's efforts in attracting a work force. It stipulates an employee selection approach in which the organization and the applicant attempt to match each other's needs, interests, and values. The first step in attracting an effective work force lies in good

Human resource planning

human resource planning. _____ is the forecasting of human resource needs and the projected matching of individuals with expected job vacancies. The HRM professional must survey competitors, technology, and expected volume of business to define the direction for the HRM strategy.

Recruiting

The next step is to recruit a pool of qualified applicants. _____ means the activities or practices that define the desired characteristics of applicants for specific jobs. HRM managers may use either *internal* recruiting (promote from within) or *external recruiting* (getting newcomers from the outside). To assess organizational needs, human resource managers conduct a job analysis, write

realistic job preview

job descriptions, and develop job specifications. A _____ is a recruiting approach that gives applicants all pertinent and realistic information about the job and the organization. It should be given to potential applicants so they can engage in self-screening and adjust more easily if hired. Many

e-cruiting

companies today use . _____, or recruiting job applicants online.

selection

Next comes _____, which is the process of determining the skills, abilities, and other attributes needed to perform a particular job. In the recruiting and selection process the manager must follow legal requirements.

job description

The _____, which is a listing of duties as well as desirable qualifications for a particular job, should be reviewed to facilitate the selection process. Other selection devices include the application form, interviews,

application form

paper-and-pencil tests, and the assessment center. The _____ is a device for collecting information about an applicant's education, previous job experience, and other background characteristics. Even though the interview is not generally a valid predictor of job performance, it seems valid to employers and is still used widely. Some companies use . _____ interviews in which the candidate meets with several interviewers to increase validity. The computer-based interview is also growing in popularity. A _____ test is a measurement of a particular attribute such as intelligence or aptitude. An _____ is a technique for selecting individuals with high managerial potential based on their performance on a series of simulated managerial tasks. All of these devices must be valid, or predict future job performance. _____ refers to the relationship between an applicant's score on a selection device and his or her future job performance.

panel

written or computer-based employment

assessment center

Validity

Developing an Effective Work Force

Effective training is needed to develop a work force. There are many training methods used, with on-the-job training (OJT) being the most popular. _____ is a type of training in which an experienced employee "adopts" a new employee to teach him or her how to perform job duties. This usually leads to a mentoring situation. Other training methods include orientation training, classroom training, self-directed learning, and computer-based training. Many companies us a _____ _____, which is an in-house training and education facility that offers broad-based learning opportunities for employees. Cross-training helps employees see the relations of jobs in meeting goals. The training method selection should be preceded by a needs analysis and followed by a training program evaluation. Promotion from within also helps companies maintain and develop worthwhile employees. Both job posting and employee resource charts facilitate promotion from within.

OJT

corporate university

_____ is the process of observing and evaluating an employee's performance, recording the assessment, and providing feedback to the employee. Performance appraisals can provide the feedback and motivation needed to produce a more effective work force. An accurate performance appraisal system needs to be developed, and appraisers need to learn how to avoid rating errors and how to conduct effective performance appraisal interviews. A recent trend is use of _____ feedback, a process that uses multiple raters, including self-rating, to appraise employee performance and guide development.

Performance appraisal

360-degree

The _____ means that a manager evaluates his or her direct reports relative to one another and categorizes each on a scale such as A, B, or C. The _____ is a type of rating error that occurs when an employee receives the same rating on all dimensions regardless of performance on individual dimensions. A method that has been developed to combat these errors is called a _____, which relates an employee's performance to specific job-related incidents.

Performance review ranking
halo error

behaviorally anchored rating scale

Maintaining an Effective Work Force

Compensation

In order to maintain an effective work force compensation has to be provided. _____ refers to the monetary payments and nonmonetary goods or commodities used to reward employees. The most common approach is .

job-based

_____ pay, which means linking compensation to the specific tasks an employee performs. In *skill-based pay systems* employees with higher skill levels receive higher pay than those with lower skill levels. _____ is

Job evaluation

the process of determining the values of jobs within an organization through an examination of job content. To maintain pay equity companies use job evaluations. *Incentive pay or pay for performance* links some portion of an employee's pay beyond base wage or salary to job performance.

exit interview

As terminations occur, managers can use exit interviews to gather useful information for the organization. An _____ which is conducted with departing employees will help to determine the reasons for their termination.

Chapter Review

Multiple-Choice Questions: Please indicate the correct response to the following questions by writing the letter of the correct answer in the space provided.

___ 1. Over the last decade human resource management (HRM)
    a. has lost some power due to downsizing.
    b. has shed its old "personnel" image.
    c. has been given a diminished role in strategic planning.
    d. has been viewed as a non-strategic element.
    e. was virtually nonexistent in corporate America.

___ 2. Which of the following is *not* an HRM activity?
    a. human resource planning
    b. recruiting potential employees
    c. selection of qualified employees
    d. training and development of employees
    e. compensation administration
    f. All of the above are HRM activities.

___ 3. Human resource planning, recruiting, selecting, and orientation are four steps involved in
    a. attracting an effective work force.
    b. developing an effective work force.
    c. maintaining an effective work force.
    d. controlling an effective work force.
    e. human resource needs assessment.

___ 4. The answer to the question, "How many senior managers will we need during this time period?" will help to
    a. pick the vice-president of human resources.
    b. define the direction for the HRM strategy.
    c. evaluate top management jobs.
    d. determine the organization's key jobs.
    e. formulate corporate marketing strategy.

___ 5. The legislation which prohibits discrimination of qualified individuals on the basis of disability and demands that reasonable accommodations be made for the disabled in the work place was is the
    a. Occupational Safety and Health Act.
    b. Vocational Rehabilitation Act.
    c. American Disabilities Act.
    d. Executive Order 11246.
    e. Civil Rights Act of 1991.

___ 6. The outside source for job applicants sometimes referred to as headhunters is (are)
   a. a newspaper ad with reference to headlines of the paper.
   b. private employment agencies.
   c. employee referrals.
   d. state employee services who count heads to maintain federal funds.
   e. colleges and universities because the company seeks management trainees there.

___ 7. Which of the following selection devices is now illegal?
   a. application form
   b. interview
   c. written or computer-based test
   d. assessment center
   e. None of the above is illegal per se.

___ 8. A person whose exclusive focuses are on recruitment of employees would be called a
   a. human resource generalists.
   b. human resource specialist.
   c. personnel specialist.
   d. people person.
   e. human resource advocate.

___ 9. The job interview has problems because
   a. of personal biases of the interviewer.
   b. it never lasts long enough.
   c. legislation has made it illegal.
   d. decision makers cannot make decisions soon enough during the interview process.
   e. interviewers tend to discount negative information.

___ 10. The _____ training method is used most frequently.
   a. on-the-job
   b. classroom
   c. computer-assisted
   d. orientation
   e. case discussion groups

___ 11. Which of the following is the first step in performance appraisal?
   a. observing
   b. assessing
   c. recording
   d. interviewing
   e. documenting

___ 12. Human capital refers to
    a. the economic value of the knowledge, experience, skills, and capabilities of employees.
    b. the cost of hiring new employees.
    c. the cost of a goods benefits package.
    d. the amount of money contributed by the owners to an enterprise.
    e. the value of the pension plan of a company.

___ 13. For an effective performance appraisal to occur a rater should
    a. tell the employee what the rating is and then sell him on this appraisal.
    b. not try to be very specific to avoid legal problems.
    c. be knowledgeable about the subordinate's job and performance level.
    d. defer all feedback until the quarterly performance appraisal review session.
    e. never give negative feedback.

___ 14. A human resource information system is
    a. something to be avoided.
    b. considered inappropriate for the human touch needed to today's organization.
    c. an integrated computer system designed to provide data and information for HR planning and decision making.
    d. a special type of computer for the human resource department.
    e. none of the above.

___ 15. Which of the following can uncover pockets of dissatisfaction that usually remain hidden in an organization?
    a. job analysis
    b. job evaluation
    c. performance appraisal interview
    d. selection interview
    e. exit interview

___ 16. After interpreting federal legislation, an HRM professional should
    a. figure out ways to get around these restrictions.
    b. implement corresponding procedures.
    c. hire legal counsel to settle lawsuits.
    d. hire lobbyists to change the legislation.
    e. hope the company never gets caught.

___ 17. The Health Insurance Portability and Accountability Act
    a. allows employees to switch health insurance plans when changing jobs and get the new coverage regardless of preexisting health conditions.
    b. does not prohibit group plans from dropping a sick employee.
    c. forces insurance companies to offer their plan in a new company an employee joins.
    d. requires a minimum amount of health insurance to be offered all employees.
    e. none of the above.

___ 18. The point of EEO legislation and Executive Orders is to
   a. provide jobs for countless numbers of bureaucrats.
   b. give minorities an advantage for a change.
   c. stop discriminatory practices that are unfair to specific groups.
   d. provide for a more liberal society.
   e. undermine morality in the United States.

___ 19. Discrimination occurs when some applicants are hired or promoted based on
   a. sexual preference.
   b. job ability alone.
   c. criteria which are not job relevant.
   d. favorable impressions.
   e. job skill tests.

___ 20. The Equal Pay Act
   a. prohibits sex differences in pay for substantially equal work.
   b. guarantees equal pay for all employees of the same company.
   c. prohibits unequal pay for noncomparable jobs.
   d. provides for the same pay in the public sector as in the private sector.
   e. was passed in 1979 as a substitute for the failed ERA movement.

___ 21. The Consolidated Omnibus Budget Reconciliation Act (COBRA)
   a. requires continued health insurance coverage (paid by the employer) following termination.
   b. requires continued health insurance coverage (paid by the employee) following termination.
   c. mandates a budget item be included for health insurance coverage of all companies.
   d. had nothing to do with health insurance.
   e. none of the above.

___ 22. _____ requires that an employer take positive steps to guarantee equal employment opportunities for people within protected groups.
   a. The Gay Rights Act of 1990
   b. Affirmative action
   c. The Civil Rights Act of 1964
   d. The Equal Pay Act
   e. The Pregnancy Discrimination Act

___ 23. The scope of equal employment opportunity legislation is
   a. increasing at the federal level but decreasing at the state level.
   b. increasing at the federal and state levels but decreasing at the municipal level.
   c. increasing at the federal level but decreasing at the state and municipal levels.
   d. increasing at the federal, state, and municipal levels.
   e. decreasing at the federal, state, and municipal levels.

___ 24.   Sexual harassment is a violation of the
a.   Civil Rights Act.
b.   Americans with Disabilities Act.
c.   Vocational Rehabilitation Act.
d.   Family and Medical Leave Act.
e.   Equal Pay Act.

___ 25.   Contingent workers are people
a.   hired on a permanent of full-time basis, if they are legal immigrants.
b.   who work for an organization, but not on a permanent or full-time basis.
c.   who come in to work only if the Internet is down.
d.   whose legal status has not yet been clarified.
e.   none of the above.

___ 26.   Employers _____ enjoy the undisputed right to fire employees.
a.   continue to
b.   in the private sector
c.   in the public sector
d.   no longer
e.   of nonprotected groups

___ 27.   In the future employers will be making _____ use of part-time employees.
a.   greater
b.   less
c.   no
d.   more cautious
e.   discriminatory

___ 28.   An exit interview refers to
a.   asking customers what they think of our business on their way out.
b.   determining why some companies went out of business.
c.   asking questions of departing employees to determine the reasons for their termination.
d.   toward industrial unions.
e.   toward managerial unions.

___ 29.   Most large companies _____ with affirmative action and EEOC guidelines.
a.   try not to comply
b.   try to comply
c.   legally avoid compliance
d.   illegally avoid compliance
e.   ignore compliance

___ 30. A valid selection procedure will provide high scores that correspond to subsequent
     a.   high scores on the same test.
     b.   interview results.
     c.   affirmative action plans.
     d.   high job performance.
     e.   managerial desires.

True/False Questions: Please indicate whether the following questions are true or false by writing a T or an F in the blank in front of each question.

___ 1. Today, HRM executives often participate directly in the formulation and implementation of corporate strategy.

___ 2. Job description is the process of obtaining accurate and complete information about jobs through a systematic examination of job content.

___ 3. Human resource planning is no longer necessary since unemployment is so low.

___ 4. Realistic job previews provide information about the job, but have not been found to reduce turnover.

___ 5. EEO laws prohibit discrimination in employment practices on the basis of sexual preference.

___ 6. Although widely used, the interview as generally practiced is a poor predictor of later job performance.

___ 7. Training usually refers to teaching managers, while development refers to teaching lower-level or technical employees.

___ 8. A needs analysis should precede the planning and execution of a training program.

___ 9. A behaviorally anchored rating scale relates an employee's performance to specific job-related incidents.

___ 10. The most commonly used training program is On-the-Job Training (OJT).

Short-Answer Questions

1.   Why is it important to include an HRM manager in the strategic planning process?

2.   Explain why a realistic job preview is so important?

3.   What are the advantages of on-the-job training (OJT)?

4.   How can compensation be used as a strategy?

Management Applications

Why Evaluate Jobs?

St. Luke's Village is a large retirement business consisting of condominiums and a rest home. It employs many persons in a variety of jobs including nurses, office personnel, food service, custodial service, maintenance, and recreation. The personnel director has asked you to come in to talk to top management. It seems that she has been trying to convince top management to formalize job descriptions, perform job evaluations, and devise a pay structure based on the job evaluations and a pay survey. You have been called in to provide an objective outsider's explanation of the advantages and disadvantages of doing this.

1.   What are the advantages and disadvantages of each of the following?

   Job descriptions

   Job evaluations

   Job evaluation-based pay structure

2. If you discovered through your job evaluations and pay structure formulation that some jobs were underpaid and some were overpaid according to their value and the prevailing market wages, what would you recommend that the company do?

Credit to Get the Job

More employers are checking credit histories of job seekers to judge the character of prospective employees. The idea is that if employees are having financial troubles, they will be more tempted to steal from the company or take other negative actions.

1. Do you think that recent legal decisions which make using a polygraph test risky have influenced the decisions of companies to use credit reports?

2. For what types of jobs do you think credit reports would be most useful in the selection process?

3.   What are the negative aspects of using credit reports?

Mini Case

Bad Attitude Billy

Even though you have only been the supervisor of the loading dock for three weeks, it is time for you to conduct annual performance appraisal review. As you are preparing for these by reading employee records, you come across Billy's file. Below are some of the things you read:

"Billy seems to have an attitude problem."

"Today Billy refused to load another box into a truck, which just reflects his bad attitude."

"Billy complained about the pay rate at the company. He is such a complainer."

"Several employees met with representatives of a union today about the possibility of forming a union. Of course, Billy took his bad attitude and went to the meeting."

Based on the above comments you are to conduct an appraisal review interview with Billy. Answer the following questions about your strategy.

1. What additional information about Billy would you want before conducting the review?

2. How well doe these comments agree with the BARS method?

Experiential Exercise

Can I Ask This?

According to EEOC guidelines, you should not ask a prospective employee any questions that are not job related and which might have adverse impact on a protected group. You have been called in as a consultant to a restaurant that is planning on hiring many new employees. It wants to know if some of the questions it plans to ask on either application blanks or during job interviews are within the EEOC guidelines.

Look at the questions below and indicate if they are "okay" or "taboo" in the space provided. If they arc "taboo," indicate the reason why. Be ready to discuss and defend your answers in class as directed.

	Okay	Taboo
1. Are you married?	____	____
2. Do you own a car?	____	____
3. Can you work evenings and weekends?	____	____
4. When did you graduate from high school?	____	____

	Okay	Taboo
5. Are you a homosexual?	_____	_____
6. Do you have any communicable diseases?	_____	_____
7. Do you have any small children at home?	_____	_____
8. Are you willing to follow our dress code?	_____	_____
9. What hobbies do you have?	_____	_____

10. Are you handicapped?   _____   _____

Study Guide Solutions

Chapter Review

Multiple-Choice Questions

1	2	3	4	5	6	7	8	9	10
b	f	a	b	c	b	e	b	a	a

11	12	13	14	15	16	17	18	19	20
a	a	c	c	e	b	a	c	c	a

21	22	23	24	25	26	27	28	29	30
b	b	d	a	b	d	a	c	b	d

True/False Questions

1	2	3	4	5	6	7	8	9	10
T	F	F	F	F	T	F	T	T	T

Short-Answer Questions

1. Because many strategic decisions require particular skills and types of employees, the HRM manager needs to be aware of and have input into these decisions. If it is not possible to carry out a given strategy with the present work force, the decision must be made to either modify the strategy or the work force. Making such a decision requires the input of the HRM professional.

2. A realistic job preview tells the prospective employee both the positive and negative aspects of the job. It allows people to refuse a job that does not fit them and also helps them to adjust more easily to the job once it is accepted.

3. OJT has fewer out-of-pocket costs for items such as training facilities, materials, or instructors. It is also easier to transfer skills learned to the actual job than with classroom training because the training takes place on the job site.

4. If an organization has a strategic goal of improving profitability, it may need to improve employee performance. One way to do this is through a compensation incentive plan.

Management Applications

Why Evaluate Jobs?

1. **Job descriptions**

   Advantages include helping in hiring decisions, serving as a self-screening device, serving as the basis for job evaluations, and clarifying the employees' role. Disadvantages are that they formalize the job, which reduces flexibility of assignments, and take time and money to develop.

   Job evaluations

   Advantages include maintaining fairness and equity in pay within the organization, basing pay on objective and legal factors, and clarifying job responsibilities. Disadvantages are that they may reveal inequities about which the employer will then have to do something, and they will no longer allow employers to show favoritism.

   Job evaluation-based pay structure

   Advantage is that pay is now based on objective, legal factors. It is also understandable and defensible to all employees. The disadvantage is that it may ignore market factors such as demand for that skill or the cost of doing business.

2. If some persons were occupying jobs that were determined as overpaid, the smart thing to do would be to not lower their pay. Instead, one should give them smaller raises than others or wait until someone else replaces them in the job to make the needed pay adjustment. Otherwise, the pay structure will be resisted and morale will decrease as indicated by factors discussed in the previous chapter on implementing organizational change. If someone is in a job that is found to be underpaid, the wise move would be to give that person a raise. This would not only be motivating, but would also decrease the probability of the person quitting for a better-paying job elsewhere.

Credit to Get the Job

1. In fact, *The Wall Street Journal* reported that the decline in the use of the polygraph test has led many companies to seek other screening devices to judge character.

2. *The Wall Street Journal* reported a jewelry store chain that used these credit histories. A department store chain also found them useful for "sensitive" jobs such as security, finance, and credit jobs. Other companies have decided to use credit histories as part of their selection procedures for all employees.

3. Some people question the legality of using such credit histories especially if the prospective employee is not told that they are being used. Another problem is that it has yet to be demonstrated that past credit history can predict future job performance. Another problem is that credit reports often contain information such as age and marital status which should not be used in the selection process.

Mini Case

Bad Attitude Billy

1. Before conducting the performance appraisal it would be important to know Billy's job performance record. It would also be important to know all of the circumstances surrounding the incidents mentioned in the quotations in the case.

2. The statements presented do not link ratings to behaviors as called for in the BARS method. Concentration on his observable behaviors, which are objective, rather than making assumptions about his attitude, which is objective, is probably wise in this case.

Experiential Exercise

Can I Ask This?

1. Taboo. This question has adverse impact on women (sexual discrimination) because it is seen as a negative employment factor for women and a positive employment factor for men.

2. Taboo. This is not job related.

3. Okay. It is job related in this type of business. It is a legitimate requirement of the job.

4. Taboo. This question is a sneaky way of determining one's age and could therefore indicate age discrimination. It is also not job related.

5. Taboo, probably. Taboo because it is not job related only. However, homosexuals are not a protected group.

6. Okay. This is job related because food handlers often pass communicable diseases. Health regulations apply here.

7. Taboo. It has adverse impact on women because it is assumed they will miss work when the children are sick. For men it is considered a positive factor because it shows they are mature and settled down.

8. Okay. This is job related.

9. Taboo. This is not job related and may reveal things such as religious or ethnic background.

10. Taboo. It would be better to ask if the applicant has any physical handicap that would impair ability to do the job. However, the employer must be willing to make "reasonable accommodations for the handicapped."

Chapter 14

Managing Diverse Employees

Chapter Summary

After you have read the text chapter, read through the summary below. Cover the left-hand margin and fill in the blanks with the appropriate terms. After you have filled in each blank, check your responses by uncovering the answer given in the margin. If you do not understand why the given answer is the correct one, refer back to the text.

Valuing Diversity

Workforce
diversity

_____ means an inclusive workforce made up of people with different human qualities who belong to various cultural groups. Diversity to an individual refers to people who are different from us. Primary dimensions of diversity are inborn differences such as age, ethnic origin, mental or physical abilities, race, gender, and sexual orientation, which have impact throughout one's life. Secondary dimensions of diversity are acquired throughout life and include education, religious beliefs, military experience, geographic location, income, work background, parental status, and marital status.

ethnocentrism

monoculture

ethnorelativism
pluralism

The belief that one's own group and subculture is inherently superior to others is called _____, and it makes valuing diversity difficult. Ethnocentric viewpoints along with a standard set of cultural practices produce a _____-_____, which is a culture that accepts only one way of doing things and one set of values and beliefs. This makes it difficult to take advantage of unique talents and abilities of those who are different. The view that groups and subcultures are inherently equal is _____. With this belief it is possible for an organization to accommodate several subcultures in what is called _____. This can be developed through effective training.

The Changing Workplace

Biculturalism

International diversity must be integrated into the organization to allow it to be effective. Workers are also now older, more likely to be women, of color, and immigrants. The majority often perceives minorities as being deficient even though it may not be intentional. Many minority workers feel they have to become bicultural to succeed. _____ can be defined as the sociocultural skills and attitudes used by racial minorities as they move back and forth between the dominant culture and their own ethnic or racial culture. Racism in the workplace is often subtle. Organizations must learn to be bias free. Top managers and educational programs can promote knowledge, acceptance, and valuing of diverse cultures.

Affirmative Action

glass ceiling

Legislation has been passed to facilitate recruitment, retention, and promotion of minorities and women. Affirmative action was developed for this purpose. The results have been mixed and the topic has been debated and reviewed. There is less support for Affirmative Action, with even minorities feeling that there is the "stigma of incompetence" associated with it. Minorities found a _____, or invisible barrier that separates women and minorities from top management. Top management tends to hire and promote those who are like them and women and minorities are also assigned to less visible projects and positions.

Current Responses to Diversity

Diversity
awareness
training

The Civil Rights Act of 1991 was designed to "provide appropriate remedies for intentional discrimination and unlawful harassment in the workplace." The organization needs to create and define a vision of the new workplace. Next an assessment of the current culture and a willingness to change must take place. To implement a truly diverse workplace the organization must value diversity; change structures, policies and systems to support diversity; and provide diversity awareness training. _____ is special training designed to make people aware of their own prejudices and stereotypes.

Defining New Relationships in Organizations

Managers are discovering that close relationships between men and women at work causes special problems. They are realizing that *nonromantic love relationships* between men and women can have a positive effect on employees. However, when the relationships become sexual or romantic, new challenges arise. These challenges are especially problematic when the relationship is between a supervisor and a subordinate.

Sexual harassment is illegal. It may be *generalized* -- sexual remarks and actions not intended to lead to sexual activity, but directed toward a group. *Inappropriate/offensive* harassment is not sexually threatening but causes discomfort in the victim. More serious forms of harassment include *solicitation with promise of reward, coercion with threat of punishment,* and *sexual crimes.* Recent court decisions have shifted the focus toward the alleged victim's feelings and away from the intent of the harasser.

Global Diversity

Expatriates

Diversity management must be broadened due to globalization.   Global diversity programs involve employee selection and training. _____ are employees who live and work in a country other than their own. Careful screening and cultural and language training of overseas candidates and families is important. Communication differences exist among cultures. In a

high-context
low-context

_____ culture communication is used to enhance personal relationships, whereas in a _____ culture communication is used to exchange facts and information.

Diversity in the New Workplace

Multicultural

Benefits of valuing diversity include improving employee morale, decreasing interpersonal conflict, facilitating progress into new markets, and increasing the organization's creativity.   One way to leverage diversity is to use a _____-_____ team which is made up of members from diverse national, racial, ethnic, and cultural backgrounds.   These teams generate more and better alternatives to problems and are more creative.   However, these teams can be more difficult to manage and sometimes have difficulty in communicating and working together.

employee network

Another mechanism is the use of _____ _____ groups which are based on social identity, such as gender or race and are organized by employees to focus on concerns of employees from that group.   The members can offer mutual support and extend influence in the organization.

Chapter Review

Multiple-Choice Questions: Please indicate the correct response to the following questions by writing the letter of the correct answer in the space provided.

___ 1. The management of diversity includes
   a. recruiting workers.
   b. training workers.
   c. full utilization of workers.
   d. the broad spectrum of society in all areas.
   e. All of the above are correct.

___ 2. Primary dimensions of diversity include
   a. religious beliefs.
   b. sexual orientation.
   c. income.
   d. work background.
   e. education.

___ 3. A secondary dimension of diversity is one that
   a. is inborn.
   b. has ongoing impact throughout one's life.
   c. has no impact on one's life.
   d. can be acquired or changed throughout one's life.
   e. All of the above are correct.

___ 4. _____ refers to the belief that one's own group and subculture are inherently superior.
   a. Ethnocentrism
   b. Monoculturism
   c. Egoism
   d. Unitarianism
   e. Geocentrism

___ 5. A monoculture is one in which
   a. everyone has only one spouse.
   b. there is only one way of doing things and one set of values and beliefs.
   c. there is only one political part.
   d. people who are different are readily accepted.
   e. a worldview of values dominates.

___ 6. The ideal employee in a monoculture is
   a. Catholic.
   b. homosexual.
   c. group oriented.
   d. one who relies on his feelings in making decisions.
   e. is like everyone else in behavior and attitudes.

___ 7. Ethnorelativism is the belief that
   a. one's culture is superior to other cultures.
   b. groups and cultures are inherently equal.
   c. hiring of relatives in a organization is a good idea.
   d. all ethnic groups are somehow related to each other.
   e. groups are superior to individuals.

___ 8. The workforce today is different in that
   a. the average worker is now younger.
   b. fewer women are working, with a return to family values.
   c. more people of color are working.
   d. fewer immigrants are entering the workforce.
   e. white males make up more than 50 percent of the workforce.

___ 9. According to the text, minorities are expected to make up _____ percent of the American workforce during the first decade of the twenty-first century.
   a. 8
   b. 15
   c. 21
   d. 40
   e. 48

___ 10. The text maintains that affirmative action programs have
   a. caused racial tensions.
   b. had mixed results.
   c. helped facilitate cultural diversity.
   d. been misunderstood by management.
   e. not gone far enough in providing legal remedies to discrimination.

___ 11. A glass ceiling refers to
   a. an invisible barrier to important lateral movement within the organization.
   b. the ability to see through false beliefs of other cultures.
   c. seeing the potential of those who are different than we are.
   d. an invisible barrier to top management positions for women and minorities.
   e. legal remedies to discrimination.

___ 12. The acceptance of homosexuality in the workplace is
   a. now widely prevalent.
   b. still a hotly debated issue.
   c. enforced by the law.
   d. opposed by the government.
   e. None of the above is correct.

___ 13. As part of the recommended response to cultural diversity, the text advises that
   a. affirmative action programs be de-emphasized since they do not work.
   b. the current culture be accepted and not be assessed.
   c. a vision for diverse workplace be created.
   d. individuals who are different be trained to fit the corporate culture.
   e. a cultural police force be established.

___ 14. To change the corporate culture to one that values diversity, the organization should
   a. ignore unwritten rules and concentrate on written policy statements that are more explicit.
   b. avoid using surveys because they can be misinterpreted.
   c. avoid structured networks among minority groups because this will be perceived as a clan.
   d. actively use symbols and signals for the new values.
   e. All of the above are recommended in the text.

___ 15. The text recommends that in the area of recruitment the company should
   a. be aware of employee demographics.
   b. ignore community demographics.
   c. ignore customer demographics.
   d. look exclusively at the dimensions of race and gender.
   e. avoid considering sexual orientation.

___ 16. One reason fewer women enter into mentoring relationships with higher-level executives is that
   a. the women believe job competency is enough to succeed.
   b. the women fear that others may view the relationship as romantic.
   c. male mentors feel more comfortable with male protégés.
   d. male mentors do not view many women as executive material.
   e. All of the above are correct.

___ 17. Many companies provide for families in which both parents work which of the following?
   a. child care
   b. maternity or paternity leave
   c. flexible work schedules
   d. part-time employment
   e. All of the above are correct

___ 18. Diversity awareness training is intended to
   a. help people become aware of prejudices and stereotypes.
   b. help minorities integrate into organizations.
   c. develop monocultural organizations.
   d. facilitate ethnocentrism.
   e. help organizations compete better with diverse firms.

___ 19. A romance that arises between a supervisor and a subordinate
   a. is desirable because each will work harder to impress the other person.
   b. is often encouraged by companies.
   c. always means that sexual harassment is occurring.
   d. requires the most attention from companies.
   e. is called a "glass ceiling."

___ 20. A multicultural team is one that
   a. investigates charges of cultural bias.
   b. is allowed to travel in many parts of the world.
   c. is made up of members from diverse national, racial, ethnic, and cultural backgrounds.
   d. is easy to manage.
   e. has no problems communicating from the very start.

___ 21. Over the past decade
   a. the number of sexual harassment claims filed annually in the U.S. has more than doubled.
   b. more men have decided to sexually harass women.
   c. women have been afraid to file lawsuits involving sexual charges.
   d. women have grown to doubt that they can receive justice for sexual harassment claims.
   e. none of the above.

___ 22. Family programs are _____ for competitive companies
   a. a necessity
   b. a luxury
   c. superfluous
   d. unheard of
   e. always present

___ 23. Nonromantic love relationships between men and women
   a. are impossible to achieve.
   b. still have negative impact on the organization.
   c. involve sex, but no divorce.
   d. is possible only for gays and lesbians.
   e. are now viewed as possible and positive.

___ 24. If a manager does something that is not sexually threatening, but it still causes discomfort in another person to the extent that the subordinate has his freedom and ability to function in the workplace limited, this is which form of sexual harassment?
   a. generalized
   b. inappropriate/offensive
   c. solicitation with promise of reward
   d. coercion with threat of punishment
   e. sexual crime or misdemeanor

___ 25. If a manager offers an employee a promotion in exchange for sex, it is
   a. legal if both are adults.
   b. generalized sexual harassment.
   c. inappropriate but not illegal.
   d. potentially a case for criminal prosecution.
   e. no concern of the company.

___ 26. Expatriates are
   a. persons who give up their citizenship to become citizens of another country.
   b. persons who relinquish their citizenship and wish to become citizens of no country.
   c. employees who live and work in a country other than their own.
   d. employees who used to be patriotic, but now consider themselves global citizens.
   e. None of the above is correct.

___ 27. When selecting persons to work abroad one should consider
   a. support of the spouse.
   b. ability to initiate social contacts in a foreign culture.
   c. ability to adjust to different living environments.
   d. ability to maintain networks to the job market back home.
   e. All of the above are correct.

___ 28. A _____ culture is sensitive to circumstances surrounding social exchanges.
   a. low-context
   b. moderate-context
   c. high-context
   d. ethnocentric
   e. ethnorelative

___ 29. Which of the following has the highest degree of context as a culture?
   a. China
   b. Greece
   c. England
   d. Vietnam
   e. Germany

___ 30. Which of the following is a benefit of valuing diversity?
  a. developing employee and organizational potential
  b. enhanced recruiting and retention
  c. successful interaction with clients/marketplace
  d. increased creativity and adaptation
  e. All of the above are benefits.

True/False Questions: Please indicate whether the following questions are true or false by writing a T or an F in the blank in front of each question.

___ 1. While diversity in North American has been a reality for years, genuine efforts to accept and manage diversity are a phenomenon of the 1990s.

___ 2. Secondary dimensions of diversity are inborn differences that have ongoing impact throughout one's life.

___ 3. In a monoculture organization the belief is that different people must change, not the organization.

___ 4. Biculturalism means that a person accepts only two cultures as legitimate.

___ 5. The Civil Rights Act of 1991 weakened the Civil Rights Act of 1964.

___ 6. Multicultural teams typically have more difficulty learning to communicate and work well together.

___ 7. For sexual harassment to be proven, evidence of the harasser's intentions must be provided.

___ 8. In a low-context culture, people use communication primarily to exchange facts and information.

___ 9. Employee network groups are formed by employers for the benefit of minorities.

___ 10. Asian and Arab countries are considered high-context cultures.

Short-Answer Questions

1. Explain what is meant by primary dimensions of diversity and give examples.

2. What is meant by the *glass ceiling*? What can companies do about it?

3. What is meant by biculturalism?

4.   What are the types of sexual harassment? Give an example of each.

5.   What are the benefits to an organization of learning to value diversity?

Management Applications

Is It Sexual Harassment?

You are the human resources manager for a large insurance company where employees want a clearer picture of what is considered sexual harassment. Accordingly, you ask them to submit a list of specific behaviors that they are unsure about. The list is below. Explain why each behavior is or is not sexual harassment.

1. Jane reports that when she arrives at work Bill frequently says, "You sure have nice-looking buns!"

2. Sally says that whenever Joe passes by her desk on the way to the copy machine, he pats her on the shoulder and says, "How are you feeling?"

3. Fred complains that Susie has a picture of a well-known male actor in the nude from *Playgirl* magazine taped to her cubicle wall.

4. Alice doesn't like the fact that her boss, James, refers to her as a "girl" instead of as a "woman."

5. Judy doesn't like Bill's comments about her sexy sweater when she wears it.

Racial, Ethnic, or Religious Harassment?

After you have resolved the previous situation regarding sexual harassment, everyone is excited about your concise and insightful information. Now several employees have come to you with questions about other types of harassment. Provide your judgments in the space after each statement.

1. Mr. Cohen, a top salesman for the company, says he is tired of hearing jokes about Jews.

2. Ray Oxendine, a full-blooded Pembroke Indian, does not like the fact that some people call him "chief."

3. Bill Goins is a Vietnam veteran. He says that some people in the company have called him a "baby killer."

4. Joshua has been attending city council meetings to seek more black representation on the civilian policy review board. Several coworkers have criticized him for doing this.

Mini Case

Women Have No Mechanical Ability

Nancy has been working as a "machine tender" for a local textile factory for a few months. The maintenance men have noticed that her machine seems to break down more often than the machines operated by her male counterparts. Upon investigation they note that the men often check oil and other fluid levels, filters, and make minor adjustments regularly. Nancy does none of this. The maintenance men have come to you as the plant manager and asked that Nancy be given work more suitable for a woman and that no other women be allowed to operate these types of machines.

1. Of what laws must you be careful in deciding what action to take?

2. What would be the appropriate action for a progressive company to take?

Experiential Exercise

Opinionnaire

Place an X in the box that best describes your opinion. Be ready to discuss your opinion in class.

	Strongly Disagree	Disagree	No Opinion	Agree	Strongly Disagree
1. You shouldn't be too quick to take offense when someone expresses a sexual interest in you.					
2. Those who sexually harass others are usually seeking power over those they bother.					
3. Women in positions of power are just as likely as men to sexually harass those who work for them.					
4. A little flirtation makes life at work more interesting.					
5. I would call something sexual harassment even if the person doing it did not mean to be offensive.					
6. People who receive annoying sexual attention have usually asked for it by their dress or behavior.					
7. Men are just as likely as women to be the victims of unwanted sexual attention.					
8. A smart woman should have no trouble handling unwanted sexual approaches.					
9. A fine line exists between casual social relationships and sexual harassment.					
10. Sexual harassment is impossible to define because what bothers one person might not bother another.					

Study Guide Solutions

Chapter Review

Multiple-Choice Questions

1	2	3	4	5	6	7	8	9	10
e	b	d	a	b	e	b	c	d	b

11	12	13	14	15	16	17	18	19	20
d	b	c	d	a	e	e	a	d	c

21	22	23	24	25	26	27	28	29	30
a	a	e	b	d	c	e	c	a	e

True/False Questions

1	2	3	4	5	6	7	8	9	10
T	F	T	F	F	T	F	T	F	T

Short-Answer Questions

1. Primary dimensions of diversity are the inborn differences that have ongoing impact throughout one's life. These include age, ethnicity, gender, physical abilities, race, and sexual orientation.

2. Glass ceilings refer to invisible barriers to top management positions that confront women and minorities. Companies must define a vision for a diverse workplace, assess the current culture, develop a willingness to change, alter policies and systems to support diversity, and provide diversity awareness training.

3. Biculturalism refers to the sociocultural skills and attitudes used by racial minorities to move back and forth between the dominant culture at work and their own ethnic or racial culture at home.

4. The first type of sexual harassment is generalized. It means making comments that reflect on the gender as a group, such as saying, "Women use their sexuality when they want to get their way." The second type is behavior inappropriate or offensive to the victims. An example would be displaying nude pictures in the office. Solicitation with promise of reward is illustrated by a boss who says, "If you will sleep with me, I'll give you that raise." Coercion with threat of punishment might be a boss saying, "If you don't sleep with me, I'll see you don't get promoted, or that you get fired." A sexual crime or misdemeanor would be any illegal activity such as sexual assault.

5. The benefits to valuing diversity include developing employee and organizational potential. As persons feel more valued they will be motivated and more productive. Enhanced recruiting and retention will also be realized because persons who are different are more likely to work for the company and less likely to leave. Successful interaction with clients/marketplace occurs because the company understands the needs of those clients better. Persons from different backgrounds will also bring innovation and fresh viewpoints that can greatly benefit the organization.

Management Applications

Is It Sexual Harassment?

1. Unwanted sexual comments about one's body is sexual harassment.

2. Unwanted touching, brushing against one's body, patting, or pinching is sexual harassment.

3. Displaying pictures or objects depicting nude or scantily clad women or men in work areas is sexual harassment.

4. Use of language implying inferiority of an employee based on sex such as "girl" or "boy," rather than "woman" or "man" is sexual harassment.

5. Unwanted sexual compliments about one's clothing is sexual harassment.

Racial, Ethnic, and Religious Harassment?

1. Telling jokes or making derisive derogatory remarks about one's ethnic background is a form of harassment because it offends and demeans the victim. Harassment of this type is considered discrimination and violates federal civil rights legislation.

2. This is the use of language implying inferiority of a race or national heritage and is also considered harassment.

3. Vietnam Veterans have protection under the law so this can be considered harassment.

4. Criticism of one's civil rights activities is considered a form of harassment.

Mini Case

Women Have No Mechanical Ability

1. Before taking any action one must realize that discrimination on the basis of sex is illegal. It might be that this job is essential to further progression in the company and barring women would be installing a glass ceiling.

2. Most women are not taught when they are young how to repair or maintain their toys, bicycles, or cars. This may seem natural to the male workers and may never have occurred to Nancy and other female workers. The prudent company should provide training and explanation to Nancy so she can do the job.

Experiential Exercise

Opinionnaire

Reactions to the statements will vary. The purpose of this discussion is to explore the concept and principles underlying sexual harassment.

Chapter 15

Foundations of Behavior in Organizations

Chapter Summary

After you have read the text chapter, read through the summary below. Cover the left-hand margin and fill in the blanks with the appropriate terms. After you have filled in each blank, check your responses by uncovering the answer given in the margin. If you do not understand why the given answer is the correct one, refer back to the text.

Organizational Behavior

Organizational behavior

organizational citizenship

_____ _____ is an interdisciplinary filed dedicated to the study of human attitudes, behavior, and performance in organizations. It relies on many social science disciplines as well as management. Understanding behavior allows managers to exercises leadership. They can foster _____ _____ which is the work behavior that goes beyond job requirements and contributes as needed to the organization's success. Different kinds of behavior partly reflect variations in employee attitudes.

attitude

job satisfaction

organizational commitment
cognitive dissonance

An _____ is an evaluation—either positive or negative--that predisposes a person to act in a certain way. An attitude has three components: cognitions (thoughts), affect (feelings), and behavior. Managers must consider all three components to understand and change attitudes. One work related attitude is _____ _____, a positive attitude toward one's job. People experience this attitude when their work matches their needs and interests, when working conditions and rewards are satisfactory, and when they like their co-workers. Another important attitude is _____ _____, which is loyalty to and heavy involvement in one's organization. When two attitudes or a behavior and an attitude conflict a person suffers from _____ _____.

Perception

perception

"Seeing" things differently is an outcome of _____, the process people use to make sense of the environment by selecting, organizing, and interpreting information for the environment. In the process of perception we

Perceptual
selectivity

observe information, screen and select items and then organize the data into meaningful patterns for interpretation and response. _____ _____ is the process by which individuals screen and select the various stimuli that vie for their attention. People focus on stimuli that satisfy their needs and are consistent with their attitudes, values, and personality. Familiarity and intensity of the stimulus will enhance the chances of a stimulus being selected. Primacy and recency can also affect selectivity

distortions

stereotyping

halo effect

Projection
perceptual defense

Perceptual _____ are errors in perceptual judgment that arise from inaccuracies in any part of the perception process. One such distortion is _____, the tendency to assign an individual to a group or broad category and then attribute generalizations about the group to the individual. The _____ _____ occurs when an overall impression of a person or situation is abased on one attribute, either favorable or unfavorable. _____ is the tendency to see one's own personal traits in other people. A _____ _____ is the tendency of perceivers to protect themselves by disregarding ideas, objects, or people that are threatening to them.

Attributions

fundamental
attribution

self-serving

_____ are judgments about what caused a person's behavior—either characteristics of the person or of the situation. Three factors that affect whether an attribution will be external or internal are distinctiveness, consensus, and consistency. Attributes often have biases. The _____ _____error is the tendency to underestimate the influence of external factor's on another's behavior and to overestimate the influence of internal factors. Another bias is the _____-_____ bias, the tendency to overestimate the contribution of internal factors to one's success and the contribution of external factors to one's failures.

Personality and Behavior

personality
big five

The set of characteristics that underlie a relatively stable pattern of behavior in response to ideas, objects, or people in the environment is known as the _____. Researchers have identified five general dimensions that describe an individual's personality. These traits are called the _____ _____ personality factors and are extroversion, agreeableness, conscientiousness, emotional stability, and openness to experience. A person may have a low, moderate, or high degree of these qualities. An individual's personality influences a wide variety of work-related attitudes and behaviors.

self-awareness

Motivating
Empathy

New insights into personality have been gained by research in the area of *emotional intelligence*, which has five components. _____ means being aware of what you are feeling. Managing emotions is the ability to balance one's moods. _____ oneself is the ability to be hopeful and to persist in the face of obstacles, setbacks, and failure. _____ is being able to put yourself in some else's shoes, to recognize what others are

Social skill	feeling without them needing to tell you. _____ _____ is the ability to connect to others, build positive relationships, respond to the emotions of others, and influence others.
locus of control	An individual's personality influences a wide variety of work-related attitudes and behaviors. One of these is the _____ _____ _____, which is the tendency to place the primary responsibility for one's success or failure either within oneself (internally) or on outside forces (externally). Another attitude is _____, the belief that power and status differences *should* exist within the organization. Another personality dimension is _____ which is the tendency to direct much of one's behavior toward the acquisition of power and the manipulation of others for personal gain.
authoritarianism	
Machiavellianism	
person-job	Managers also need to understand that individuals differ in the way they go about gathering and evaluating information for problem solving and decision making. Carl Jung identified four functions related to this process: sensation, intuition, thinking, and feeling. It is important for managers to try to match employees with job characteristics. The extent to which a person's ability and personality match the requirements of a job is called _____ fit.

Learning

Learning	_____ is a change in behavior or performance as a result of experience. The learning process as been depicted as a four-stage cycle: concrete experience, reflective observation, abstract conceptualization, and active experimentation. People have different learning styles. The dominant learning styles are the diverger, assimilator, converger, and accommodator. To thrive both individuals and organizations must be continuous learners.

Stress and Stress Management

Stress	_____ is a physiological and emotional response to stimuli that place physical or psychological demands on an individual. People respond and cope with stress differently. The stress response follows a pattern known as the _____ _____ Syndrome (GAS). This is the physiological response to a stressor, beginning with an alarm response, continuing to resistance, and sometimes ending in exhaustion if the stressor continues beyond the person's ability to cope. _____ _____ Behavior is a pattern characterized by extreme competitiveness, impatience, aggressiveness, and devotion to work. _____ _____ behavior is a pattern that lacks Type A characteristics and includes a more balanced, relaxed lifestyle.
General Adaptation	
Type A	
Type B	

Role ambiguity

conflict

Work stressors have been placed in four categories: task demands, physical demands, role demands, and interpersonal demands. _____ _____ is the uncertainty about what behaviors are expected of a person in a particular role. Role _____ occurs when an individual perceives incompatible demands from others. Many coping devices have been developed to deal with stress, but the method chosen varies by individuals. At the company level, managers can adopt sound corporate practices to ease employee stress.

Chapter Review

Multiple-Choice Questions: Please indicate the correct response to the following questions by writing the letter of the correct answer in the space provided.

___ 1. Organizational behavior relies on the discipline of
    a. psychology.
    b. sociology.
    c. cultural anthropology.
    d. industrial engineering.
    e. all of the above.

___ 2. When an employee does work that goes beyond job requirements we call it
    a. stupid.
    b. "brown nosing."
    c. organizational citizenship.
    d. organizational behavior.
    e. cognitive dissonance.

___ 3. When an employee says, "I love this job," he is exhibiting the _____ component of an attitude.
    a. cognitive
    b. affective
    c. behavioral
    d. rational
    e. opinion

___ 4. An employee is likely to experience high job satisfaction when
    a. personal needs are met more than organizational needs.
    b. he or she likes his or her coworkers.
    c. working conditions are challenging.
    d. pay is not equitable, thus providing motivation.
    e. the work is not interesting, thereby allowing time to daydream.

___ 5. Which statement indicates loyalty and heavy commitment to the organization?
    a. "We are the best restaurant in town."
    b. "This is a nice place to work."
    c. "I try hard to do my job."
    d. "Management tries to keep us happy."
    e. "I'd rather be fishing."

___ 6. When your boss asks you to work on the weekend and you have a family camping trip planned and you cancel the trip to work, you will probably experience
   a. cognitive dissonance.
   b. a personality disorder.
   c. a mental breakdown.
   d. emotional dysentery.
   e. a divorce.

___ 7. Which of the five is NOT one of the big five personality traits?
   a. extroversion
   b. agreeableness
   c. conscientiousness
   d. sociability
   e. emotional stability

___ 8. Internal locus of control refers to
   a. having a strong ego.
   b. having a strong and dominant personality.
   c. being able to overcome cognitive dissonance.
   d. the tendency to place the responsibility for one's success or failure on outside forces.
   e. the tendency to place the responsibility for one's success or failure within oneself.

___ 9. "The job of the boss is to be tough," is a belief of someone subscribing to
   a. authoritarianism.
   b. cognitive dissonance.
   c. egalitarianism.
   d. achievement-orientation.
   e. participative management.

___ 10. "If you have to choose between being loved and being feared, it is better to be feared," is a statement that agrees with
   a. socialism.
   b. communism
   c. Republicanism
   d. Machiavellianism.
   e. all of the above

___ 11. According to Carl Jung's typology, a person who is decisive and an applied thinker has the _____ personal style.
   a. sensation-thinking
   b. intuitive-thinking
   c. sensation-feeling
   d. intuitive-feeling
   e. sensation-intuitive

___   12.   A thinking-type person evaluates information by
a.   using personal values.
b.   relying on emotional aspects of the situation.
c.   considering the probability of approval from others.
d.   using reason and logic.
e.   considering harmony of the group.

___   13.   If you put a highly social person into a job having little contact with others you are ignoring
a.   cognitive dissonance.
b.   the big five personality theory.
c.   Jung's typology.
d.   economies of scale.
e.   person-job fit.

___   14.   While watching television with a friend you ask the friend what the first commercial was about during the last break in your show. The fact that your friend cannot tell you what the commercial was about illustrates
a.   his stupidity.
b.   perceptual contrast.
c.   perceptual selectivity.
d.   perceptual familiarity.
e.   perceptual learning.

___   15.   When a stimulus is not new or different from stimuli previous perceived, it has
a.   contrast.
b.   familiarity.
c.   intensity.
d.   novelty.
e.   motion.

___   16.   When a person pays relatively greater attention to stimuli near the beginning of an event he is exhibiting the characteristic of
a.   primacy.
b.   recency.
c.   personality.
d.   novelty.
e.   learning.

___   17.   The ability to balance one's moods is called
a.   self-awareness
b.   managing emotions
c.   motivating oneself
d.   empathy
e.   social skill

___ 18. Studies have found a _____ relationship between job performance and high degrees of emotional intelligence.
   a. positive
   b. negative
   c. inverse
   d. small
   e. negligible

___ 19. If you are in a line at a movie theater and see someone break in line in front of you and then say, "He must be trying to catch a movie that is about to start," because that is the only reason you would break into line, you are using
   a. stereotyping.
   b. the halo effect.
   c. projection.
   d. a perceptual defense.
   e. learning.

20. If you are in a line at a movie theater and see someone break in line in front of you and then say, "He must be an impatient person," you are making a(n)
   a. stereotyping.
   b. attribution.
   c. cognitive decision.
   d. perceptual defense.
   e. learning.error (type I).

___ 21. When a other people tend to respond to similar situations in the same way attribution theory calls this
   a. distinctiveness.
   b. consensus.
   c. consistency
   d. the fundamental attribution error.
   e. maverick behavior.

___ 22. Sally said, "I did well on the Biology test because I studied so hard, but my grade on the Philosophy test was low because the instructor just doesn't like me." Sally is exhibiting
   a. cognitive dissonance.
   b. learning.
   c. maverick behavior.
   d. knowledge patterns.
   e. the self-serving bias.

___ 23. In the experiential learning cycle, after concrete experience what comes next?
   a. abstract conceptualization
   b. reflexive experimentation
   c. concrete conceptualization
   d. reflective observation
   e. active experimentation

___ 24. The _____ is good at generating ideas, seeing a situation from multiple perspectives, and being aware of meaning and value.
   a. diverger
   b. assimilator
   c. converger
   d. accommodator
   e. maverick

___ 25. For individuals, continuous learning entails looking for _____ to learn from classes, reading, and talking to others.
   a. reasons
   b. time
   c. mistakes
   d. repetition
   e. opportunities

___ 26. In biological terms, the stress response follows a pattern know as the
   a. stress model
   b. physiological stress pattern
   c. general adaptation syndrome
   d. physical stress syndrome
   e. biological stress syndrome

___ 27. The behavior pattern characterized by extreme competitiveness, impatience, aggressiveness, and devotion to work is known as
   a. workaholism
   b. type A behavior
   c. type B behavior
   d. machiavellianism
   e. maverick behavior

___ 28. _____ are stressors associated with the setting in which an individual works.
   a. role ambiguity
   b. interpersonal demands
   c. role demands
   d. physical demands
   e. task demands

___ 29. When your boss asks you to work on the weekend and you have a family camping trip planned and you cancel the trip to work, you will probably experience
    a. role conflict.
    b. an interpersonal crisis.
    c. a conflicting task demand.
    d. an impossible task demand.
    e. extreme dizziness.

___ 30. Organizations that want to challenge their employees and stay competitive will want the environment to be
    a. stress-free.
    b. somewhat stressful, but not too much so.
    c. very stressful.
    d. devoid of all stress.
    e. highly structured.

True/False Questions: Please indicate whether the following questions are true or false by writing a T or an F in the blank in front of each question.

____   1.   The concepts and principles of organizational behavior are important to managers because people make decisions about how resources are used in the organization.

____   2.   Changing one component of an attitude—cognitions, affect, or behavior—cannot contribute to an overall change in attitude.

____   3.   Research shows that the link between satisfaction and performance is very strong.

____   4.   The degree to which a person is sociable, talkative, assertive, and comfortable with interpersonal relationships is called extroversion.

____   5.   A person who feels like a pawn of fate has a high internal locus of control.

____   6.   It is impossible to measure a person's Machiavellianism (Mach) orientation.

____   7.   Even though we are bombarded by a lot of sensory data, we can perceive and understand it all.

____   8.   Experience with similar stimuli teaches people what it is important for them to pay attention to.

____   9.   People tend to perceive the sensory data they are most attentive to as standing out against the background of sensory data to which they are less attentive.

____   10.   People's responses to stressors vary according to their personality, resources available to cope, and the context of the stress.

Short-Answer Questions

1. What is an attitude and what are its major components?

2.   What are the Big Five personality factors? Do you think other factors should be included or that these five are sufficient?

3.   Why is it that we do not all perceive things the same way?

4. Why is it that some people learn better by having something explained to them, while others need to see a task demonstrated to learn how to do it?

5. Explain why a mother of three children who has a full-time job may feel stress?

Management Applications

The Employee with the Bad Attitude

You have just been appointed the night shift supervisor for your part-time job while going to college. It is a fast food restaurant. When you were given this promotion you were warned about one employee, Jack. You were told that Jack has a *bad attitude*.

1. You have been observing Jack for the last few days and have noticed the following events. Which component of an attitude (cognitions--thoughts, affective--feelings, or behavior) is illustrated by each event?

Event	Attitude Component Illustrated
Jack is frequently late in coming to work.	
When a coworker asks Jack to help out, he snaps at them and says something like, "That's your problem! Leave me alone!"	
You overhear Jack saying to a friend, who has come into the restaurant, "I hate this place."	
When a customer spills a soft drink while taking his tray to a booth, Jack laughs at him.	
When you confront Jack for some of his inappropriate behavior he says, "That's typical of management, always looking for something to bug workers about."	

2. Most likely you had problems in classifying each event as just one single component of an attitude. What does this illustrate?

Designing a Stress Management Workshop

You have been asked by a local telemarketing firm to design a stress management workshop for its employees. Since the job pays well and you are still in college, you take on the contract.

1. What components would you put into the workshop?

2. What stress management techniques would you teach the participants?

3. What type of stress might you experience in preparing for and presenting this workshop? How would you manage this stress?

Mini Case

A New Dean

You are now a professor of Management at Mountain University where you have been teaching for ten years. You have tenure and have the respect of both your students and colleagues. Recently the University hired a new dean to run the School of Management. This dean has a national reputation as a Cost Accountant and a major university. Since he has taken over you have had the following situations occur.

1. You got into an argument with him during a staff meeting about grading. He says you are giving too many A's because you cannot discriminate between good students and poor students. You said your job was to expect and encourage excellence in all your students and that you want as many of the m to get A's as possible.
2. One day the Dean visited your class. A student group was assigned to present a case analysis during that class period. The group finished their presentation early and you let the class go about 15 minutes early. The Dean got after you for letting them go early. He said that 15 minutes times 20 students equaled 300 minutes wasted and that the students were getting cheated out of their tuition. He says you should have planned a short lecture in case the student group finished early.
3. You arrived at campus 20 minutes late because you were doing a workshop for a local business. When you arrive at your office, the Dean is waiting at your door. He scolds you for being 20 minutes late for your office hours.

Answer the following questions regarding these situations:

1. What is the basic problem here? How does perception play a role?

2. What can you do to improve your relationship with the Dean?

Experiential Exercise

World Trade Center Perceptions

We all engaged in perceptual distortions although we may not be aware of it. Reflect on the terrorist attacks of the World Trade Center. Comment on the perceptual distortions of both the Americans and the Muslim world to this event as applied to the following types of distortions.

Type of Distortion	Americans	Muslim World
Stereotyping		
The Halo Effect		
Projection		
Perceptual Defense		

Study Guide Solutions

Chapter Review

Multiple-Choice Questions

1	2	3	4	5	6	7	8	9	10
e	c	b	b	a	a	d	e	a	d

11	12	13	14	15	16	17	18	19	20
a	d	e	c	b	a	b	a	c	b

21	22	23	24	25	26	27	28	29	30
b	e	b	a	e	c	b	d	a	b

True/False Questions

1	2	3	4	5	6	7	8	9	10
T	F	F	T	F	F	F	T	T	T

Short-Answer Questions

1. An attitude is a cognitive and effective evaluation that predisposes a person to act in a certain way. An attitude has three components: cognitions (thoughts), affect (feelings), and behavior.

2. The Big Five personality factors are personality factors extroversion, agreeableness, conscientiousness, emotional stability, and openness to experience. While most experts feel that these five summarize the important traits, one could easily make a case for other factors.

3. We do not all perceive things the same way because of perceptual selectivity, which means that we screen and select the various stimuli that vie for our attention. Individual characteristics of the perceiver such as your own needs, values, and personality also influence how you perceive stimuli.

4. We all have different learning styles that we have developed in our lives. These differences occur because individual needs and goals direct the learning process.

5. A working mother of three children would certainly feel stress. The primary reason would be due to a role conflict. The demands of her work will undoubtedly conflict with the demands of her family causing her stress.

Management Applications

The Employee with the Bad Attitude

Event	Attitude Component Illustrated
Jack is frequently late in coming to work.	Behavior and Affective
When a coworker asks Jack to help out, he snaps at them and says something like, "That's your problem! Leave me alone!"	Behavior and Affective
You overhear Jack saying to a friend, who has come into the restaurant, "I hate this place."	Affective
When a customer spills a soft drink while taking his tray to a booth, Jack laughs at him.	Behavior and Affective
When you confront Jack for some of his inappropriate behavior he says, "That's typical of management, always looking for something to bug workers about."	Cognition and Affective

2. The fact that you had problems in classifying each event as just one single component of an attitude illustrates that the components are interrelated. You need to consider all three components and not just one component in analyzing any situation.

Designing a Stress Management Workshop

You have been asked by a local telemarketing firm to design a stress management workshop for its employees. Since the job pays well and you are still in college, you take on the contract.

1. The components would you put into the workshop is up to you. A good outline of the program would probably include the following items:
    * The sources of stress
    * How to cope with the various sources of stress
    * Practicing techniques to reduce stress

2. The stress management techniques would you teach are those you are most comfortable with and feel would be the most useful. The following are the most commonly used techniques:
    * Exercising
    * Getting plenty of rest
    * Eating a healthful diet
    * Relaxation
    * Meditation
    * Taking regular breaks
    * Recreation

3. You might experience role conflict in preparing for and presenting this workshop. You would also feel stress due to the fact that you want to do a good job and probably have very little experience in doing this sort of thing. To manage this stress you would probably pick from the list of techniques listed above the one that works best for you.

Mini Case

A New Dean

1. The basic problem seems to be one of perceptions. The Dean comes from a cost accounting background and you come from a management background and you both see things differently. He is looking for ways to improve efficiency and is very conscious of the facts as calculated quantitatively. You are concerned with effectiveness and quality and are willing to let things slide sometimes. You truly do see things differently.

2. The way you decide to solve this problem is probably a matter of individual preferences. However, a meeting with the Dean to discuss differences is in order. You should discuss with him your perceptions as to grading, the relationship between quality and length of a class and the value of doing workshops off campus. In addition to these specific issues you probably need to discuss how the differences in your backgrounds make you see things differently.

Experiential Exercise

World Trade Center Perceptions

The answers you come up with will vary. The following are examples of what may be provided.

Type of Distortion	Americans	Muslim World
Stereotyping	Those who attacked the World Trade Center must be terrorists to kill innocent civilians	Those who attacked the World Trade Center are patriots who are giving America what it deserves in light of its policies.
The Halo Effect	Since those who attacked were Muslims, any subsequent act by Muslims will also be bad.	Since American policies toward the Muslim world have had negative impact, any actions they now take are aimed at inflicting more injuries.
Projection	Anyone who would attack a civilian target is wicked.	Americans want to blame Muslims for their own misdeeds.
Perceptual Defense	We are not attacking the Islamic religion, just trying to get the terrorists who did this act.	Those who attacked the WTC did so out of feelings of patriotism and self defense.

Chapter 16

Leadership in Organizations

Chapter Summary

After you have read the text chapter, read through the summary below. Cover the left-hand margin and fill in the blanks with the appropriate terms. After you have filled in each blank, check your responses by uncovering the answer given in the margin. If you do not understand why the given answer is the correct one, refer back to the text.

The Nature of Leadership

Leadership
Power

legitimate

reward

coercive
Expert
Referent

_____ is the ability to influence people toward the attainment of organizational goals. _____ is the potential ability to influence others' behavior. There are five bases of power a leader may use. Power that stems from a formal management position in an organization and the authority granted to it is called _____ power. Power that results from the leader's authority to reward others is _____ power. If power stems from the leader's authority to punish or recommend punishment, it is _____ power. _____ power is that which stems from the leader's special knowledge of or skill in the tasks performed by subordinates. _____ power results from leader characteristics that command subordinates' identification with, respect and admiration for, and desire to emulate the leader. The use of this power may result in commitment, compliance, or resistance by subordinates. Recently top executives have moved to *empower* lower employees. This means they encourage more participation, consensus building, and communication.

Leadership Traits

trait

Trait theories of leadership sought to find the personal characteristics of a leader. A _____ is the distinguishing personal characteristics of a leader such as intelligence, values, and appearance. Research has shown that the type of trait that a leader needs depends on the situation. This applies to personality traits as well as physical, social, and work-related traits.

Autocratic versus Democratic Leaders

autocratic

democratic

Several studies have centered on autocratic versus democratic leaders. A(n) _____ tends to centralize authority and rely on legitimate, reward, and coercive power to manage subordinates. This type of leader has been found to be effective in certain situations. A(n) _____ delegates authority to others, encourages participation, and relies on expert and referent power to manage subordinates. This type is more effective in different situations. Tannenbaum and Schmidt demonstrated that one need not be at one of these two opposites in leadership style, but could be somewhere in between.

Behavioral Approaches

consideration

initiating structure

leadership grid

The Ohio State studies, the Michigan studies, and Blake and Mouton's leadership grid all conclude that a leader can either be more concerned with the people or with the task to be performed. Although each labeled these concerns differently, they each support each other. In the Ohio State studies _____ was the label given to the type of leader behavior that describes the extent to which a leader is sensitive to subordinates, respects their ideas and feelings, and establishes mutual trust. The label of _____ referred to a type of leader behavior that describes the extent to which a leader is task oriented and directs subordinates' work activities toward goal achievement. In the University of Michigan studies the terms *employee-centered leaders* and *job-centered* leaders were used for the same factors. Blake and Mouton developed the _____, which measures a leader's concern for people and concern for production.

Contingency Approaches

contingency approach
LPC scale

situational

Fiedler determined that the best leadership style depends on the favorableness of the situation. His theory is part of the _____, which descries the relationship between leadership styles and specific organizational situations. He measured leadership style by using the _____, which is a questionnaire designed to measure relationship-oriented versus task-oriented leadership style according to the leader's choice of adjectives for describing the "least preferred co-worker." In a very favorable or very unfavorable situation, the most effective leader is task oriented. In a moderately favorable situation, an effective leader is people oriented. The favorableness of the situation depends on *leader-member relations, task structure,* and *position* power. Hersey and Blanchard developed the _____ theory of leadership, which links the leader's two-dimensional style with the task readiness of subordinates. They identified four styles of leadership: telling, selling, participating, and delegating.

path-goal

The _____ approach to leadership suggests that the leader should increase subordinates' motivation by clarifying the behaviors necessary for task accomplishment and rewards. These actions will result in increased job satisfaction and job performance. One contingency approach holds that situational variables can be so powerful that they substitute for or neutralize the need for leadership. A _____ is a situational variable that makes a leadership style redundant or unnecessary. A _____ is a situational variable that counteracts a leadership style and prevents the leader from displaying certain behaviors.

substitute
neutralizer

Change Leadership

transactional

Managers have been described as transactional leaders. A _____ leader is one who clarifies subordinates' role and task requirements, initiates structure, provides rewards, and displays consideration for subordinates. The two types of leadership that can have a substantial impact on change are charismatic and transformational. A _____ leader is one who has the ability to inspire and motivate subordinates to transcend their expected performance despite obstacles and personal sacrifice. Charismatic leaders are often skilled in _____ leadership that speaks to the hearts of employees, letting them be part of something bigger than themselves. A _____ leader is distinguished by a special ability to bring about innovation and change. They focus on intangible qualities such as vision, shared values, and ideas to build relationships, give larger meaning to diverse activities, and find common ground to enlist followers in the change process.

charismatic

visionary
transformational

Leading the New Workplace

humility

A Level 5 leader builds an enduring great organization through a combination of personal _____ and professional resolve. Women's ways of leading focuses on minimizing personal ambition and developing others by motivating, fostering communication, and listening. This approach has also been called _____ leadership since the leader favors consensual and collaborative processes, and has influence based on relationships. _____ leadership set clear goals and timelines and are very explicit about how people will communicated and coordinate their work while allowing the employees to determine the details of their day-to-day activities. This requires the leader to be open-minded and flexible, focus on solutions, and have strong communication, coaching, and relationship-building skills. A _____ leader is one who works to fulfill subordinates' needs and goals as well as to achieve the organization's larger mission.

interactive
Virtual

servant

Chapter Review

Multiple-Choice Questions: Please indicate the correct response to the following questions by writing the letter of the correct answer in the space provided.

___   1.   Leadership
    a.   is a people activity.
    b.   is static in nature.
    c.   does not need compliance to occur.
    d.   should not rely on power.
    e.   can pertain to administrative paper shuffling.

___   2.   _____ power comes from a formal management position in an organization and the authority granted to it.
    a.   Referent
    b.   Expert
    c.   Coercive
    d.   Reward
    e.   Legitimate

___   3.   When workers obey orders they may disagree with and lack enthusiasm, they are exhibiting
    a.   commitment.
    b.   compliance.
    c.   resistance.
    d.   consideration.
    e.   referent power.

___   4.   A democratic leader relies on _____ power to influence subordinates.
    a.   expert
    b.   referent
    c.   both a and b
    d.   legitimate
    e.   reward

___   5.   A vision is
    a.   an attractive, ideal future that is credible and readily available.
    b.   an attractive, ideal future that is credible and yet not readily available.
    c.   something leaders should avoid talking about.
    d.   not part of charismatic leadership.
    e.   never found in the real world.

___   6.   A leader is exhibiting initiating structure when he or she
    a.   emphasizes deadlines.
    b.   is mindful of subordinates.
    c.   establishes mutual trust.
    d.   provides open communication.
    e.   is friendly.

___   7.   The leader-member relations can be seen in
    a.   how well defined the task is.
    b.   how much authority the leader has to reward subordinates.
    c.   specific procedures.
    d.   the evaluation of subordinates.
    e.   the members' attitude and acceptance of the leader.

___   8.   A person-oriented leader is most effective in a situation where
    a.   the task is clear.
    b.   he supervises jobs that contain some ambiguity.
    c.   everyone gets along.
    d.   the leader has power.
    e.   all that is needed is for someone to take charge.

___   9.   Which of the following is *not* one of the types of leader behavior from the path-goal theory?
    a.   autocratic
    b.   supportive
    c.   directive
    d.   achievement-oriented
    e.   participative

___   10.   _____ is/are (an) element(s) of the environmental contingencies.
    a.   Ability of subordinates
    b.   Motivations of followers
    c.   Needs of followers
    d.   The nature of the formal authority system
    e.   all of the above

___   11.   According to the path-goal theory of leadership, when there is a lack of challenge on the job, the leader should
    a.   increase confidence to achieve the work outcome.
    b.   clarify the path to the reward.
    c.   be achievement oriented.
    d.   use participative leadership.
    e.   use directive leadership.

___ 12. When subordinates are highly professional and experienced,
   a. a people-oriented style is better.
   b. a task-oriented style is better.
   c. both leadership styles are unimportant.
   d. a substitute leadership style must be developed.
   e. a neutralizer approach should be used.

___ 13. A transactional leader
   a. clarifies subordinates' roles.
   b. does not initiate structure but lets it develop.
   c. avoids showing consideration for subordinates.
   d. receives rewards.
   e. does not clarify task requirements.

___ 14. Charismatic leaders
   a. can only exist in religious organizations.
   b. are usually lacking in vision.
   c. get subordinates to look out for their own interests.
   d. are more predictable than transactional leaders.
   e. may have visionary ideas.

___ 15. Expert power and referent power are most likely to elicit _____ from workers.
   a. commitment
   b. compliance
   c. resistance
   d. complaints
   e. efficiency

___ 16. When executives share power and are more participatory, they are said to _____ employees.
   a. pamper
   b. patronize
   c. baby
   d. empower
   e. enrich

___ 17. The leadership grid was developed by
   a. Ohio State.
   b. the University of Michigan.
   c. Fred Fiedler.
   d. Blake and Mouton.
   e. Hersey and Blanchard.

___ 18. The point of Hersey and Blanchard's situational theory of leadership is that subordinates vary in their
a. individual situations.
b. task readiness.
c. desire for responsibility.
d. motivational level.
e. hair styles.

___ 19. Hersey and Blanchard's approach as compared to Fiedler's model is
a. more difficult to understand.
b. more difficult to apply.
c. casier to understand.
d. more complex.
e. not a contingency approach.

___ 20. The impact from charismatic leaders is normally from
a. stating a lofty vision of an imagined future with which employees identify.
b. shaping a corporate value system for which everyone stands.
c. trusting subordinates.
d. earning subordinates' complete trust.
e. all of the above

___ 21. A leader who works to fulfill subordinates' needs and goals as well as to achieve the organization's larger mission is called a (an) _____ leader.
a. autocratic
b. servant
c. democratic
d. ineffective
e. maverick

___ 22. A level 5 leader
a. is a productive contributor who offers talent, knowledge, skills, and good work habits.
b. contributes to the achievement of team goals and works effectively with others in a group.
c. sets plans and organizes people for the efficient and effective pursuit of objectives.
d. builds widespread commitment to a clear and compelling vision while stimulating people to high performance.
e. builds an enduring great organization through a combination of personal humility and professional resolve.

___ 23. At top management, it may be that leaders lack _____ power because subordinates know more about technical details than they do.
   a. legitimate
   b. reward
   c. coercive
   d. expert
   e. referent

___ 24. Leaders use power to affect the _____ and _____ of followers.
   a. psychology, makeup
   b. psychology, performance
   c. performance, attitudes
   d. behavior, attitudes
   e. husbands, wives

___ 25. _____ power most often generates resistance.
   a. Coercive
   b. Legitimate
   c. Expert
   d. Referent
   e. Reward

___ 26. Blake and Mouton's leadership grid presents concern for production, which is the same as _____ in the Ohio State model.
   a. consideration
   b. initiating structure
   c. task orientation
   d. relationship orientation
   e. behavior by objectives

___ 27. The LPC scale of Fiedler stands for
   a. Leadership Potential Characteristics
   b. Likely Power Core
   c. Least Preferred Co-worker
   d. Leadership Power Curve
   e. Leader Preference Caliber

___ 28. In the Hersey and Blanchard model the style indicated as S2 is the _____ style.
   a. selling
   b. telling
   c. participating
   d. delegating
   e. maturing

___   29.   According to Hersey and Blanchard, if one or more of the followers are low in task readiness, the leader must
    a.   delegate to them.
    b.   tell them exactly what to do.
    c.   sell them on his ideas.
    d.   use a participative leadership style.
    e.   tell them to grow up.

___   30.   Servant leaders tend to
    a.   have an inappropriate style for today's corporate environment.
    b.   be too "soft" to be effective.
    c.   give things away—power, ideas, information, recognition.
    d.   discourage empowerment.
    e.   overcompensate in aggressiveness.

True/False Questions: Please indicate whether the following questions are true or false by writing a T or an F in the blank in front of each question.

___   1.   Expert power depends on the leader's personal characteristics rather than formal title, knowledge, or skills.

___   2.   When leaders use legitimate power and reward power, the most likely outcome will be commitment.

___   3.   Research has found a strong relationship between personal traits and leader success.

___   4.   The Ohio State research found that the high consideration-high initiating structure style achieved better performance and greater satisfaction.

___   5.   Contingency approaches to leadership explain that the relationship between leadership styles and specific situations are related.

___   6.   Task-oriented leaders are less effective than a relationship-oriented leader in a highly favorable situation according to Fiedler.

___   7.   Fiedler suggests that if a leader finds that his or her style does not match the situation, the leader should try to change styles.

___   8.   Situational variables can be so powerful that they actually substitute for or neutralize the need for leadership.

___   9.   The traditional management function of leading has been called transactional leadership.

___   10.   The servant leader will help employees become empowered.

Short-Answer Questions

1.   What is the difference between reward power and coercive power?

2. Do you agree with the original Ohio State studies that concluded that high consideration and high initiating structure are always the best? Why or why not?

3. Why is the Hersey and Blanchard approach to leadership better for practicing managers than the Fiedler model?

4.   What is the basic assumption of the path-goal theory of leadership?

5.   Does the new organization change the role of leadership?

Management Applications

Great Leaders

In the text leadership was defined along two dimensions, a task orientation or a people orientation. When asked which of these two dimensions is most important in leadership, most persons will say the people orientation. Listed below are some famous leaders. For the ones you are familiar with indicate whether you feel they were more people or task oriented by placing a check in the appropriate space.

Leader	Task	People
Sadam Hussein	_____	_____
George W. Bush	_____	_____
General Patton	_____	_____
Margaret Thatcher	_____	_____
Gandhi	_____	_____
Cleopatra	_____	_____
Julius Caesar	_____	_____
Napoleon	_____	_____
The Pope	_____	_____

1.   How many did you classify as task oriented? _____

     How many did you classify as people oriented? _____

     Explain this outcome.

2.   What do the task leaders have in common?

Decide How to Lead

The best leadership style often depends on the situation. In the following situations explain which leadership style you feel would be the best and explain why.

1. You are the production manager in a manufacturing company and receive notice from your boss that a very important customer has an order that must be filled within 24 hours. In other words, this is a rush job!

    ___ Task or ___ People   Why?

2. You are the production manager in a manufacturing company and receive notice from your boss that a very important customer has an order that must be of the highest quality possible. It does not have to go out really soon, but must meet the quality specifications.

    ___ Task or ___ People   Why?

3. You are the office manager for an insurance company and come to work one morning and find Frank and Stan, two of your subordinates, in a fist fight right there in the office.

    ___ Task or ___ People   Why?

Mini Case

A New Commander

Lt. Paris has just been assigned to be the Flight Commander for the 8369th Squadron stationed at Elmendorf Air Force Base in Anchorage, Alaska. This squadron was an intelligence unit. Included in the unit were Russian linguists and Electronic Code operators. Lt. Paris has just graduated from the Air Force Academy with a degree in Russian studies. While he was required to take several Russian language classes, most of his studies dealt with Russian politics, culture, geography, and history. He was required to learn the basics of Electronic Coding as part of his basic training, but has forgotten most of it. This is his first assignment and he is anxious to do well.

1. What type of power should Lt. Paris expect to have over the group and why?

2. If you were Lt. Paris, what would you say to the squadron at the first formal meeting?

Experiential Exercise

What Type of Director of Nursing?

Assume that you are the hospital administrator for a medium-sized hospital. You are in the process of hiring a new director of nursing. In deciding on the type of director you want you have discovered a list of possible adjectives. From the list below pick the adjectives that would describe the type of person you would want. Put the items in rank order. Place a "1" in the blank of the characteristic you feel would be most important, a "2" in front of the one you feel would be second most important, and so on to "10".

___	Decisive	___	Good organizer
___	Understanding	___	Take-charge type
___	Effective	___	Sympathetic
___	Good listener	___	Fair
___	Technically competent	___	Friendly

Now assume that you are a nurse working in this hospital. You have been asked by the hospital administrator to look at the list of adjectives below and to check off the characteristics that you think the new director of nursing should have. You will be working for this new director yourself. Put the items in rank order. Place a "1" in the blank of the characteristic you feel would be most important, a "2" in front of the one you feel would be second most important, and so on to "10".

___	Decisive	___	Good organizer
___	Understanding	___	Take-charge type
___	Effective	___	Sympathetic
___	Good listener	___	Fair
___	Technically competent	___	Friendly

1. Did you rank the items differently in the above two lists? If so, why did you do so?

2. In the list of items a classification has been made to determine if the adjectives apply more to a task orientation or a people orientation. Here is the classification.

Decisive = task

Understanding = people

Effective = task

Good listener = people

Technically competent = task

Good organizer = task

Take-charge type = task

Sympathetic = people

Fair = people

Friendly = people

Score your two lists above for task versus people orientation. Give your number one ranking in each list 10 points, your number two ranking 9 points, your number three ranking 8 points, and so on to the number 10 ranking receiving 1 point. Then count up the number of points the task orientation received for the administrator and for the nurse and record your scores below.

Administrator

Task score = _____

People score = _____

Nurse

Task score = _____

People score = _____

3. Why do you have different task and people scores for the administrator than for the nurse?

4. What does this difference in scores tell you about the pressures that a middle manager leader may face?

Study Guide Solutions

Chapter Review

Multiple-Choice Questions

1	2	3	4	5	6	7	8	9	10
a	e	b	c	b	a	e	b	a	d

11	12	13	14	15	16	17	18	19	20
c	c	a	e	a	d	d	b	c	e

21	22	23	24	25	26	27	28	29	30
b	e	d	d	a	b	c	a	b	c

True/False Questions

1	2	3	4	5	6	7	8	9	10
F	F	F	T	T	F	F	T	T	T

Short-Answer Questions

1. Reward power is the ability to influence others because of the rewards you have to offer them such as praise, attention, and recognition. Coercive power refers to the ability to influence others because of the leader's authority to punish them by firing, demotions, criticism, or withdrawing a pay increase. Reward power is positive by nature, while coercive power is negative.

2. New research has shown the effective leadership style depends on the situation, and the high consideration and initiating structure is not the best in every situation.

3. The Hersey and Blanchard model is easier to understand than the Fiedler model. It is also easier to apply because it describes the best leadership for the manager to take.

4. The path-goal theory of leadership emphasizes the leader's responsibility in increasing subordinates' motivation toward goals by clarifying the path to the rewards or increasing the desired rewards.

5. In today's organizations, leaders learn to thin in terms of "controlling with" rather than having "control over" others. To "control with" others, leaders build relationships based on a shared vision and shape the culture that can help achieve it. They help people see the whole system, facilitate teamwork, initiate change, and expand the capacity of people to shape the future.

Management Applications

Great Leaders

1. Most persons classify the following persons as task oriented: Sadam Hussein, Patton, Thatcher, Cleopatra, Caesar, and Napoleon. Sometimes George W. Bush is also classified here. People-oriented leaders are usually as follows: Gandhi, the Pope, and sometimes Bush.

2. The task leaders all have a crisis situation in common, either military or economic. This exercise illustrates how important the task is in determining the appropriate leadership style.

Decide How to Lead

1. This situation has a time limit and can be classified as a crisis. It calls for a task orientation.

2. This situation is more difficult to classify. One could make the argument that since the specifications must be met so exactly that a task orientation would be best. On the other hand, one needs a people orientation to gain the cooperation of the workers to insure quality. Perhaps a middle-range position between these two extremes would be most appropriate.

3. This situation requires a people orientation first to break up the fight. This is definitely a crisis situation. After the fighting has stopped, an effective leader will switch to a people orientation to solve this people-based "personality" conflict.

Mini Case

A New Commander

1. Lt. Paris can expect to have legitimate power over the group because of his rank in the military. He will also have reward power since he can promote the airmen as well as provide praise and other intangible rewards. He has coercive power since he can punish or recommend punishment. He may have referent power over some of the personnel who also wish to become officers someday. He will not have expert power since they are the technical experts and their knowledge exceeds his.

2. At the first formal meeting Lt. Paris should recognize the expertise of the group. He should probably state his goals and try later to influence the group towards those goals. He must be careful not to talk down to the group since their technical abilities exceed his.

Experiential Exercise

What Type of Director of Nursing?

1. Most persons will mark the lists differently. The reason is that you are looking at the position from different perspectives. In the position of the hospital administrator you are most concerned about getting the job done. From the perspective of the nurse who will be working for the director of nursing, you are most concerned with getting along with your new boss.

2. Most persons will have a higher task score for the hospital administrator and a higher people score for the nurse.

3. The reasons for the difference in scores are due to the different perspectives and expectations from the director of nursing of the persons involved. The administrator is most concerned with effectiveness or a task orientation. The nurse is most concerned about her relationship with the new boss.

4. The middle manager quite often is expected to have a task orientation from superiors and to have a people orientation from subordinates. This manager must develop the skill to use both these orientations for the various situations that will be faced on the job.

Chapter 17

Motivation in Organizations

Chapter Summary

After you have read the text chapter, read through the summary below. Cover the left-hand margin and fill in the blanks with the appropriate terms. After you have filled in each blank, check your responses by uncovering the answer given in the margin. If you do not understand why the given answer is the correct one, refer back to the text.

The Concept of Motivation

Motivation

intrinsic
extrinsic

_____ refers to the arousal, direction, and persistence of behavior. The basic notion of motivation is that needs are translated into an internal tension which motivates people to fulfill the need. If the need is satisfied, the person is rewarded. An _____ reward is received as a direct consequence of a person's actions, whereas an _____ reward is given by another person.

Foundations of Motivation

Traditionally, managers led by Frederick W. Taylor and others believed that employees were motivated primarily by money. It was concluded from the Hawthorne studies that workers were motivated by social factors. The human resource approach suggested that employees should be viewed as whole *persons* and are motivated by many diverse factors. The contemporary approaches group the factors into content theories, process theories, and reinforcement theories.

Content Perspectives on Motivation

Content
hierarchy of
  needs theory
ERG theory

frustration-
  regression

_____ theories emphasize the fulfillment of needs in motivation. Maslow developed a _____, which proposes that people are motivated by five categories of needs—physiological, safety, belongingness, esteem, and self-actualization—that exist in a hierarchical order. The _____ is a modification of the needs hierarchy theory that proposes three categories of needs: existence, relatedness, and growth. This theory also espouses the _____ principle, which is the idea that failure to meet a higher-order need may cause a regression to an already satisfied lower-order need.

hygiene factors

Herzberg's two-factor theory categorizes needs into two types. The first group is called _____ and involves the presence or absence of job dissatisfiers including working conditions, pay, company policies, and interpersonal relationships. The second group is called _____, which are factors that

motivators

influence job satisfaction based on fulfillment of higher-level needs such as achievement, recognition, responsibility, and opportunity for growth. McClelland adds to needs theories the notion that needs can be acquired throughout life. These needs include the need for achievement, affiliation, and power.

Process Perspectives on Motivation

Process

_____ theories are a group of theories that explain how employees select behaviors with which to meet their needs and determine whether their

Equity theory

choices are successful. _____ focuses on individuals' perceptions of how fairly they are treated relative to others. If they perceive an imbalance in this perception, they are motivated to change something in the situation.

Equity

_____ exists when the ratio of one person's outcomes to inputs equals that of another's. _____ proposes that motivation depends on

Expectancy
theory

individuals' expectations about their ability to perform tasks and receive desired rewards. The probabilities that effort will result in high performance, that high performance will result in outcomes, and the desirability of the outcomes all

E ➜ P

combine together to affect motivation. _____ expectancy is the expectation that putting effort into a given task will lead to high performance.

P ➜ O
valence

_____ expectancy is the expectation that successful performance of a task will lead to the desired outcome. The _____ is the value of outcomes for the individual.

Reinforcement Perspective on Motivation

Reinforcement

_____ theory is based on the relationship between a given behavior and its consequences. Several tools have been developed to change behavior by

Behavior
modification
law of effect

changing the consequences. _____ is the set of techniques by which reinforcement theory is used to modify human behavior. The _____ is the assumption that positively reinforced behavior tends to be repeated and unreinforced or negatively reinforced behavior tends to be inhibited.

Reinforcement

_____ is anything that causes a given behavior to be repeated or inhibited. Reinforcement can be positive, negative, punishment, or extinction. The timing of the reinforcement can also affect the learning of behaviors. The

schedule of
reinforcement
continuous
partial

_____ is the frequency with and intervals over which reinforcement occurs. The schedule could be one of continuous reinforcement or of a partial reinforcement. A _____ reinforcement schedule is one in which every occurrence of the desired behavior is reinforced. A _____ reinforcement schedule is one in which only some occurrences of the desired behavior are reinforced. Partial reinforcement includes the fixed-interval, fixed-ratio, variable-interval, and variable-ratio schedules.

Job Design for Motivation

Job design

_____ is the application of motivational theories to the structure of work for improving productivity and satisfaction. The number of tasks and the nature of those tasks one has on a job affect the motivational level of workers. Several techniques have been developed to change these factors.

Job simplification

_____ is a job design whose purpose is to improve task efficiency by reducing the number of tasks a single person must perform. While job simplification reduces the number of tasks by specialization, it often results in boredom and reduced motivation.

Job rotation

_____ systematically moves employees from one job to another to provide them with variety and stimulation. Job rotation increases the number of tasks over time and can be motivational if the jobs are challenging.

Job enlargement

_____ combines a series of tasks into one new, broader job to give employees variety and challenge.

Job enrichment

_____ incorporates achievement, recognition, and other high-level motivators into the work. Job enrichment adds more responsibility to the job and thereby has more motivational potential. Hackman and Oldham developed

job, model

the _____ characteristics _____, which is a model of job design that comprises core job dimensions, critical psychological states, and employee growth-need strength.

Work redesign

_____ involves the changing of jobs to increase the quality of work life and the productivity of workers. Core job dimensions are *skill variety, task identity, task significance, autonomy,* and *feedback.* These dimensions produce *meaningful work, a feeling of responsibility,* and *knowledge of results.* These lead to positive personal and work outcomes. The effectiveness of each of these programs depends on the types of perceived needs that the workers have.

Motivation in the New Workplace

empowerment

A recent trend in motivation is _____, which is the delegation of power and authority to subordinates. This releases motivation within employees. Empowered employees must receive information about company performance, have knowledge and skills to contribute to company goals, have power to make substantive decisions, and be rewarded based on performance.

Chapter Review

Multiple-Choice Questions: Please indicate the correct response to the following questions by writing the letter of the correct answer in the space provided.

___ 1. An example of contemporary approaches to employee motivation is (are)
a.   content theories.
b.   the economic man theory.
c.   scientific management.
d.   the human relations approach.
e.   all of the above

___ 2. Content theories emphasize the _____ that motivate people.
a.   expectancies
b.   rewards
c.   equities
d.   needs
e.   valences

___ 3. The most basic needs according to Maslow's hierarchy are _____ needs.
a.   physiological
b.   safety
c.   belongingness
d.   esteem
e.   self-actualization

___ 4. According to Herzberg's two-factor theory, _____ is a hygiene factor, not a motivator.
a.   achievement
b.   pay
c.   recognition
d.   responsibility
e.   work itself

___ 5. McClelland describes the need for _____ as the desire to accomplish something difficult.
a.   affiliation
b.   attention
c.   power
d.   achievement
e.   self-actualization

___   6.   According to equity theory, which of the following is an input?
      a.   experience
      b.   recognition
      c.   pay
      d.   promotions
      e.   all of the above

___   7.   In a situation where one perceives unfavorable inequity, he is likely to
      a.   increase effort.
      b.   quit the union.
      c.   distort others' perceived rewards.
      d.   stay on the job longer to improve equity.
      e.   all of the above

___   8.   For the expectancy that effort will lead to performance to be high, the individual must have
      a.   ability.
      b.   previous experience.
      c.   necessary tools.
      d.   opportunity to perform.
      e.   all of the above

___   9.   To increase motivation managers can
      a.   conceal the outcomes available to provide the "surprise" effect.
      b.   withdraw support so the individual must grow.
      c.   clarify individual needs.
      d.   deemphasize individual ability.
      e.   ignore the match between abilities and job demands so subordinates can develop new skills.

___   10.   The removal of an unpleasant consequence following a desired behavior is called
      a.   positive reinforcement.
      b.   negative reinforcement.
      c.   punishment.
      d.   extinction.
      e.   positive extinction.

___   11.   A farm worker who is paid $2.00 for picking 20 pounds of peppers is being reinforced according to a _____ schedule.
      a.   fixed-interval
      b.   fixed-ratio
      c.   variable-interval
      d.   variable-ratio
      e.   continuous

___ 12. The most powerful reinforcement schedule is the _____ schedule.
   a. fixed-interval
   b. fixed-ratio
   c. variable-interval
   d. variable-ratio
   e. continuous

___ 13. Job rotation has greater motivational potential when jobs are
   a. simplified.
   b. challenging.
   c. boring.
   d. longer lasting.
   e. well structured.

___ 14. The core job dimension from the job characteristics model which is the degree to which an employee performs a total job with a recognizable beginning and ending is
   a. skill variety.
   b. task identity.
   c. task significance.
   d. autonomy.
   e. feedback.

___ 15. Which of the following is true of empowered employees?
   a. they receive little information about company performance to reduce anxiety
   b. they make only minor decisions
   c. they do not really have the skills and abilities to contribute to company goals, but are made to feel that they do
   d. they are rewarded based on company performance
   e. all of the above are true

___ 16. _____ is an example of an extrinsic reward.
   a. A good feeling
   b. A promotion
   c. Enjoying the job
   d. A sense of accomplishment
   e. all of the above

___ 17. The highest level of needs according to Maslow is developing one's full potential. Maslow named this set of needs
   a. physiological.
   b. safety.
   c. belongingness.
   d. esteem.
   e. self-actualization.

___ 18. According to the frustration-regression principle,
    a. failure to have an adequate sexual relationship may lead to rape.
    b. failure to have one's needs met on the job may lead one to be more aggressive on the job.
    c. failure to meet a higher-order need may trigger a regression to an already fulfilled lower-order need.
    d. frustration is a good thing because it makes us more assertive.
    e. when we are frustrated, we begin to act like babies.

___ 19. According to Herzberg, making the work more safe will
    a. result in increased motivation of the workers.
    b. increase the level of satisfaction.
    c. decrease the level of dissatisfaction.
    d. make the workers want to work harder.
    e. make the workers want higher pay.

___ 20. The desire to influence or control others is the _____ need.
    a. esteem
    b. achievement
    c. affiliation
    d. expectancy
    e. power

___ 21. _____ is the value of the outcomes for the individual.
    a. Expectancy
    b. Valence
    c. E$\rightarrow$P
    d. P$\rightarrow$O
    e. Achievement

___ 22. Reinforcement theory focuses on changing _____ through the appropriate use of immediate rewards and punishments.
    a. attitudes
    b. opinions
    c. expectancies
    d. behavior
    e. organizational structure

___ 23. Frances Flood, CEO of Gentner Communications
    a. allowed employees to become part owners.
    b. gave managers authority to make many of their own decisions.
    c. required managers to make a $25,000 investment.
    d. required engineers to sign a five-year contract.
    e. offered engineers a stake in the company's profits if they met targets for getting new products to market faster.

___ 24. Which of the following refers to the degree to which an employee performs a total job with a recognizable beginning and end?
   a.   skill variety
   b.   task significance
   c.   task identity
   d.   autonomy
   e.   feedback

___ 25. At Ralcorp's cereal manufacturing plant in Sparks, Nevada, enriched jobs
   a.   refer to the fiber put into the cereal.
   b.   ended up costing the company lots of money.
   c.   were phased out in favor of enlarged jobs.
   d.   were declared illegal by the state legislature.
   e.   have improved employee motivation and satisfaction.

___ 26. Which core job dimension refers to the degree to which a job is considered important and having an impact?
   a.   task significance
   b.   task identity
   c.   skill variety
   d.   autonomy
   e.   feedback

___ 27. Autonomy refers to
   a.   the degree to which a job is considered important and having impact.
   b.   the degree to which an employee performs a total job with a recognizable beginning and end.
   c.   the degree to which an employee has freedom and discretion in planning and carrying out tasks.
   d.   the degree to which a job provides information to the employee regarding performance.
   e.   none of the above.

___ 28. Giving an employee control over resources, decision making, the pace of work, and providing growth is called
   a.   job enlargement.
   b.   task significance.
   c.   task identity.
   d.   job enrichment.
   e.   psychological fulfillment.

— 29. If a person chooses to increase his inputs to the organization without an increase in income, it is because he or she has perceived
   a. equity.
   b. inequity.
   c. valence.
   d. a continuous reinforcement schedule.
   e. a pay-for-performance plan.

— 30. Job simplification is based on principles drawn from
   a. adolescent psychology.
   b. social psychology.
   c. the human relations movement.
   d. industrial engineering.
   e. Elton Mayo.

True/False Questions: Please indicate whether the following questions are true or false by writing a T or an F in the blank in front of each question.

— 1. An extrinsic reward is one received as a direct consequence of a person's actions.

— 2. Work redesign is the altering of jobs to increase the quality of the work experience and worker productivity.

— 3. According to Maslow's theory, higher-level needs take priority over the lower-level needs.

— 4. The ERG model is more rigid than Maslow's need hierarchy.

— 5. Good hygiene factors can cause people to become highly satisfied and motivated in their work.

— 6. Equity theory focuses on individuals' perceptions of how fairly they are treated compared to others.

— 7. Expectancy theory is concerned with identifying types of needs, not with the thinking process that individuals use to achieve rewards.

— 8. Valence is the value of outcomes for the individual.

— 9. Reinforcement theory sidesteps the issues of employee needs and thinking processes.

— 10. Punishment is the withdrawal of a positive reward.

Short-Answer Questions

1. Is there a relationship between Maslow's hierarchy of needs theory and Herzberg's two-factor theory?

2. What is the relationship between effort and outcome?

3. Explain how each of the four types of reinforcement might be used to deal with an employee who is always coming in late?

4.   Explain how you might use job enlargement and then job enrichment on the job of a custodian?

5.   To which motivational theory is pay for performance related?

Management Applications

Miss Peppy Paula

Paula is an attractive 22-year-old woman going through a divorce. She works in the office of a large insurance company. Recently, she has been transferred to a new job. She is a naturally friendly, happy, outspoken person and likes to talk. Despite her divorce, she is not bitter about men. In fact, she is dating one of the men in the division she now works for.

1. Which of Maslow's needs are most important to Paula?

2. Do you think Paula will have any problems in the office where she works? If so, what type would you predict?

Should I Study for the Exam?

Fred is trying to decide whether to study for the next management exam. The exam is on Monday morning and it is now early Friday evening. As he is thinking about this important decision, he remembers that he spent ten hours studying for the last examination. He still only made a D minus on the exam.

1.   Do you think Fred will study for this exam?

2.   Which motivational theory influences your answer to the first question?

While contemplating this decision, Fred receives two telephone calls. The first call is from his father, who wants Fred to do well in college. He offers Fred $100 if he gets a B on the next management exam and $200 if he gets an A.

3.   Do you think Fred will now study hard for this exam? Explain your answer.

The second telephone call is from Suzanne. She is a very attractive young woman that Fred has had his eye on for some time. He has been trying to get up the courage to ask her out. She asks Fred to spend the weekend with her at her folks' cabin.

4.   Do you think Fred will now study hard for this exam? Explain your answer.

Mini Case

Slothful Sally

You are a shift supervisor at the local hospital. One of the nurses on your shift, Sally, has been worrying you lately. She saunters down the hall, works slowly, and has a poor personal appearance. She also seems to be bored or depressed most of the time and does the job without enthusiasm or in a routine manner only. You've noticed the effect Sally has had on patients and other nurses. Even your department head has remarked about Sally's attitude and performance. You decided that Sally needs some motivation. You call Sally into a conference room to talk. You want to discover what the problem is and to figure out a way to motivate Sally. You ask her what is wrong and she gives you the following reply:

"When I graduated from college two years ago, I was really looking forward to a career in the health care field. I knew I'd have to start out doing mundane tasks, but felt that as soon as my true capabilities were recognized; I'd be given more challenging work. Now I see things differently. I've been stuck on the same job assignment for two years now. The job seems pretty routine and boring to me. I find that I am not very excited about coming to work and that even getting ready for work is a chore. I've been thinking lately about changing to a more challenging and rewarding career."

1. According to Maslow's hierarchy of needs theory, which level is Sally on? How can you tell?

2. According to Herzberg's two-factor theory, what needs are not being met as described by Sally? Does this explain her apparent lack of motivation?

3. What job design technique might help to make Sally more motivated? Explain why.

Experiential Exercise

In May of 1990 New York City hosted the 52nd annual Premium Incentive Show. It showcased items meant to be used as sales incentives or worker incentives. Some of the items are listed below. In the blank to the right indicate the motivational theory on which each item is based. Be ready to explain your choice in a class discussion led by the instructor.

Source: *The Wall Street Journal*, May 4, 1990, pages A1, A7.

Item	Theory on Which It Is Based
Vacuum-packed smoked salmon to be given for ace salesmen contests.	
The Congratulator—a device that pats you on the back when you pull a string—for workers to give themselves the recognition they don't get from others.	
Tapes of relaxing sounds packaged together with massage oil for overstressed salesmen.	
The Citizen Defense Shield, a bulletproof line for luggage.	
A bingo game with five balls with numbers being drawn for every week of no defects or no accidents. Bingo winners receive prizes.	
A tiny Sony Watchman television to be given to salespeople who exceed quotas.	

Study Guide Solutions

Chapter Review

Multiple-Choice Questions

1	2	3	4	5	6	7	8	9	10
a	d	a	b	d	a	c	e	c	b
11	**12**	**13**	**14**	**15**	**16**	**17**	**18**	**19**	**20**
b	d	b	b	d	b	e	c	c	e
21	**22**	**23**	**24**	**25**	**26**	**27**	**28**	**29**	**30**
b	d	e	c	e	a	c	d	b	d

True/False Questions

1	2	3	4	5	6	7	8	9	10
F	T	F	F	F	T	F	T	T	F

Short-Answer Questions

1. It seems that Herzberg's hygiene factors are related to the lower-level needs of Maslow. The motivators seem to be the higher-level needs of Maslow.

2. The relationship between effort and outcome is indirect according to expectancy theory. Effort leads to performance and performance leads to the outcome.

3. Positive reinforcement could be used to reinforce the employee on those occasions when he does come in on time. Avoidance learning or negative reinforcement might be used by not being nasty to the employee when he does come in on time. Punishment might be used by making the employee stay late when he comes in late. Extinction could be used by not rewarding his coming in late with extra attention.

4. To enlarge the job of a custodian you might assign him to clean more rooms. You might also require him to mop floors in addition to cleaning them. To enrich the job of the custodian you might assign him to do maintenance work or be in charge of building security in addition to his cleaning duties.

5. Pay for performance is related to expectancy theory and reinforcement theory. Pay raises are tied to work behavior with the pay raises being the desired outcome and the close linking of them to performance increasing the degree of expectancy. The pay raise is also a reinforcement of the desired behavior.

Management Applications

Miss Peppy Paula

1. It seems that the social need is most important to Paula at this time as she is concerned with working through her divorce, dating other men, and getting along in her new office.

2. Paula may run into problems from other employees who have different needs or even the same needs. She is young and attractive. This may spawn jealousy among the other women in the office as Paula is asked out by men in the office. Her high social need may also cause her to socialize too much and not do very well in performing assigned tasks.

Should I Study for the Exam?

1. Fred is not likely to study hard for the exam given his past experience. It does not seem to pay for him to study.

2. The expectancy theory comes into play here. The probability that effort will lead to high performance seems to be very low.

3. If the expected outcome ($100 or $200) is highly valued by Fred, he may now be motivated to study hard. This may be enough to overcome the low probability of effort leading to performance which will also influence him.

4. If the valence of the weekend with Suzanne is higher than that of the money offered by Fred's father (which is most likely the case), he will not study hard.

Mini Case

Slothful Sally

1. Sally is pretty high on Maslow's hierarchy. She could be concerned with esteem. She longs for more self-respect. It could be argued that she is even at the self-actualization stage and seeking more fulfillment from the job.

2. The need for recognition is definitely not being met. Responsibility also seems to be lacking. Most importantly is the need for growth, which she really indicates is not present. The work itself is also not motivating to her. It is no wonder that she is not motivated.

3. Job rotation would certainly alleviate the boredom, but not provide the chance for growth. The same holds for job enlargement. It seems that job enrichment is needed the most in this situation. This would add the opportunities for growth and give the responsibility she needs.

Experiential Exercise

Item	Theory on Which It Is Based
Vacuum-packed smoked salmon to be given for ace salesmen contests.	Reinforcement theory and a bit of the lump-sum bonus plan. Economic man.
The Congratulator—a device that pats you on the back when you pull a string—for workers to give themselves the recognition they don't get from others.	Maslow's hierarchy and Herzberg's two-factor theory.
Tapes of relaxing sounds packaged together with massage oil for overstressed salesmen.	Hygiene factor of Herzberg's theory. Also physiological needs of Maslow.
The Citizen Defense Shield, a bulletproof line for luggage.	Maslow's safety need.
A bingo game with five balls with numbers being drawn for every week of no defects or no accidents. Bingo winners receive prizes.	Scientific management and economic man assumptions. Also reinforcement theory.
A tiny Sony Watchman television to be given to salespeople who exceed quotas.	Reinforcement theory and a bit of the lump-sum bonus plan. Economic man.

Chapter 18

Communicating in Organizations

Chapter Summary

After you have read the text chapter, read through the summary below. Cover the left-hand margin and fill in the blanks with the appropriate terms. After you have filled in each blank, check your responses by uncovering the answer given in the margin. If you do not understand why the given answer is the correct one, refer back to the text.

Communication and the Manager's Job

Communication

_____ is the process by which information is exchanged and understood by two or more people, usually with the intent to motivate or influence behavior. Managers spend much of their time communicating. The communication process consists of encoding, message formulation, picking a channel, decoding by the receiver, and feedback to the sender. _____ means to select symbols with which to compose a message. The _____ is the tangible formulation of an idea to be sent to a receiver. The _____ is the carrier of a communication. To _____ is to translate the symbols used in a message for the purpose of interpreting its meaning, and _____ is a response by the receiver to the sender's communication.

Encoding
message
channel
decode
feedback

Communicating among People

Channel richness

The type of channel chosen affects communication. _____ refers to the amount of information that can be transmitted during a communication episode. Selection of the appropriate channel depends on the nature of the message. *Routine messages* convey data that are easily understood and do not require a very rich channel. *Nonroutine messages*, which are more likely to be misinterpreted, require richer channels. Communication is used not only to convey information, but to persuade and influence people. To persuade and influence, managers connect with others on an emotional level by using symbols, metaphors, and stories. Nonverbal actions and behaviors have more effect on whether communication takes place than do the actual words spoken. _____ is a communication transmitted through actions and behaviors rather than through words. The listening skill of the receiver is also a major

Nonverbal
communication

Listening

factor affecting communication. _____ is the skill of receiving messages to accurately grasp facts and feelings to interpret the genuine meaning.

Organizational Communication

formal

A _____ organizational channel is one which flows within the chain of command or task responsibility defined by the organization and uses downward communications for topics such as goals, job instructions, procedures, feedback, and indoctrination. _____ communication refers

Downward

to messages sent from top management down to subordinates. It is used for implementation of goals and strategies, job instructions, procedures and practices, performance feedback, and indoctrination. _____

Upward

communication means that messages are transmitted from the lower to the higher level in the organization's hierarchy. Upward communication is used for problems, suggestions, performance reports, grievances, and accounting information. Horizontal communication is used for interdepartmental problem solving and coordination as well as for change initiatives and improvements.

Horizontal
informal
communication
channel
wandering around

_____ communication is the lateral or diagonal exchange of messages across peers or co-workers. An _____ is one that exists outside formally authorized channels without regard for the organization's hierarchy of authority. Informal communication channels exist in every organization. Management by _____ (MBWA) has become a popular concept that involves direct interaction of management with workers to exchange infor-

grapevine

mation. The _____ is an informal, personal communication network which is not officially sanctioned by the organization. It is always present, is usually accurate, and is very fast in transmitting information.

centralized
network
decentralized
network

A _____ means that team members communicate through a single person to solve problems or make decisions. In a _____ team members communicate freely with each other and arrive at decisions together. The centralized network is faster and is more appropriate for less complex tasks. The decentralized network is better for more complex tasks.

Communicating in the New Workplace

open
communications
dialogue

A recent trend for empowering employees is _____, which means sharing all types of information throughout the company, across functions and hierarchical levels. A way of creating team spirit is _____, a group communication process in which people together create a stream of shared meaning that enables them to understand each other and share a view of the world.. In the new workplace, feedback occurs when managers use evaluation and communication to help individuals and the organization learn and improve.

Managing Organizational Communication

Semantics

Several barriers negatively affect communication. Individual barriers include emotions and perceptions, choosing the wrong channel, poor semantics, and sending inconsistent cues. _____ refers to the meaning of words and the way they are used. Organizational barriers include status and power differences, dissimilar goals, wrong communication flow, and the absence of formal channels.

These barriers to communication can be overcome by individual and organizational actions. Individually, listening is the most important skill to develop. Choice of the correct channel and understanding the other person's perspective are also important. Management by wandering around can also overcome barriers to effective communication. Organizational actions include the creation of a climate of trust and openness. Managers should use the formal channels in all directions and encourage the use of multiple channels. One must also be sure that the structure fits the communication needs.

Chapter Review

Multiple-Choice Questions: Please indicate the correct response to the following questions by writing the letter of the correct answer in the space provided.

___ 1. The tangible formulation of an idea to be sent to a receiver is called
   a. encoding.
   b. the message.
   c. the channel.
   d. decoding.
   e. feedback.

___ 2. Which of the following is an example of "noise" which impedes communication?
   a. lack of knowledge
   b. negative attitude
   c. different backgrounds of sender and receiver
   d. all of the above
   e. a and b only

___ 3. Which of the following is *not* a communication channel?
   a. telephone
   b. memo
   c. newsletter
   d. letter
   e. perceptual background

___ 4. The richest communication channel is a
   a. telephone.
   b. memo.
   c. face-to-face talk.
   d. flyer.
   e. letter.

___ 5. _____ is a characteristic of a nonroutine message.
   a. Simplicity
   b. Prior agreement
   c. Pertaining to statistics
   d. Dealing with a novel event
   e. Straightforwardness

___ 6. Open communications means
   a. the same as having an open door policy.
   b. sharing company information throughout the organization.
   c. getting rid of informatl communications.
   d. allowing managers to use electronic mail.
   e. providing company information to users of the World Wide Web.

    7. If a girl hugs a boy tighter at the door after a date while saying, "You'd better go now," this is an example of
      a. a grapevine.
      b. a nonverbal message contradicting the verbal.
      c. noise.
      d. feedback.
      e. femininity.

    8. An effective listener
      a. does not show interest until the other stops talking.
      b. listens for facts.
      c. listens for central themes.
      d. judges by the quality of the delivery.
      e. never asks questions.

    9. Which type of downward communication is illustrated by the following words: "Sally, you need to improve your typing skills."?
      a. indoctrination
      b. performance feedback
      c. procedures and practices
      d. job instructions
      e. implementation of goals

   10. Recently, a manager received the following note on his desk: "The main computer just went down. We expect to have it fixed in about two hours." What type of communication is this?
      a. downward
      b. upward
      c. horizontal
      d. rumor
      e. grapevine

   11. Which of the following would *not* facilitate upward communication?
      a. suggestion box
      b. employee survey
      c. open-door policy
      d. management by wandering around
      e. All of the above would facilitate upward communication.

   12. The grapevine
      a. will not exist in a well-run company.
      b. usually carries inaccurate information.
      c. usually circulates nonbusiness-related matters.
      d. fills in information gaps in the organization.
      e. usually is inactive during a period of change.

___   13.   When the complexity of a department task is high, a(n) _____ communication process works best.
a.   decentralized
b.   centralized
c.   wheel
d.   "Y"
e.   informal

___   14.   Attaching different meanings to words is a communication problem pertaining to
a.   interpersonal dynamics.
b.   channels and media.
c.   semantics.
d.   inconsistent cues.
e.   linguistics.

___   15.   To improve organization communication the organization should
a.   allow subordinates to transmit only positive messages to managers.
b.   use formal information channels in one direction only.
c.   use only the formal communication channel.
d.   create a climate of trust and openness.
e.   never change the organizational structure.

___   16.   About _____ minutes of every working hour is spent communicating by managers.
a.   10
b.   22
c.   36
d.   48
e.   54

___   17.   The message, "We are streamlining the company travel procedures and would like to discuss them with your department," is an example of _____ communication.
a.   downward
b.   upward
c.   horizontal
d.   vertical
e.   informal

___   18.   When the audience is widely dispersed, _____ communications should be used.
a.   informal
b.   nonroutine
c.   written
d.   verbal
e.   perceptual

___ 19. If your supervisor stays behind her desk and you sit in a straight chair on the opposite
side, to most people it would mean
  a. the supervisor is afraid of you.
  b. the supervisor wants you to know she is in charge.
  c. the supervisor wants you to know this is serious business.
  d. the supervisor wants to create a casual, friendly atmosphere.
  e. the supervisor is expecting someone else to join you.

___ 20. Most executives now believe that important information
  a. flows from the top down.
  b. flows from the bottom up.
  c. flows in both directions.
  d. comes only from suppliers.
  e. comes only from computers.

___ 21. The book *In Search of Excellence* advises managers to
  a. avoid asking dumb questions.
  b. not join casual get-togethers with employees.
  c. force themselves to get out and about.
  d. never take notes to improve listening.
  e. not promise feedback because you may not be able to deliver.

___ 22. Which of the following is evidence of a good listener?
  a. laid back
  b. listens for facts
  c. prefers recreational material rather than difficult material
  d. judges content and skips over delivery errors
  e. does not ask questions

___ 23. The major problem with downward communication is drop-off, which means
  a. the tendency of employees to drop off to sleep while listening.
  b. the distortion or loss of message content.
  c. using poor grammar or slang.
  d. the incongruency with the informal communication channel of the message content.
  e. the conflict between verbal and nonverbal messages.

___ 24. In reference to teams, a *dialogue* refers to
  a. efforts to improve collaboration, trust, and commitment to strategic goals.
  b. productive arguments between team members.
  c. communication between two different teams.
  d. minor disagreements between management and the team.
  e. none of the above.

___ 25.   The informal communication channel is called the grapevine because it
    a.   links employees in all directions together.
    b.   is too strong to be cut.
    c.   can be tapped into for the "wine of the message."
    d.   contains "grapes" of information.
    e.   only exists when employees have drunk a little wine.

___ 26.   In a highly competitive global environment, organizations use _____ to deal with complex problems.
    a.   the grapevine
    b.   fax machines
    c.   groups and teams
    d.   formal communication channels
    e.   brokers

___ 27.   To overcome the barrier of inconsistent communication cues the text recommends
    a.   active listening.
    b.   selection of an appropriate channel.
    c.   knowledge of others' perspectives.
    d.   MBWA.
    e.   creation of a climate of trust.

___ 28.   Structure should reflect
    a.   group information needs.
    b.   the grapevine.
    c.   the informal communication channel.
    d.   the competitor's mission.
    e.   nonverbal communication.

___ 29.   Without feedback communication is
    a.   two-way.
    b.   one-way.
    c.   informal
    d.   bottom up.
    e.   most effective.

___ 30.   Communications can break down if sender and receiver do not _____ or _____ language in the same way.
    a.   send, receive
    b.   encode, decode
    c.   semanticize, interpret
    d.   implicate, replicate
    e.   synthesize, empathize

True/False Questions: Please indicate whether the following questions are true or false by writing a T or an F in the blank in front of each question.

___ 1. Managers spend about 20 percent of every working day communicating.

___ 2. Communication means essentially the same as sending information.

___ 3. The more similar the frames of reference between people, the more easily they can communicate.

___ 4. A task force is an example of an informal communication channel.

___ 5. Major parts of the shared understanding from communication come from the nonverbal messages of facial expression, voice, mannerisms, posture, and dress.

___ 6. Management by wandering around only works on the lower levels of management.

___ 7. Listening requires attention, energy, and skill.

___ 8. A research and development department should be organized for centralized communications.

___ 9. People with different backgrounds or knowledge may interpret communications in different ways.

___ 10. The least important individual communication skill is active listening.

Short-Answer Questions

1. Explain why feedback is an essential part of the communication process.

2.   How does nonverbal behavior affect the communication process?

3.   Which is the richest communication channel and when should it be used?

4. Since informal communication is so powerful, fast, and accurate, why do organizations need formal channels of communication?

5. Which type of network would be most appropriate for a team assigned to come up with new ideas?

Management Applications

Which One Is Motivated?

Listed below are adjectives given by actual supervisors describing employees. Read through the lists and then answer the questions that follow.

Employee A	**Employee B**
Independent thinker	Unresponsive to management
Creative	Refuses to use new procedures
Makes close friends with most fellow workers	Rudely ignores nearly half of her fellow employees
Willing to point out areas that need improvement and offer suggestions	Demands action on her need grievances
Experienced	
Gets the job done	

1. What should an effective manager do with Employee A?

2.   What should an effective manager do with Employee B?

3.   In reality, these descriptions were from different supervisors, but were describing the same employee. How do you explain the difference in description?

Nonverbal Cues

It is important to understand what nonverbal cues mean. In the following scenarios, explain what the nonverbal cue means and how it affects the verbal message.

1. "I just *love* doing homework!" Cindy yelled as she threw her calculus book into the trash can.

2. "Your report is certainly complete," said the boss with a frown on his face as he pushed the 500-page report aside having not even read it.

3. "Isn't my idea great?" asked Sally. "Sure," replied Jack as he continued dialing the telephone.

4. "No more applause, please!" said David Letterman as he waved his hands in a "come on and give me more" fashion.

5. "That politician sure knows what he wants to do," said Ted as he rubbed his fingers together as if handling some coins.

Mini Case

So That's What We Are Supposed to Be Doing!

"Did you read the President's letter about the new Dean?" Pablo asked Stan.

"You mean the one describing all of the areas of international expertise that we in the School of Business have?" queried Stan.

"Si, that is the one. I did not know that the President wanted us to emphasize international business, did you?"

"No, I didn't. I wonder if the new Dean feels the same way."

1. Based on the foregoing conversation, what actions would you take if you were the new Dean of the School of Business?

2.   What explanation could there be for the apparent lack of communication between the President and the faculty in the School of Business?

Experiential Exercise

Listening or Faking It?

Choose a partner for this exercise. Between the two of you decide who will be the listener and who will be the talker. The person who is to be the listener should flip a coin. If the coin lands as "heads," that person is to really listen to what you say. If the coin lands as "tails," that person is to fake listening. In faking the listening try to do all of the nonverbal things you usually do when listening. For example, maintain eye contact, smile occasionally, and sometimes nod your head. The talker is not allowed to ask the listener for verbal feedback, just to talk.

1. When the instructor says, "Go!" the talker is to speak for two minutes on "the most important person to me in my life."

2. At the end of the two-minute speaking period the instructor will ask each talker to tell the class if the person was listening or faking it. The instructor will then ask the listener to reveal the truth. If the listener was supposed to be faking it, but ended up listening, the instructor will keep a tally on the board of the number who were not able to fake it while nonverbally listening. The instructor will also keep a tally of correct and incorrect answers by the talker on the board.

The theory is that one way to improve listening skills is to pay attention to the nonverbal behaviors that indicate listening. If you do all of those nonverbal things, you will find yourself listening. If you do not listen, you are not doing all of the nonverbal behaviors correctly, and the listener will be able to detect the fact that you are faking it. Discuss the validity of this theory in light of the results of this activity as indicated by the tallies on the board.

Study Guide Solutions

Chapter Review

Multiple-Choice Questions

1	2	3	4	5	6	7	8	9	10
b	d	e	c	d	b	b	c	b	b

11	12	13	14	15	16	17	18	19	20
e	d	a	c	d	d	c	c	b	b

21	22	23	24	25	26	27	28	29	30
c	d	b	a	a	c	d	a	b	b

True/False Questions

1	2	3	4	5	6	7	8	9	10
F	F	T	F	T	F	T	F	T	F

Short-Answer Questions

1. Feedback is necessary for the sender to know that the receiver grasped the intended message. It can tell the sender if improper encoding took place, if the channel was improper, or if noise impeded the communication process.

2. Nonverbal behavior is the most important part of the communication media. It is more powerful than the words or the voice. It can override or completely change the meaning of words.

3. The richest communication channel is face-to-face discussion because it permits direct experience, multiple information cues, immediate feedback, and personal focus. When the communication is very important and emotion must also be shared, this channel is appropriate.

4. Formal communication channels are needed to implement goals; to give job instructions and rationale; to communicate procedures, practices, performance feedback, and indoctrination; to deal with problems; to provide suggestions and performance reports; and as a means of airing grievances and officially providing financial information.

5. The decentralized network would be the best structure for a team assigned to come up with new ideas. It allows members to communicate freely with each other and would therefore facilitate brainstorming and piggy-backing on the ideas of others, thus fostering creativity.

Management Applications

Which One Is Motivated?

1. Most persons would answer that employee A should be rewarded or even promoted. This employee seems to be a valuable resource to the organization.

2. It would appear that Employee B needs either some training or motivation. Some persons would even say that this employee should be fired.

3. The difference in description is probably due to the different perceptions that the two supervisors have of this employee. Based on these perceptions they attach labels to her behavior, which imply the motivation behind her actions.

Nonverbal Cues

1. The major nonverbal cue is Cindy's throwing her calculus book into the trash can. The fact that she yelled and emphasized the word "love" also adds to the meaning. Obviously, she hates homework, at least calculus homework. The nonverbal cue in this case gives the verbal statement the opposite meaning.

2. Both the frown on the face and the pushing aside of the report without reading it are nonverbal cues. They seem to be saying that the report is too long to read and be understood. In this case they seem to be explaining that it is too complete.

3. In this case the fact that Jack keeps on dialing the phone is contradicting his statement that he agrees that Sally's idea is great. It says in essence that it is not so great or important.

4. Again in this case the nonverbal cue is contradicting the verbal. The nonverbal cue will be stronger usually as it generally is in this situation.

5. In this case the nonverbal cue is explaining what is meant by the verbal, namely that the politician only wants money.

Mini Case

So That's What We Are Supposed to Be Doing!

1. If I were the new Dean, I would first meet with the President to discover if this is the direction he wants to go. Then I would communicate this clearly to the faculty and ask for their input on ways to accomplish this. I would also make sure that the communication link between the President and the Business faculty is clearly established and used in the future.

2. If the School of Business had no dean or an acting dean prior to this incident, the communication link could have been broken. This points out the importance of a formal channel of communication.

Experiential Exercise

Listening or Faking It?

The results for this exercise will vary with each class. However, if the listener really fakes it without listening, the speaker can usually tell. If the listener who was supposed to fake it really ends up listening, the speaker can usually detect this also. Both of these results would support the theory.

Chapter 19

Teamwork in Organizations

Chapter Summary

After you have read the text chapter, read through the summary below. Cover the left-hand margin and fill in the blanks with the appropriate terms. After you have filled in each blank, check your responses by uncovering the answer given in the margin. If you do not understand why the given answer is the correct one, refer back to the text.

Teams at Work

team

For a _____ to exist two or more persons must interact and coordinate their work to accomplish a specific goal. The effectiveness of a team is determined by its productive output and the personal satisfaction of team members. Factors that influence team effectiveness include the context within which the team exists, the type of team it is, its characteristics, and composition. All these factors affect team process, which in turn affects team effectiveness.

Types of Teams

formal
vertical

horizontal

special-purpose

committee

Teams that are _____ are created by the organization as part of the formal organization structure. One type of formal team is the _____ team, which refers to the manager and his subordinates in the organization's formal chain of command. A _____ team is also a formal team, but one that is composed of employees from about the same hierarchical level but from different areas of expertise. A _____ team is created outside the formal organization to undertake a project of special importance or creativity and is sometimes called a project team. The _____ is a long-lasting, sometimes permanent team in the organization structure created to deal with tasks that recur regularly.

problem-solving

self-directed

A _____ team typically consists of 5 to 12 hourly employees from the same department who meet to discuss ways of improving quality, efficiency, and the work environment. A _____ team consists of 5 to 20 multiskilled workers who rotate jobs to produce an entire product or service and perform managerial duties, often supervised by an elected member. One

virtual team

global

type of self-directed team in the new workplace is the _____, which uses advanced information and telecommunications technologies so that geographically distant members can collaborate on projects and reach common goals. A _____ team is a cross-border work team made up of members of different nationalities whose activities span multiple countries.

Team Characteristics

The best size for a work team seems to be 5 to 12 persons. Large teams provide a diversity of skills, but smaller teams provide more personal satisfaction for members.

task specialist
socioemotional

dual
nonparticipator

There are four basic roles that members in teams may assume. The _____ role in which the individual devotes personal time and energy to helping the team accomplish its task. The _____ role in which the individual provides support for team members' emotional needs and social unity. A person assuming a _____ role tries to meet both of these needs and is often chosen as the leader of the team. The _____ does not foster either the task or social goals of the team.

Team Processes

forming
storming
norming

performing
adjourning

Teams go through five stages of development. The first stage is _____, which is characterized by orientation and acquaintance. During the _____ stage individual personalities and roles, and resulting conflicts, emerge. In the _____ stage conflicts are resolved and team harmony and unity emerge. The problem is solved and the task is accomplished during the _____ stage. After the task is completed, if it is a temporary team, the _____ stage occurs next, in which members prepare for the team's disbandment.

cohesiveness

Team _____ is the extent to which team members are attracted to the team and motivated to remain in it. The cohesiveness of the team depends on the amount of member interaction, the degree to which goals are shared, personal attraction, the competition that exists, and how outsiders evaluate the team. Team cohesiveness can affect both the morale and the productivity of the team.

norms

Team _____ are the standards of conduct shared by team members which guide their behavior. They are established by critical events or may be formed by simple precedent, depending on what was done first. Norms also may be carried over from one team to another. Making explicit statements is often an effective way to change team norms.

Managing Team Conflict

Conflict

_____ is the antagonistic interaction in which one party attempts to thwart the intentions or goals of another. It may be due to competition for scarce resources or debate over responsibilities. It may result from a communication breakdown or personality clash. Differences in power, status, or goals can also cause conflicts to occur. Five styles of conflict are available to choose from. The *competing* style reflects assertiveness. The *avoiding* style means not being assertive or cooperative. The *compromising* style reflects a moderate amount of both assertiveness and cooperativeness. An *accommodating* style reflects a high degree of cooperativeness and the *collaborating* style reflects both a high degree of assertiveness and cooperativeness. The appropriateness of these styles depends on the situation. One way to resolve conflict is to appeal to a _____, which is a goal that cannot be reached by a single party. One may also attempt to negotiate or mediate the dispute. _____ is the process of using a third party to settle a dispute. Often, one only needs to facilitate communication to ensure that conflicting parties hold accurate perceptions.

superordinate

Mediation

Benefits and Costs of Teams

Social facilitation

One benefit of a team is that it may lead to increased effort and improved performance. _____ is the tendency for the presence of others to influence an individual's motivation and performance. Persons also can fill their needs for belongingness and affiliation. Teams also provide a broader range of skills and knowledge for task accomplishment. If an employee involvement team is used, workers have the skills to do a greater variety of jobs, providing more organizational responsiveness for the future.

free rider

coordination costs

When teams are used, fewer supervisors are needed requiring a power realignment. Another problem with work teams is the tendency to take a free ride or to put forth less effort than one would alone. A _____ is a person who benefits from team membership but does not make a proportionate contribution to the team's work. Another disadvantage is _____, which refer to the time and energy needed to coordinate the activities of a team to enable it to perform its task. One other disadvantage of teams is that no one person is responsible for the output of the team. Some workers feel that the team concept is a management ploy to kill unions.

Chapter Review

Multiple-Choice Questions: Please indicate the correct response to the following questions by writing the letter of the correct answer in the space provided.

___ 1. Which of the following factors affect(s) team effectiveness?
- a. organizational context
- b. team type
- c. team characteristics
- d. team composition
- e. all of the above

___ 2. The most frequent topic of management training is
- a. teamwork.
- b. motivation.
- c. communication.
- d. leadership of teams.
- e. mediation.

___ 3. Horizontal teams
- a. reflect the organization's command structure.
- b. have an indefinite life span.
- c. may be drawn from several departments.
- d. are run by autocrats.
- e. may have no real purpose at all.

___ 4. A characteristic of a small team is
- a. that it has more disagreement than larger teams.
- b. that fewer questions are asked.
- c. that fewer opinions are offered.
- d. that more satisfaction is enjoyed by members.
- e. that subteams form rather easily.

___ 5. The role of the task specialist may involve
- a. proposing new solutions to team problems.
- b. being warm and receptive to the ideas of others.
- c. reconciling team conflicts.
- d. telling jokes.
- e. shifting one's own opinion to maintain team harmony.

___ 6. Another word for team as used in the text is
- a. informal gathering.
- b. group.
- c. party.
- d. athletic club.
- e. purposeful grouping.

___ 7. Which stage of team development is characterized by cooperation and problem solving?
   a. forming
   b. storming
   c. norming
   d. performing
   e. adjourning

___ 8. In the _____ stage of team development many people disagree over their perceptions of the team's mission.
   a. forming
   b. storming
   c. norming
   d. performing
   e. adjourning

___ 9. Why is morale higher in cohesive teams?
   a. because of less communication to waste time
   b. because one doesn't have to feel so loyal to the team
   c. because less participation is needed in decision making
   d. because of a friendly climate
   e. all of the above

___ 10. The highest productivity in a team occurs when the team is _____ in cohesiveness and has a(n) _____ performance norm.
   a. high, high
   b. low, low
   c. high, low
   d. low, high
   e. high, average

___ 11. Team norms
   a. are formal.
   b. are usually written down by a team member called the "secretary" by sociologists.
   c. make life harder for team members because they must now conform.
   d. provide a frame of reference for members.
   e. do not tell members what is acceptable behavior, only what is unacceptable.

___ 12. Which of the following is *not* a cause of conflict among people as described in the text?
   a. communication overload
   b. scarce resources
   c. jurisdictional ambiguities
   d. power and status differences
   e. goal differences.

___ 13. If individuals can set aside personal animosities and deal with the conflict in a businesslike way, the _____ approach to conflict resolution will work well.
   a. superordinate goal appeal
   b. bargaining or negotiation
   c. providing of well-defined tasks
   d. facilitating communication
   e. mediation

___ 14. Social facilitation refers to the
   a. orientation of new members into the team.
   b. teaching of social norms to new team members.
   c. tendency for the presence of others to influence individual motivation and performance.
   d. ease with which a new member learns social norms.
   e. person who enforces team norms by social sanctioning within the team.

___ 15. A _____ team is sometimes called a functional team or a command team.
   a. horizontal
   b. vertical
   c. matrix
   d. task force
   e. cross-functional

___ 16. A cross-functional team is a type of _____ team.
   a. horizontal
   b. vertical
   c. matrix
   d. functional
   e. command

___ 17. Membership on a committee is usually decided by a person's
   a. area of expertise.
   b. functional specialty.
   c. individual qualifications.
   d. title or position.
   e. supervisor.

___ 18. The new-venture team is an example of a _____ team.
   a. special-purpose
   b. committee
   c. task force
   d. problem-solving
   e. vertical

___ 19. The purpose of self-directed teams is to
   a. make lower-level employees feel good.
   b. make top management feel more humanitarian.
   c. increase the participation of lower-level workers in decision making.
   d. let employees determine their own pay levels.
   e. let employees pick their own supervisors.

___ 20. Which of the following is/are true of problem-solving teams?
   a. They consist of 5 to 12 volunteer hourly employees.
   b. They meet two hours a week.
   c. They discuss ways of improving quality.
   d. Their recommendations are proposed to management for approval.
   e. All of the above are true.

___ 21. Which of the following is/are true of self-directed teams?
   a. They consist of 5 to 20 multiskilled employees.
   b. They meet two hours a week.
   c. They discuss ways of improving quality.
   d. Their recommendations are proposed to management for approval.
   e. All of the above are true.

___ 22. The supervisor of a self-directed team
   a. must do very little work.
   b. only makes sure that the work is completed on time.
   c. is often elected by the team.
   d. can only hire and fire new team members.
   e. is only needed to work out the vacation schedule.

___ 23. A team member who plays the task specialist role would display which of the following behaviors?
   a. initiation
   b. encourage
   c. harmonize
   d. compromise
   e. reduce tension

___ 24. A team member who plays the socioemotional role would display which of the following behaviors?
   a. initiation
   b. give opinions
   c. seek information
   d. energize
   e. follow

___ 25. A critical event in a team's history will
   a. help determine group norms.
   b. usually lead to the group's demise.
   c. destroy the group's norms.
   d. occur during the storming stage.
   e. require a critical mass manager.

___ 26. An explicit statement has _____ impact on group norms.
   a. adverse
   b. inverse
   c. considerable
   d. negligible
   e. no

___ 27. Of all the skills required for effective team management, none is more important than
   a. conducting meetings effectively.
   b. learning to play the task specialist role.
   c. learning to play the socioemotional role.
   d. learning to handle conflicts.
   e. communicating effectively.

___ 28. A virtual team is a group which
   a. almost acts like a team.
   b. is geographically dispersed, but linked by technology.
   c. exists only in the mind of the creator.
   d. only imaginary characters exist.
   e. none of the above.

___ 29. Which conflict handling style reflects a moderate amount of both assertiveness and cooperativeness?
   a. competing
   b. avoiding
   c. compromising
   d. accommodating
   e. collaborating

___ 30. One advantage of employee involvement teams is an increase in organizational
   a. communication.
   b. responsiveness.
   c. identity.
   d. morale.
   e. pride.

True/False Questions: Please indicate whether the following questions are true or false by writing a T or an F in the blank in front of each question.

___ 1. People standing in line at a lunch counter constitute a team.

___ 2. Satisfaction pertains to the team's ability to meet the personal needs of its members.

___ 3. Primacy means that the first behaviors that occur in a team often set a precedent for later team expectations.

___ 4. Making explicit statements is probably the most ineffective way for managers to change norms of an established team.

___ 5. The ideal size of a team is four persons or less.

___ 6. Large teams make need satisfaction for individuals easier.

___ 7. Nonparticipators are typically held in high esteem by the team because they do not cause trouble.

___ 8. Competition can have a healthy impact on teams because it energizes people toward higher performance.

___ 9. During the performing stage of team development members solve the team's problem.

___ 10. High cohesiveness is normally considered an unattractive feature of teams.

Short-Answer Questions

1. What is the difference between a vertical team and a horizontal team?

2. Why would an organization want to form a problem-solving team?

3. During the norming stage of team development, how are norms established?

4.   Why is team cohesiveness important?

5.   How can a team overcome a conflict due to differences in power or status?

Management Applications

Playing the Role without a Script

A role is the expected behavior of a person because of the position he or she occupies. In life we all play many roles because we occupy many positions. In the following situations indicate the expected behavior or role of the persons involved.

1.   The professor of your management class walks into the class the day of the final exam. You are the student. Explain the expected behavior for the professor and for the student.

2.   As the basketball game is about to begin, the cheerleaders run out onto the floor, followed by the players and the referees. What roles are each of these persons expected to fulfill?

3. The chairman of the board walks into the crowded boardroom. All the board members are present and the executive secretary is seated next to the chairman's seat. What role do these persons play?

4. The manager trainee is introduced to the loan officer by the branch manager of the bank. The trainee is told to remain with the loan officer for the next few days. What are the expected behaviors for the trainee and the loan officer?

The Pros and Cons

There are both advantages and disadvantages of teams. Listed below are the benefits and drawbacks of teams along with several types of teams.

1. Explain the extent of the advantages and disadvantages for each team by writing in high, medium, or low in the blank provided.

Team Type	Member Satisfaction	Skill Diversity	Free Riding	Coordination Costs	Responsibility Diffusion
Baseball Team	_____	_____	_____	_____	_____
Dance Clean-up Committee	_____	_____	_____	_____	_____
"Chain Gang"	_____	_____	_____	_____	_____
NASA Launch Team	_____	_____	_____	_____	_____
U.S. Senate	_____	_____	_____	_____	_____

2. Take one of the teams above and explain the reasons for your answers.

Mini Case

Flirty Francis

Francis is a secretary for a brokerage firm. The office manager, Mrs. Matronly, has noticed that Francis spends a lot of time flirting with the customers and the other male employees. Since Francis is a very attractive young woman, this has been very detracting to the work environment. Mrs. Matronly has even noticed several of the male employees going to Francis for help or to get questions answered that Mrs. Matronly has routinely handled in the past. After a few flirting moments these men end up being sent to Mrs. Matronly for help. Lately, the atmosphere between Francis and Mrs. Matronly has become very stiff and filled with tension. You are the operations manager, and when you came into work this morning, you found the two of them yelling at each other about who should make the coffee.

1. What is the cause of this conflict? Try to apply each cause of conflict listed in the text to this situation.

2. Below are several conflict resolution techniques from the text. Indicate how each one might be or might not be appropriate for this situation.

Superordinate goals

Bargaining/Negotiation

Mediation

Providing well-defined tasks

Facilitating communication

Experiential Exercise

The Best Artwork for the White House

For this exercise you should be divided up into teams of four to five persons as directed by your instructor. Each team is to assign one person to be an observer. Each team has the same assignment. Using just the pens, pencils, or markers, and paper you have with you in class today, you are to sketch out or make a prototype of what you consider the best art work for the White House. The President has just called and asked your class to provide the best artwork for today's times. Being a politician he has refused to be more specific. Before reading the rest of the exercise form your teams and develop the artwork. The observer is to take notes on the roles played by team members. Identify the task specialist, the socioemotional role, and any nonparticipators.

DESIGN THE ARTWORK NOW!!

After about five minutes the instructor will ask you to appoint one person to represent each team. The team representatives will line up chairs in front of the room in single file facing the class to form a Super Team. They will then present the artwork to each other and decide which one artwork to present to President Bush as the best artwork for the White House.

Team members may pass notes to team representatives through their observer. No verbal comment is allowed. No guidelines are provided on how the decision is to be reached by the Super Team.

PICK THE BEST ARTWORK NOW!!

After the team has picked the best artwork, answer the following questions as a class:

1. Was there a storming stage by the Super Team? What are some of the things that were said or done to indicate this stage?

2. How were norms arrived at and what were some of the norms?

3. Did the Super Team finally perform its assigned task? Are there other ways that teams sometimes use to arrive at decisions?

4.   Identify who played the roles of task specialist, socioemotional specialist, and nonparticipator in the Super Team.

Study Guide Solutions

Chapter Review

Multiple-Choice Questions

1	2	3	4	5	6	7	8	9	10
e	a	c	d	a	b	d	b	d	a

11	12	13	14	15	16	17	18	19	20
d	a	b	c	b	a	d	a	c	e

21	22	23	24	25	26	27	28	29	30
a	c	a	e	a	c	d	b	c	b

True/False Questions

1	2	3	4	5	6	7	8	9	10
F	T	T	F	F	F	F	T	T	F

Short-Answer Questions

1. A vertical team consists of the manager and subordinates in the formal chain of command. It is the organizational structure one would normally expect molded into a team. The horizontal team includes workers from different areas of expertise. This provides the team with different viewpoints and abilities.

2. A problem-solving team works voluntarily and therefore will have a different motivation. They will help to improve quality, efficiency, and the work environment. These teams have been very successful in some organizations.

3. Norms can be established by discussion to clarify values, roles, and goals. Critical events can also help to establish norms. The first behavior which occurs, becoming a precedent for other norms, or an explicit statement from top management can determine the norms. Carryover behavior from previous teams can also influence the formation of norms in a team.

4. Cohesiveness is needed to attract new members and to maintain members. It builds commitment and motivation to accomplish a task, especially if the task is difficult and opposition to the team is strong. It provides satisfaction and morale in the team.

5. More clearly defining the roles of individuals or departments can help to overcome this type of conflict. Helping persons to understand the importance of teamwork and concepts such as synergism can also be useful.

Management Applications

Playing the Role without a Script

1. The professor is expected to hand out the exams, remind the students not to cheat and do their best, then walk around the room looking for cheaters. The student is expected to be nervous, answer the questions, not cheat, be quiet, and hand in the paper when finished.

2. The cheerleaders are expected to jump up and down, yell, be excited, and generally lead the fans in support of the team. The players are expected to play basketball to the best of their ability. The referees are expected to call fouls, make sure rules are followed, keep the game under control, and leave town alive.

3. The chairman is expected to take charge of the meeting, asking for reports and opinions, giving out assignments, and asking for votes when needed. The board members are expected to participate in the meeting in the style dictated by the chairman. The executive secretary is expected to take notes of the proceedings and to keep her mouth shut.

4. The loan officer is expected to be the trainer for the management trainee and teach him about the loan officer's job. The manager trainee is expected to ask appropriate questions and to learn the job of the loan officer.

The Pros and Cons

1. The answers provided will vary according to each person's perception and past experiences. For example, the degree of member satisfaction resulting from a baseball team will depend on one's feelings toward baseball and how much satisfaction one has received in the past from being on a baseball team.

2. The answers to this question will also depend on personal perceptions and experiences. If you were able to answer these two questions, you should have a good understanding for the advantages and disadvantages of teams.

Mini Case

Flirty Francis

1. The cause of this conflict may be viewed several ways. Most people would probably simply say that Mrs. Matronly is just jealous of Francis. Applying the causes of conflict listed in the book to this situation could result in the following analysis.

    a. Scarce resources = There are not enough men to go around.

    b. Jurisdictional ambiguities = dispute over who is responsible for making the coffee.

    c. Communication breakdown = poor communications between the two parties have resulted in misperceptions of each other.

    d. Personality clash = These two have very different values and traits.

    e. Power and status differences = Francis is trying to increase her status by flirting.

    f. Goal differences = Francis' goal is to be popular with the men, and Mrs. Matronly's goal is to keep the department running smoothly.

2. **Superordinate goals**

    You might appeal to the higher goal of the need to get the office work done. Since this does not deal directly with the problem, its probability of success is low.

    Bargaining/Negotiation

    This means that you try to get the two parties to act more businesslike. Then you logically work out the problem. While this may have a better chance of success than the previous method, it probably will not work either because it assumes that they can set aside personal animosities.

    Mediation

    You might try to mediate the dispute yourself. This probably has a greater chance of success than the previous two methods, but the two parties would have to agree to do this in advance. Since the issue is deeper than who makes the coffee, this method does not seem to be the best solution.

    Providing well-defined tasks

    This technique may truly have a chance of success. Not only can you determine who is responsible for making coffee, but also just what both parties are supposed to be doing. If this decision is communicated throughout the organization, then maybe the male employees will quit talking to Francis so much. This, however, may be a little too optimistic of an assumption.

Facilitating communication

This method may work the best since it could help the parties to improve their perceptions of each other. Perhaps some sessions could be arranged for these two to just talk and try harder to understand each other.

Experiential Exercise

The Best Artwork for the White House

The results of this exercise will vary for each class.

Chapter 20

The Importance of Control

Chapter Summary

After you have read the text chapter, read through the summary below. Cover the left-hand margin and fill in the blanks with the appropriate terms. After you have filled in each blank, check your responses by uncovering the answer given in the margin. If you do not understand why the given answer is the correct one, refer back to the text.

The Meaning of Control

Organizational
Control

_____ is the systematic process of regulating organizational activities to make them consistent with the expectations established in plans, targets, and performance standards.

Organizational Control Focus

feedforward
control

concurrent
Feedback

Control can focus on events before, during, or after production. _____ control focuses on human, material, and financial resources flowing into the organization. Control that consists of monitoring ongoing employee activities to insure their consistency with established performance standards is _____ control. _____ control focuses on the organization's outputs, especially the quality of an end product or service.

Feedback Control Model

The elements of feedback control include establishing standards of performance, measuring actual performance, comparing performance to standards, and taking corrective action if needed.

responsibility
center
expense budget

revenue budget
cash budget
capital
expenditure
top-down

A major tool for control used by managers is a budget. A _____ is any organizational department under the supervision of a single individual who is responsible for its activity. The _____, which outlines the anticipated expenses for each responsibility center and for the organization as a whole. The _____ indicates the forecasted and actual revenues of the organization. The _____ projects the cash flows on a daily or weekly basis to ensure that the company has sufficient cash to meet its obligations. The _____ budget is the plan for future investments in major assets to be paid for over several years.
One method of arriving at a budget is called _____ budgeting, in

bottom -up

which middle and lower-level managers set departmental budget targets in accordance with overall company revenues and expenditures specified by top management. In _____ budgeting the lower levels of management determine their budgets first and then pass them up to management for approval

Financial Control

balance
sheet
income
statement
Liquidity
Activity
Profitability
Leverage

Financial analysis is accomplished by the analysis of financial ratios based on the balance sheet and the income statement. The _____ _____ shows the firm's financial position with respect to assets and liabilities at a specific point in time. The _____ _____ summarizes the firm's financial performance for a given time interval, usually one year.. _____ ratios tell how well the company can meet its current debt obligations. _____ ratios indicate the firm's internal performance with respect to key activities defined by management. _____ ratios describe the firm's profits or losses. _____ ratios indicate how well the company uses debt.

The Changing Philosophy of Control

Bureaucratic

Decentralized

After deciding on what to focus, an organization must determine the approach to control it wishes to take so that the approach agrees with the corporate culture. _____ control uses rules, policies, hierarchy of authority, a quality control department, selection and training, technology, reward systems, and other formal devices to influence employee behavior and assess performance. _____ control relies on social values, traditions, common beliefs, and trust to generate compliance with organizational goals. The trend is for more companies to use decentralized control. Decentralized control is based on knowledge, experience and empowerment.

Total Quality Management

Total quality

quality circle

_____ management (TQM) which is an organization-wide effort to infuse quality throughout every activity in a company through continuous improvement.. Although it was originally American educators who introduced the concept, the Japanese have made it popular today. TQM focuses on teamwork, increasing customer satisfaction, and lowering costs. This is a more participative approach to control and often requires a change of corporate culture. One approach to implementing the decentralized approach of TQM is to use the _____, a group of 6 to 12 volunteer employees who meet regularly to discuss and solve problems that affect their common work activities. TQM relies on the empowerment of employees, as well as the contributions of suppliers and customers in the decision-making process. The continuous process of measuring products, services and practices against the

benchmarking

six sigma

cycle time

continuous
   improvement

toughest competitors or those companies recognized as industry leaders is a known as _____. This is needed to devise a strategy for implementing improved procedures. General Electric introduced a program called _____ _____ to achieve defect-free production 99.9997 percent of the time. This has evolved into a term for quality control that takes nothing for granted and emphasizes a disciplined and relentless pursuit of higher quality and lower costs. Companies try to reduce _____, which is the steps taken to complete a company process. Often improvement comes by _____, which is the implementation of a large number of small, incremental improvements in all areas of the organization on an on-going basis.

Trends in Quality and Financial Control

ISO 9000

economic value-
added systems

Market value
added
Activity-based
costing (ABC)

Many countries have endorsed a universal framework for quality assurance called _____, a set of international standards for quality management. Companies that adopt these standards benefit from the rigorous analysis of their manufacturing and service processes. Another innovation is the concept of _____(EVA), in which a company's net operating profit after taxes and after deducting the cost of capital. These systems capture all the things a company can do to add value from its activities and measure each job, department, or process by the value added. _____ (MVA) measures the stock market's estimate of the value of a company's past and projected capital investment projects. _____ is a control system that identifies the various activities needed to produce a product or service, determines the cost of these activities, and allocates financial resources according to the true cost of each product or service.

Control in the New Workplace

Open-book
   management

balanced scorecard

To complement teamwork and participative management styles, new financial controls techniques are being used. _____ refers to the sharing of financial information and results with all employees in the organization. The _____ _____ is a comprehensive management control system that balances traditional financial measures with operational measures relating to a company's critical success factors.

Chapter Review

Multiple-Choice Questions: Please indicate the correct response to the following questions by writing the letter of the correct answer in the space provided.

___ 1. Feedforward control focuses on
   a. human resources.
   b. material resources.
   c. financial resources.
   d. inputs into the organization.
   e. all of the above

___ 2. Conducting a survey to determine customer satisfaction is an example of _____ control.
   a. feedback
   b. total quality
   c. statistical
   d. concurrent
   e. feedforward

___ 3. Feedback control is
   a. a focus on the transformation process.
   b. a focus on organizational outputs.
   c. a focus on organizational inputs.
   d. sometimes called preliminary control.
   e. sometimes called preventative control.

___ 4. _____ is/are *not* (an) element(s) of bureaucratic control.
   a. Rules
   b. Written documentation
   c. Reward systems
   d. Social values
   e. Hierarchy of authority

___ 5. Activity-based costing allocates financial resources according to
   a. the true cost of each product or service.
   b. a zero base.
   c. strategic considerations.
   d. the number of activities associate with production of a product or service.
   e. none of the above.

___ 6. The current ratio is found by dividing _____ by _____.
   a. current assets, current liabilities
   b. current liabilities, current assets
   c. current assets, fixed assets
   d. current liabilities, long-term liabilities
   e. current assets, current revenue

___ 7. Which type of control relies on the use of social values and trust to control?
a. decentralized control
b. bureaucratic control
c. feedback control
d. concurrent control
e. feedforward control

___ 8. Rewards in a bureaucratic control system are based on
a. an employee's achievement in his or her own job.
b. group achievements.
c. equity across employees.
d. informal evaluations of performance.
e. none of the above

___ 9. Decentralized control is preferred when
a. management style is directive.
b. tasks are quantifiable.
c. corporate culture supports participation.
d. subordinates desire not to participate.
e. the company is owned by a family.

___ 10. The first step in the control process is
a. establish standards.
b. measure actual performance.
c. compare performance to standards.
d. take corrective action.
e. use feedback.

___ 11. The _____ budget estimates the cash flows on a daily or weekly basis.
a. capital
b. balance sheet
c. bottom-up
d. cash
e. expense

___ 12. In top-down budgeting
a. lower-level managers are more likely to be committed to achieving budget targets.
b. lower-level managers are included in the process.
c. the budget developers lack reliable information.
d. lower-level managers pass to higher levels their anticipated resource needs.
e. the budget is imposed on lower-level managers.

___ 13. _____ measures the stock market's estimate of the value of a company's past and projected capital investment projects.
   a. Activity Based Costing
   b. Economic Value Added
   c. ISO 9000
   d. Market Value Added
   e. TQM

___ 14. A disadvantage of budgets is that they
   a. can cause perceptions of unfairness.
   b. decrease communications with employees.
   c. worsen resource allocation.
   d. ignore strategic plans.
   e. hinder coordination among departments.

___ 15. The term EVA refers to
   a. economic variance analysis.
   b. economic value-added systems.
   c. expected value analysis.
   d. expected variance adjustment.
   e. economic variation adjustment.

___ 16. The selection and hiring of new employees involves _____ control.
   a. total quality
   b. statistical process
   c. feedforward
   d. concurrent
   e. feedback

___ 17. A financial ratio is
   a. the relationship between a manager and the chief financial officer of the company.
   b. the relationship between the president of the company and the bank.
   c. how one financial item influences another.
   d. the comparison of two financial numbers.
   e. the amount of leverage a firm has.

___ 18. The conversion ratio is _____ divided by _____.
   a. purchase orders, customer inquiries
   b. customer inquiries, purchase orders
   c. competitive customers, newly acquired customers
   d. proselytes, new members
   e. soft currency, hard currency

___ 19. Frito-Lay's use of handheld computers to monitor daily sales activities is an example of _____ control.
    a.   total quality
    b.   statistical process
    c.   feedforward
    d.   concurrent
    e.   feedback

___ 20. Bureaucratic control relies on the cultural value of
    a.   employee participation.
    b.   top-down control.
    c.   flexibility.
    d.   informal communications.
    e.   self-control.

___ 21. As part of bureaucratic control the management control systems may include which of the following?
    a.   detailed rules
    b.   detailed procedures
    c.   job descriptions
    d.   measurable standards
    e.   all of the above

___ 22. The relationship between decentralized control and bureaucratic control is
    a.   direct.
    b.   that decentralized control is bureaucratic control applied to a family-owned business.
    c.   that they are opposites.
    d.   through the grapevine.
    e.   parallel.

___ 23. The status of decentralized control can be said to be
    a.   poor because of impending federal legislation.
    b.   unsure due to the influence of Japanese management on American management thought and practices.
    c.   the wave of the future with more companies adopting it.
    d.   an outmoded practice to be replaced by more useful techniques.
    e.   none of the above

___ 24. In deciding whether revenues will be large enough to pay for annual operating expenses and the purchase of a major asset, management needs to develop a _____ budget.
    a.   cash
    b.   revenue
    c.   cost
    d.   profit
    e.   capital expenditure

___ 25. _____ is/are (a) characteristic of bureaucratic control, while _____ is/are (a) characteristic of decentralized control.
   a. Employee compliance, tall structure
   b. Formal authority, flexible authority
   c. Self-control, mutual influence
   d. Formalization, rules
   e. Grievance procedures, measurable standards

___ 26. The total quality management approach was conceived by
   a. the Japanese.
   b. the Germans.
   c. American researchers and consultants
   d. Frederick W. Taylor.
   e. Donald Trump.

___ 27. In open-book management
   a. any employee is allowed to initiate a complaint.
   b. the public has full access to financial records.
   c. the salaries of top managers is posted on bulletin boards.
   d. financial information and results are shared with all employees in the organization.
   e. none of the above.

___ 28. Under total quality management the responsibility for quality rests with
   a. managers, where it belongs.
   b. the entire company.
   c. the control system.
   d. the control department.
   e. the computer system.

___ 29. When an organization uses quality circles, it is most likely that
   a. management expectations will be too low.
   b. middle managers will be highly satisfied.
   c. union leaders will be included in quality circle discussions.
   d. problem-solving skills are improved for team participants.
   e. those plants that are highly automated will experience the greatest improvements in personal productivity.

___ 30. Which of the following is a characteristic of six sigma?
   a. taking nothing for granted
   b. an emphasis on higher quality
   c. an emphasis on lower costs
   d. a methodology called DMAIC
   e. all of the above

True/False Questions: Please indicate whether the following questions are true or false by writing a T or an F in the blank in front of each question.

___ 1. Capital expenditures are minor purchases that are paid for over several months.

___ 2. Feedforward control is anticipatory and attempts to identify and prevent deviations before they occur.

___ 3. Under bureaucratic control job descriptions are generally very specific and task related.

___ 4. The purpose of bureaucratic control is to establish employee commitment.

___ 5. The more a manager prefers to make decisions alone, the more appropriate is the decentralized control style.

___ 6. An activity ratio measures how active the firm's stock has been on the stock market.

___ 7. One problem with bottom-up budgeting is that managers' estimates of future expenditures may be unrealistic.

___ 8. Value-added is a company's net operating profit after taxes and after deducting the cost of capital.

___ 9. A quality circle consists of three to four persons assigned to the task of improving quality in their work areas.

___ 10. A financial budget defines where the organization will receive its cash and how it will spend it.

Short-Answer Questions

1. Which is the first component of the feedback control model, and why is it first?

2.   Which focus is most important to have for an organization--feedforward, concurrent, or feedback control?

3.   Why is a fundamental unit of analysis of a budget control center called a *responsibility* center?

4.   Why is total quality management so important to North American managers?

5.   Explain how poor quality of goods and services is an indicator of an inadequate control system.

Management Applications

Control of the Football Team

The Catawba College football team began preparing for its game with Carson-Newman College the week before the game. First, team members all read a scouting report with particular emphasis on the effects of Carson-Newman's style of play on each player's assignment. In practice that week adjustments were made on play executions both defensively and offensively based on the scouting report.

During the game the coach sent in plays by rotating players in and out of the game. Occasionally, he called a time-out and brought his quarterback to the sidelines for a little chat. At half-time the coach gave his fiery, emotional speech. After this he and the assistant coaches talked to the players about how they could be more effective in the second half.

On the day after the game, Sunday, the team had a meeting to view the film of the game. The coaches pointed out mistakes that had been made and praised good plays also. On Monday several changes in plays and personnel were made based on the game.

1. What are some examples from the foregoing story of feedforward control?

2. How was concurrent control used?

3. Explain how feedback control was used.

4. Was bureaucratic or decentralized control used?

Anna's Turn to Do the Dishes

Delores checked her chores chart and discovered that it was Anna's turn to do the dishes. "It's time to do the dishes now, Anna. Make sure you do a good job!"

"Yes, Mother," replied Anna as she headed for the stack of dirty dishes next to the kitchen sink.

Thirty minutes later Anna reported the dishes done and went into the family room to watch her favorite television show. Delores went into the kitchen just before going to bed for a drink of water. She picked up a glass from the drain rack and was repulsed. It still was filthy. She checked a few other dishes and found many of them to be dirty also. Then she looked at the kitchen counter and the dining room table and noticed that they had not been properly cleaned off either. She was mad!!

Delores stormed into Anna's room, threw on the light switch, and yelled, "I thought I told you to do the dishes, young lady! Now get out of that bed and get in there and do the job right!"

What followed was not a pretty sight. The entire family became involved in a major dispute, and it was two hours before Dad—as a gesture of peace—finished the dishes and everyone went to bed. Everyone was now in a bad mood, and Delores was wondering where she had gone wrong.

1. Where did Delores go wrong?

2. Would feedforward, concurrent, or feedback control have solved this problem?

Mini Case

Foray Incorporated

Bud was excited about the opportunity to consult with Foray, Inc., about its situation. After all, Bud was a management consultant with considerable experience. He spent the first week analyzing reports, talking to people, and observing the operation of the plant. The company manufactured agricultural equipment. Below are some of the notes that Bud made. Read the notes, write out a sentence or two summarizing the general problem, and make specific suggestions for one of the problems noted.

- Everyone I talked to seemed to be worried about his or her own future with the company. There have been recent layoffs, and everyone is worrying about who will be next. Many are searching for jobs on their own.

- The shipping department says it is hard to get orders out on time because so many orders are being returned. An analysis reveals that the orders are being incorrectly filled with the wrong equipment or with the wrong sizes.

- Jeff, the production manager, says that it is very difficult to meet production schedules. It seems that there is a large number of absences each day.

- Foray's market share has slipped from 22 percent three years ago to 14 percent today. Foreign competition has been the main reason according to management.

1. What is the general problem of Foray, Inc.?

2.   What specific recommendations can you make for one of the above problems?

Experiential Exercise

Rational Ratios

Listed below are the abbreviated balance sheets for Angelo's Pizza Palace. Look them over and then answer the questions that follow.

Angelo's Pizza Palace
Balance Sheet
December 31, 2002

Assets		Liabilities and Owners' Equity	
Current Assets	$ 20,000	Current Liabilities	$ 15,000
Fixed Assets	100,000	Long-term Liabilities	42,000
– Accumulated Depreciation	10,000	Owners' Equity	53,000
Total Fixed Assets	90,000		
TOTAL ASSETS	$110,000	TOTAL ASSETS AND NET WORTH	$110,000

Angelo's Pizza Palace
Income Statement
For the Year Ended December 31, 2002

Net Sales	$300,000
Less: Cost of Goods Sold	200,000
Gross Revenue	100,000
Less: Selling and Administrative Expenses	18,000
Operating Profit	82,000
Less: Interest Expense	2,000
Income before Taxes	80,000
Less: Taxes	40,000
Net Income	$ 40,000

1. Listed below are the three ratios to be calculated for Angelo's, the budget target, and the industry average. Make the calculations for Angelo's. Then evaluate Angelo's ratios as "Good," "Satisfactory," or "Poor."

Ratio	Angelo's	Budget Target	Industry Average	Evaluation
Current ratio	_____	2.3	2.8	_____
Profit margin on sales	_____	10%	12%	_____
Return on total assets	_____	23%	25%	_____

2. What changes, if any, does Angelo's need to make?

Study Guide Solutions

Chapter Review

Multiple-Choice Questions

1	2	3	4	5	6	7	8	9	10
e	a	b	d	a	a	a	a	c	a

11	12	13	14	15	16	17	18	19	20
d	e	d	a	b	c	d	a	d	b

21	22	23	24	25	26	27	28	29	30
e	c	c	e	b	c	d	b	d	e

True/False Questions

1	2	3	4	5	6	7	8	9	10
F	T	T	F	F	F	T	T	F	T

Short-Answer Questions

1. The first component of the feedback control model is the strategic plan, which consists of the organization's strategic objectives. It specifies where the company wants to go and therefore determines the items that need to be controlled by the organization.

2. It is impossible to say which type of control focus is the most important. Often, all three are equally important. The relative importance of focus depends on the nature of the organization and its strategic objectives.

3. The term responsibility center is used because it tells the manager who is responsible for that particular operating unit. The type of responsibility center (i.e., cost, revenue, profit, or investment) also tells the manager the area of primary responsibility.

4. Total quality management is important to North American managers because of the increased importance of worldwide competition. It is believed that quality is the dominate factor in the success of the Japanese in world markets. To achieve this type of quality requires companywide commitment.

5. If the company has poor quality goods and services, that means that control is lacking in some area. Perhaps feedforward control is not adequate in picking skilled and motivated workers. Maybe the incoming materials are below standard. If concurrent control is not adequate, workers

may be slack in their work or the equipment may be below standard. Feedback control should be catching these problems before they reach the customer in any event.

Management Applications

Control of the Football Team

1. Feedforward control was exhibited in all the things the team did to prepare for the game. This includes scouting the opponent, going over the scouting report, making adjustments, and practicing accordingly.

2. Concurrent control was used during the game. It consisted of sending in plays, making substitutes, talking to the quarterback during time-outs, giving a half-time speech, and talking to individual players on improving effectiveness.

3. Feedback control was used in viewing the film of the game with the corresponding comments and by making changes in plays and personnel in the next practice on Monday.

4. There are elements of both control systems here. Rules are in place for any football team, the authority of the coach's position is used, and some rewards such as playing time are based on individual achievement. These are all elements of the bureaucratic control system. Peer pressure is also used, and higher performance is also expected. The goal of winning is shared, and the authority of the coaches is based on their knowledge and expertise. The reward of winning is based on the group's achievements. These are all items which are associated with decentralized control.

Anna's Turn to Do the Dishes

1. Delores should have explained more in advance what her expectations were in doing the job (feedforward control). She should have checked up while Anna was still doing the dishes to make sure they were being done correctly (concurrent control). She should have checked up immediately upon Anna's reporting that the job was done to make sure the job met her standards (feedback control).

2. All three types of control would have helped in this situation as illustrated in the answer to the previous question.

Mini Case

Foray Incorporated

1. Foray's general problem seems to be the lack of adequate controls. All of the notes correspond to the list in the text of signs of inadequate controls.

2. The first problem is low morale of the workers. Management could alleviate this problem somewhat with assurances that future layoffs will be very limited or that there will be no more. This should only be done if management truly can stand behind the statement, however.

    The second problem can be addressed by providing for the inspection of all outgoing orders to make sure the shipment has been properly filled.

    The third problem is also an indicator of poor morale. The solution to the first problem will also help to solve this problem. The company might also consider offering incentives for improved attendance.

    The loss of market share is critical. First, the company must determine the reason that foreign competition has gained market share. It could be due to quality differences, price differences, or even service differences. After the reason has been discovered, the company will need to introduce controls to improve that area.

Experiential Exercise

Rational Ratios

1. Angelo's current ratio is 1.33 and should be evaluated POOR.
    Angelo's profit margin is 13 percent and is SATISFACTORY.
    Angelo's return on total assets is 36 percent and is GOOD.

2. Angelo's probably needs to either reduce current liabilities or increase current assets.

Chapter 21

Information Technology and E-business

Chapter Summary

After you have read the text chapter, read through the summary below. Cover the left-hand margin and fill in the blanks with the appropriate terms. After you have filled in each blank, check your responses by uncovering the answer given in the margin. If you do not understand why the given answer is the correct one, refer back to the text.

Information Technology

Information technology

data

information

_____ is the hardware, software, telecommunications, database management, and other technologies used to store data and make it available in the form of information for organizational decision making. To be considered information, _____ or raw facts must be converted into a useful form for managers. Data that are meaningful and alter the receiver's understanding are called _____. Useful information must be accurate or portray reality. It must also be timely, complete, concise, relevant, accurate, and in a form that is easy for the use to understand and that meets the user's needs for the level of detail.

Types of Information Systems

Management information
Operations information
transaction

process control
automation
information
reporting

Since managers at different levels in the organization perform different functions, strategic planning at the top and operational control at operations level, different types of decisions are made by them. _____ system typically supports the strategic decision-making needs of higher-level managers. _____ system is a computer-based information system that supports a company's day-to-day operations. At the operations level _____ processing systems perform the organization's routine tasks. A _____ system monitors and controls ongoing physical processes such as temperature or pressure changes. Office _____ systems transform manual office procedures to electronic media and an _____ system organizes information in the form that managers use in day-to-day decision making.

decision support
executive

An interactive system that uses decision models and specialized databases to support organization decision makers is called a _____ system. An _____ retrieves, manipulates, and displays information tailored to the information   needs of top-level managers.

The Internet and E-Business

Internet   The _____ is a global collection of computer networks linked together
World Wide Web   for the exchange of data and information. The _____ _____
                           _____ is a collection of central servers for accessing information on
                           the Internet.   The Internet and World Wide Web have been helpful in
E-business   developing _____, any business that takes place by digital processes
E-commerce   over a computer network rather than in physical space. _____ refers
                           to business exchanges or transactions that occur electronically. An
intranet   _____ is a network that uses Internet technology but limits access to
                           all or some of the organization's employees. An _____ uses Internet
extranet   technology but links authorized users inside the company with certain outsiders
Electronic data   such as customers or vendors. _____ _____ interchange
                           (EDI) networks link the computer systems of buyers and sellers to allow the
                           transmission of structured data primarily for ordering, distribution, and
                           payables and receivables.

                           There are different E-business strategies a company may follow. One is setting
in-house   up an _____ Internet division which offers tight integration between
                           the Internet operation and the organization's traditional operation. To give the
                           Internet operation greater organizational focus, autonomy, and flexibility, some
spin-off   organizations choose to create a separate _____ company. Another
strategic   strategy is a _____ _____ that allows companies to combine
partnership   their core strengths with a company having complementary strengths.

business   The biggest boom in e-commerce is _____ to _____ (B2B)
  business   transactions, or buying and selling between companies.
Enterprise
resource planning   _____ _____ _____ (ERP) systems integrate and
                           optimize all the various business processes across the entire firm. Another
customer   approach is a c_____ r_____ m_____ (CRM)
relationship   system that helps companies track customers' interactions with the firm and
management   allows employees to call up a customer's past sales and service records,
                           outstanding orders, or resolved problems.

                           Companies have found that information technology can be used strategically
Knowledge   also. Improved operational efficiency, coordination, and flexibility are possible.
  Management   _____is an effort to systematically gather knowledge, make it widely
                           available, and foster a culture of learning. The use of a huge database that
                           combines all of a company's data and allows users to access the data directly,
data warehousing   create reports, and obtain answers to what-if questions is called _____
data mining   _____.   Often this use requires _____ _____,
                           software that uses sophisticated decision-making processes to search raw data
                           for patterns and relationships that may be significant. Many companies are
knowledge   building a _____ management portal which is a single point of access

for employees to multiple sources of information.

Management Implications of Information Technology

learning

Information technology and e-business help achieve improved employee effectiveness, erase time and geographic boundaries, empower employees, increase efficiency, and enhanced collaboration.   It also contributes to organizational _____ by making it possible to more rapidly identify problems and opportunities, as well as facilitating faster decision making..

IT Trends in the New Workplace

Instant messaging

wireless

peer, peer

_____ _____ technology provides a way to zap quick notes from PC to PC over the Internet and thus facilitate instantaneous communication. The _____ Internet is also growing in popularity because it can serve up information any place at any time while bypassing the Web. _____–to– _____ (P2P) allows PCs to communicate directly over the Internet, bypassing central databases, servers, control points, and Web pages.

Chapter Review

Multiple-Choice Questions: Please indicate the correct response to the following questions by writing the letter of the correct answer in the space provided.

___ 1. Quality of information means that it is
   a. the most expensive information available.
   b. accurate and portrays reality.
   c. from a well-known source.
   d. free of subjective interpretations.
   e. relevant to the problem.

___ 2. Which of the following is *not* true of an information system?
   a. It is responsible for the collection of data.
   b. It organizes data that have been collected.
   c. It distributes data throughout the organization.
   d. It makes decisions for managers.
   e. All of the above are true.

___ 3. The global collection of computer networks linked together for the exchange of data and information is called
   a. an intranet.
   b. an extranet.
   c. the Internet.
   d. the global Internet.
   e. the Global Web.

___ 4. A collection of central servers for accessing information on the Internet is called
   a. an intranet.
   b. an extranet.
   c. the Internet.
   d. the global Internet.
   e. the World Wide Web.

___ 5. Information technology includes
   a. hardware.
   b. software.
   c. telecommunications.
   d. database management.
   e. all of the above.

___ 6. Which type of computer-based information systems are designed to aid middle managers?
a. transaction processing systems
b. management information systems
c. decision support systems
d. expert systems
e. billing systems

___ 7. An example of transactions performed by transaction processing systems is
a. placing orders.
b. developing a marketing plan.
c. new-product development.
d. design of a merger plan.
e. all of the above

___ 8. One aspect of the content dimension of quality of information is that
a. it is being provided when needed.
b. it is free of error.
c. it can be provided in detail or summary form.
d. it is up to date when provided.
e. all of the above.

___ 9. Which of the following is an operations information system?
a. executive information system
b. decision support system
c. group decision support system
d. .information reporting system
e. transaction processing system

___ 10. Any business that takes place by digital processes over a computer network rather than in physical space is called
a. e-business
b. e-commerce
c. electronic data interchange
d. intranet commerce
e. extranet commerce

___ 11. _____ refer(s) to facts that are meaningful and change the understanding of the manager.
a. Data
b. An information system
c. Information
d. Intelligence
e. Wisdom

___ 12. _____ is a system that records and processes routinely occurring transactions.
    a. Transaction processing
    b. Office automation
    c. Process control
    d. Decision support
    e. Information reporting

___ 13. Business exchanges or transactions that occur electronically are called
    a. e-business
    b. e-commerce
    c. electronic data interchange
    d. intranet commerce
    e. extranet commerce

___ 14. Linking the computer systems of buyers and sellers to allow the transmission of structured data primarily for ordering, distribution, and payables and receivables is called
    a. e-business
    b. e-commerce
    c. electronic data interchange
    d. intranet commerce
    e. extranet commerce

___ 15. A network that uses Internet technology but limits access to all or some of the organization's employees is called a(n)
    a. limited Internet.
    b. intranet.
    c. extranet.
    d. local area network.
    e. wide area network.

___ 16. Bricks and clicks refers to
    a. a traditional organization establishing an Internet division.
    b. contrasting websites on the Internet.
    c. having a webpage for a construction business on the Web.
    d. getting mad at your computer and throwing a brick through the monitor—computer rage.
    e. none of the above.

___ 17. When a company decides to set up its own dot-com division it is called a(n)
    a. strategic alliance
    b. spin-off
    c. in-house Internet division
    d. strategic partnership
    e. intranet

___ 18. A spin-off is
    a. a company that does fraudulent business on the Internet.

    b.   a stand-alone company that is separate from the parent organization.

    c.   the dizzying graphics on some websites.

    d.   an Internet company that relocates offshore to avoid federal regulations.

    e.   a peer-to-peer system.

19. Another name for a group decision support system is
    a. collaborative work system.
    b. expert system.
    c. artificial intelligence.
    d. PC network.
    e. database management system.

20. An Executive Information System is designed to
    a. help in making more strategic decisions.
    b. help increase the speed of computerization of organizations.
    c. more than pay for itself in one year.
    d. be a career of increasing value in the future.
    e. become irrelevant as world markets increase in importance.

21. The major contribution of transaction processing was to
    a. allow managers to make better decisions.
    b. help top managers make nonprogrammed decisions.
    c. address strategic issues.
    d. reduce costs and improve efficiency at lower organization levels.
    e. more rapidly respond to external changes.

22. When Toys "R" Us partnered with Amazon.com it was using a(n)
    a. web alliance
    b. spin-off
    c. in-house Internet division
    d. strategic partnership
    e. intranet

23. A collaborative work system is also called
    a. group decision support system
    b. executive information system
    c. management information system
    d. office automation
    e. transaction processing

___ 24. B2B marketplace refers to
a. the marketplace for alternative rock music.
b. an electronic flea market.
c. an aeronautical website for giant bombers.
d. the most famous electronic auction
e. the business-to-business marketplace.

___ 25. ERP stands for
a. Enterprise Resource Planning.
b. Electronic Replacement Positioning.
c. Entry Restricted Placement.
d. Empty Resources Posturing.
e. Electronic Research Planning.

___ 26. Customer Relationship Management (CRM)
a. teaches employees how to interact with customers.
b. helps companies track customers' interactions.
c. provides feedback on interpersonal relationships via the Internet.
d. gives managers a personality inventory for each employee.
e. tells a company what the customer really wants.

___ 27. Which of the following was NOT listed as an advantage of CRM?
a. increase in customer loyalty
b. lower costs to customers
c. improved privacy of transactions
d. more precisely defined procedures
e. all of the above were listed in the textbook

___ 28. A system that links together people and departments within or among organizations to share information resources is called a
a. management information system.
b. network.
c. group decision support system.
d. transaction processing system.
e. none of the above.

___ 29. The Internet is
a. a web of computer networks around the world.
b. a company specializing in groupware.
c. an E-mail software program.
d. a government entity.
e. a subsidiary of Microsoft.

___ 30. Knowledge management refers to
    a. supervisor computer programmers.
    b. systematically gathering and disseminating information.
    c. controlling the types of knowledge employees are allowed to acquire.
    d. attempts by the government to control the Internet.
    e. teaching novices to use computer programs.

True/False Questions: Please indicate whether the following questions are true or false by writing a T or an F in the blank in front of each question.

___ 1. Information refers to raw, unsummarized, and unanalyzed facts.

___ 2. Data warehousing is the use of a huge database that combines all of a company's data and allows business users to access the data directly.

___ 3. Information technology and e-business have changed the way people and organizations work.

___ 4. The World Wide Web is made up of independently owned computers.

___ 5. Operations personnel are concerned mainly with information from the past.

___ 6. One reason for the development of management information systems is that managers needed information in summary form.

___ 7. One drawback of decision support systems is the fact that they are not interactive.

___ 8. Computer-based technologies have had their greatest impact on top management.

___ 9. Effective CIOs focus on information design.

___ 10. Merrill Lynch uses office automation to electronically manage consultants' travel and entertainment expenses.

Short-Answer Questions

1.   Why is timeliness an important characteristic of information for a manager?

2.   Why does top management require an executive information system rather than a transaction processing system or a management information system?

3.   Why is networking becoming so important to organizations today?

4. Which management functions are affected the most by information technology?

5. For what type of task would a computer-based information system be unsuitable?

Management Applications

Is This an Information System?

Professor Hiatt invited the college's management information system manager to come speak to his class. The manager began by saying that a check register in a checkbook is an information system. For this to be so it would have to provide useful information and have all the components of an information system. Explain below if a check register has the characteristics of an information system and the necessary components.

1. Quality information

2. Timely information

3. Complete information

4. Relevant information

5.   Inputs

6.   Processing

7.   Storage

8.   Control

9.   Output

I Really Don't Know!

Frank was called on the carpet by the president of the consulting firm for which he worked. Frank's division, which provided public workshops nationwide, had not been doing well lately. While sitting in the office of the president, Frank was asked how much it cost him to put on his latest five workshops. To this Frank gave the following reply:

"I really don't know how much it cost for the latest workshops. If you were to ask me about earlier workshops, I could give you an idea. We get printouts from the accounting department at the end of each month telling us how much was spent for printing and mailing out brochures, running advertisements, providing workshop materials and refreshments. The only figures I am sure of at this point are how much revenue we received and how much we paid each presenter. Even for the older workshops I am not sure that I could give you accurate numbers since the postage charges are all charged to our department and not broken down by workshop."

1.   In what areas is the information system of Frank's company inadequate?

2.   How could the information system be improved?

Mini Case

What Does a Computer Know about Toys?

Don Seibel had been a wholesale buyer for about 40 years. He had the reputation for being a very good buyer. One might classify him as a loyal buyer because he was very loyal to his suppliers. "If I am good to them, they will be good to me," he would often say.

Don's company bought many items for resale to retail grocery or drug store customers. Don was the toy buyer. His company had installed a computerized system to help the buyers do their jobs. Each morning Don would get a computer printout with information about suppliers that he was scheduled to buy from that day. The printout told Don how many items of each kind he had left in inventory for each supplier. It also told him how many had been sold each week for the last four weeks. Based on the amount of inventory left, the sales pattern, the amount of time needed to get in more products from that particular supplier, and minimum quantities the supplier would ship, the computer would suggest the quantity of each item to order. Each buyer had the option of accepting the quantity suggested by the computer, if any, or of modifying or even canceling the amount ordered. Often buyers would know of a sale or other change in the marketplace the computer did not know about.

Each buyer was to review this printout daily and hand it in to the order department by ten o'clock in the morning. While most buyers were hard-pressed to meet this deadline, Don Seibel had no trouble making it at all. When asked how he did it so fast, he replied, "I don't look at that printout at all. I make up my own order as I have for years. After all, what does a computer know about toys?"

1.   Why did Don not use the information supplied by the computer?

2.   If you were Don's boss, what action would you take if you overheard his comments?

Experiential Exercise

King Arthur's Information System

Since you have watched so much television and so many movies, you will have an easy time accepting this exercise. Through a freak opening in the space-time continuum you and your portable personal computer have been transported back to King Arthur's days. You arrive in King Arthur's court, and everyone is frightened of you because of your appearance and your PC. Merlin, the Magician, is called in and you and he become friends. Merlin has discovered batteries and how to recharge them. He frequently uses batteries for his magic. He can recharge the batteries for your portable PC and portable printer that goes with it. You tell him and King Arthur that your PC is a great tool that can help the King run the kingdom. Your hard disk has several programs such as Excel, Word, and Access on it. You ask the King to describe how he runs things now and what some of his problems are. Based on his descriptions below, suggest how you might use your PC to develop a Computer-based information system for King Arthur.

- The King's major source of revenue is taxes from the people. However, he is never sure that they pay taxes owed and that the tax collectors hand in everything they collect.

- The King has many expenses. He must make sure that all his servants, knights, and army are paid. He says trying to keep track of whom has been paid, the amount to pay, and how much is left in the royal treasury is a pain in the neck.

- King Arthur spends a lot of time trying to keep track of activities, alliances, and wars in the surrounding areas and all over Europe.

After you have suggested how a computer-based information system might help the King in the areas above, indicate what problems of implementation might arise.

Be prepared to discuss your answers in groups if so assigned by your instructor or with the class if requested.

Study Guide Solutions

Chapter Review

Multiple-Choice Questions

1	2	3	4	5	6	7	8	9	10
b	d	c	e	e	b	a	b	e	a

11	12	13	14	15	16	17	18	19	20
c	a	b	c	c	a	c	b	a	a

21	22	23	24	25	26	27	28	29	30
d	d	a	e	a	b	a	b	a	b

True/False Questions

1	2	3	4	5	6	7	8	9	10
F	T	T	T	T	T	F	F	T	T

Short-Answer Questions

1. If the information is slow in coming to a manager, it may be too late to take appropriate action. To find out that a competitive price change has occurred *after* losing one's customers does not help a manager, for example.

2. Transaction processing systems are designed to cope with routine, recurring transactions. These are not of major concern to top management. A management information system is designed to help managers in performing their management functions. They are usually not flexible and do not help top managers to cope with unstructured problems. An executive information system helps managers in making unstructured decisions by providing decision support.

3. Networks link together people and departments and allow them to share information. This facilitates communication and decision making. It makes firms more flexible and able to respond to changes in the environment more rapidly. It also fits with the more participative management styles of modern organizations.

4. The management functions of decision making and control are the most affected by information technology. More information and more timely information help managers to perform in both of these areas, and these are provided by information technology.

5. Any situation requiring rich face-to-face communications would be unsuitable for a computer-based information system. For example, interviewing prospective employees or conducting a

performance appraisal review would probably not be suitable for a computer-based information system.

Management Applications

Is This an Information System?

1. Quality information: The information should be reliable and accurate if the person owning the checking account remembers to write down the checks and subtract the amounts each time a check is written.

2. Timely information: The information on the account balance should be available soon after each check is written so it will be timely.

3. Complete information: The information is enough for the purpose intended and not too much to overburden the check writer.

4. Relevant information: The information provided is relevant because it tells the check writer his current balance so the decision can be made whether to write a check for a certain amount or not.

5. Inputs: The raw data entered into this system include the date, the check number, to whom it was written, and the amount of the check.

6. Processing: Calculations are performed by this system when the amount of the check written is subtracted from the previous balance to give the new balance.

7. Storage: The information about the check is stored in written form in the check register until needed later.

8. Control: Some control is provided in the instructions in the front of most check registers on how to use the system. Another means of control is the monthly statement. This statement allows the owner of the checking account to correct mistakes.

9. Output: The output for this system is the new balance. The monthly statement could perhaps also be considered output.

I Really Don't Know

1. The current information system fails in two areas. The information provided Frank is not timely. He needs to know the costs allocated to each workshop more often than once a month. The information's quality is also in doubt.

2. Frank's company needs to set up an account number for each workshop so that all costs can be designated to that account. It also needs to provide interim reports to Frank so that he will know these costs in a more timely manner.

Mini Case

What Does a Computer Know about Toys?

1. Don probably resisted using the information system provided because he did not trust the system. He felt his experience could not be put into a computer. He may have also thought that if he went along with the computerized system that the computer might someday replace him.

2. If Don were nearing retirement age, I would probably have done nothing. That is what really happened in this case. Another action that might have been taken is to explain to Don in more detail how the entire system worked, emphasizing the important role of the buyers in the system. The boss must allay Don's fears of being replaced by the computer in this process.

Experiential Exercise

King Arthur's Information System

To solve the problem of keeping track of revenues and expenses the King needs a computerized accounting system. One could be built using your Excel program. Either Excel or Access could be used to set up a file of the population and its assets so taxes due could be more accurately collected and accounted for. You may also want to suggest that the functions of assessment of taxes and collection of taxes be separated so controls could be instituted.

A payroll program could be developed in Excel for the King to make the payment of expenses less of a problem for him. At least he doesn't have to worry about the IRS.

The King can use Word to make his written communication with other kingdoms more efficient. He can also use dBase to build files on the activities of the various kingdoms and to help in his analysis of events.

Problems of implementation will be a major hurdle. Many would see the computer as a magical tool not to be trusted. Some would even view it as a threat. (Is that much different than today?) Another problem would be with the quality and speed of data that are given to you to put into the computer. The old saying, "Garbage In—Garbage Out," really applies here.

Chapter 22

Operations and Service Management

Chapter Summary

After you have read the text chapter, read through the summary below. Cover the left-hand margin and fill in the blanks with the appropriate terms. After you have filled in each blank, check your responses by uncovering the answer given in the margin. If you do not understand why the given answer is the correct one, refer back to the text.

Organizations as Production Systems

Operations
management
technical core

manufacturing
service

_____ is the field of management that specializes in the physical production of goods or services and uses quantitative techniques for solving manufacturing problems. It focuses on the _____, which is the heart of the organization's production of its product or service. This can be applied both to _____ organizations which produce physical goods as well as to _____ organizations which produce nonphysical goods that require customer involvement and cannot be stored in inventory.

Operations
Strategy

supply chain

_____ is the recognition of the importance of operations to the firm's success and the involvement of operations managers in the organization's strategic planning. There are four stages of involvement of operations management in an organization's strategy. The first stage is no involvement. Stage two involves keeping current to industry practice. In stage three operations management closely follows and supports the organization's competitive strategy. During the fourth stage operations management initiates competitive advantage itself. Operations managers must be involved in _____ _____ management, which is managing the sequence of suppliers and purchasers covering all stages of processing. Internet technologies are now being used to achieve the right balance of low inventory levels and customer responsiveness. Enterprise integration through the use of electronic linkages can create a high level of cooperation and more rapid responses. Instead of an *arm's length* approach, companies are choosing a *partnership* approach which involves cultivating intimate relationships with a few suppliers.

Designing Operations Management Systems

Design for manufacturability and assembly (DFMA) makes products easier and less expensive to manufacture. In designing a product or service one must consider its producibility, cost, quality, reliability, and timing. The purchasing of supplies, services, and raw materials for use in the production process is **procurement** known as _____. The Internet and business-to-business (B2B) commerce are having a tremendous impact on procurement, often leading to *direct* procurement. After the product or service has been designed and systems set up for procurement of materials, the facilities layout needs to be **process** determined. A _____ layout involves machines that perform the same function being grouped together in one location. The product is brought to each group of machines for production. In the _____ layout the machines **product** and tasks are arranged according to the sequence of steps in the production of a **cellular** single product. The _____ layout groups machines dedicated to sequences of production into cells in accordance with group-technology **fixed-position** principles. The _____ layout allows the product to remain in one location and the tasks and equipment are brought to it.

Flexible Automation technologies are increasing, especially in the service industry. **manufacturing** _____ systems refer to small or medium-size automated production **Computer-aided** lines that can be adapted to produce more than one product. _____ is a **design** production technology in which computers perform new product design. After **computer-aided** they have been designed with the aid of computers, _____ systems **manufacturing** may be used in which computers help guide and control the manufacturing system.

Facility location decisions are generally based on a cost-benefit analysis. **Capacity planning** _____ is the determination and adjustment of the organization's ability to produce goods or services to match customer demand. Often, organizations wish to increase capacity without excess. They may do this with additional shifts, overtime, by subcontracting, or expanding plant or equipment.

Inventory Management

Inventory _____ refers to the goods that the organization keeps on hand for use in the production process. Inventory can consist of finished goods, work in **Finished-goods** process, or raw materials. _____ inventory consists of items that have passed through the complete production process but have yet to be sold. **Work-in-process** _____ inventory is composed of the materials that are still moving through the stages of the production process. _____ inventory is the **Raw materials** basic inputs to the organization's production process. Too much inventory is an unproductive asset. Several methods have been developed which minimize **economic order quantity**

reorder point
dependent demand
  inventory
Material
  requirements
  planning

inventory levels. The _____ is a technique designed to minimize the total of ordering and holding costs for inventory items. It helps the manager to determine the _____, the most economical level at which an inventory item should be reordered. The EOQ formula does not work well with _____ in which an item demanded is related to the demand for other inventory items. _____ is a dependent demand inventory planning and control system that schedules the precise amount of all materials required to support the production of desired end products. It results in precise coordination between inventory requirements and production schedules based on future orders. MRP eventually evolved into enterprise resource planning (ERP) which linked more functions via computers to integrate, track, and optimize functions across the entire organization. _____ inventory systems seek a zero level of inventory by having the needed supplies arrive at the point of production at the exact moment they are needed on a production line. Such a system requires accurate scheduling and excellent employee motivation. . _____ refers to the activities required to physically move materials into the company's operations facility and to move finished products to customers. . _____ or *order fulfillment* is the moving of finished products to customers. This can reduce costs and improve customer returns. The Internet is helping companies find better ways of doing this.

Just-in-time

Logistics

Distribution

Managing Productivity

Productivity
Total factor

partial
  productivity

_____ is the output of the organization divided by the input. _____ productivity is the ratio of total outputs to the inputs from labor, capital, materials, and energy. Even more useful for assigning managerial responsibility is the _____, which is a ratio of total outputs to the inputs from a single major input category. It is important to improve quality when improving productivity also. One should consider these two concepts complementary, not opposites. There are three places to look to improve productivity: technological productivity, worker productivity, and managerial productivity.

Chapter Review

Multiple-Choice Questions: Please indicate the correct response to the following questions by writing the letter of the correct answer in the space provided.

___ 1. Inputs into the technical core of an organization include
    a. goods.
    b. services.
    c. people.
    d. feedback.
    e. transportation.

___ 2. Which of the following is *not* a service company?
    a. United Airlines
    b. McDonald's
    c. Joe's Barbershop
    d. Metro Medical Clinic
    e. Ford Motor Company

___ 3. In the _____ stage of operations strategy, operations management closely follows and supports the organization's competitive strategy.
    a. first
    b. second
    c. third
    d. fourth
    e. fifth

___ 4. Many orders are lost by
    a. having quality too high.
    b. having prices too low.
    c. delivering products too late.
    d. trying to be too responsive to customer needs.
    e. all of the above

___ 5. Producibility means the ability to
    a. copy a competitor's product design.
    b. have outputs exceeding inputs.
    c. get the job done.
    d. make the product with existing capacity.
    e. make hit movies.

____ 6. Which facilities layout type groups machines together which perform the same function?
   a. process
   b. product
   c. clan
   d. fixed-position
   e. assembly line

____ 7. CAD stands for
   a. computer-analyzed demand.
   b. computer-assisted design.
   c. computerized analog digits.
   d. cost associated delay.
   e. cost allied delivery.

____ 8. Which type of inventory is composed of materials that are still moving through the production process?
   a. finished-goods
   b. production-processing
   c. raw materials
   d. fixed-position
   e. work-in-process

____ 9. When inventory can be kept at an absolute minimum, operations management is considered
   a. astoundingly weak.
   b. better than average.
   c. cost excessive.
   d. demand derived.
   e. excellent.

____ 10. The EOQ formula includes
   a. economic costs.
   b. operations costs.
   c. holding costs.
   d. quantity of costs.
   e. engineering costs.

____ 11. MRP stands for
   a. major reorder point.
   b. mandated research plan.
   c. mistaken resource protection.
   d. materials requested proposal.
   e. material requirements planning.

___ 12. A just-in-time inventory system
   a. can work even if scheduling is sloppy.
   b. is a batch push system.
   c. is also called a "stock full" system.
   d. ignores sales demand.
   e. requires excellent employee motivation.

___ 13. When comparing services with manufacturing, one difference is that
   a. services do not need to be concerned with scheduling.
   b. only manufacturing needs to obtain materials and supplies since services are intangible.
   c. services need to be concerned with quality but not productivity because of their nature.
   d. customers are involved in the production process of services.
   e. inventory control is more important for services.

___ 14. The difference between total factor productivity and partial productivity lies in
   a. the number of outputs considered.
   b. the number of inputs considered.
   c. applying productivity to the whole organization or just to one subunit.
   d. measuring productivity during or after the production process.
   e. semantics since there is no real difference.

___ 15. The approach in which a company cultivates intimate relationships with a few carefully-selected suppliers is called _____ approach.
   a. arm's length
   b. pimp
   c. close operations
   d. partnership
   e. collaboration

___ 16. The acronym DFMA stands for
   a. design for manufacturability and assembly.
   b. designated for manufacturing acquisition.
   c. delegation for management accuracy.
   d. development of foreign materials alliances.
   e. department for manufacturing accuracy.

___ 17. The watchword for DFMA is
   a. complexity.
   b. simplicity.
   c. participation.
   d. quality.
   e. efficiency.

____ 18. Reliability refers to
   a. the degree to which a product or service can actually be produced.
   b. the relationship between cost and product design.
   c. the serviceability of the product.
   d. the degree to which customers can count on the product to fill its intended function.
   e. the value that customers gain by purchasing the product.

____ 19. A cellular layout refers to
   a. grouping employees together in a small cluster isolated from distractions.
   b. grouping machines dedicated to sequences of operations into cells.
   c. arranging machines and tasks according to the progressive steps in producing a single (cellular) product.
   d. grouping together divisions of similar manufacturing technology.
   e. requiring each worker to concentrate on one machine in his cell.

____ 20. A flexible manufacturing system
   a. is a large assembly-line type of operation.
   b. is a small or medium-size automated production line.
   c. does not use computers to enhance flexibility.
   d. uses manual labor for loading and unloading and computerizes the rest of the process.
   e. is restricted to a single product.

____ 21. CAM is most similar to
   a. process layout.
   b. product layout.
   c. cellular layout.
   d. fixed-position layout.
   e. flexible manufacturing.

____ 22. Relating to capacity planning, the biggest problem for most organizations is
   a. how to add capacity.
   b. excess capacity.
   c. partial capacity.
   d. not enough capacity.
   e. incapacity.

____ 23. Work-in-process inventory refers to
   a. items that have been produced but not yet sold.
   b. materials moving through the stages of production but not yet completed.
   c. basic inputs into the production process.
   d. the amount of time used to produce inventory.
   e. the amount of worker time available for production not yet scheduled.

___ 24. The MRP system is meant for _____ inventory.
    a. independent
    b. random
    c. dependent demand
    d. economically adjusted
    e. work-in-process

___ 25. On average, a manufacturing company spends _____ percent of its revenues to buy materials and supplies.
    a. 10 - 20
    b. 30 - 40
    c. 40 - 50
    d. 50 – 60
    e. 70 - 80

___ 26. Productivity is nothing more than
    a. output divided by input.
    b. how hard the workers try.
    c. how many units are produced.
    d. how many hours employees work per week.
    e. how many units are defective out of 100.

___ 27. Total factor productivity refers to
    a. the ratio of total outputs to the inputs from labor, capital, materials, and energy.
    b. the total amount of goods produced.
    c. the accumulated effort of the work force.
    d. the total number of hours worked divided by the number of employees.
    e. the total number of goods passing final inspection as compared to the total number which fail.

___ 28. Partial productivity
    a. measures productivity of only a part of the economy.
    b. is the ratio of total outputs to a major category of inputs.
    c. is never used for direct labor.
    d. is that part of productivity that produces high-quality goods.
    e. refers to the productivity of part-time workers.

___ 29. Direct procurement initiatives refers to
    a. materials and supplies that go into the company's products.
    b. materials and supplies that go all over the company for use.
    c. buying from manufacturers rather than wholesalers.
    d. buying on a face-to-face basis.
    e. none of the above.

___   30.   Using a CAD/CAM system can influence _____ productivity.
   a. technological
   b. worker
   c. managerial
   d. partial
   e. complete

True/False Questions: Please indicate whether the following questions are true or false by writing a T or an F in the blank in front of each question.

___   1.   Using MRP, inventory levels are based on past consumption.

___   2.   Today, approximately 25 percent of all businesses are service organizations.

___   3.   Service outputs can be stored in inventory just like manufactured goods.

___   4.   Superior operations effectiveness can support existing strategy and contribute to new strategic directions that can be difficult for competitors to stop.

___   5.   Increased managerial productivity simply means that managers do a better job of running the business.

___   6.   The product layout is efficient when the organization produces huge volumes of identical products.

___   7.   With a flexible manufacturing system, a single line can be readily adapted to different products based on computer instructions.

___   8.   The least common approach to selecting a site for a new location is to do a cost-benefit analysis.

___   9.   Today, a firm's wealth is measured by its inventory.

___   10.   Holding costs are the costs associated with keeping the item on hand.

Short-Answer Questions

1. Explain what operations management is and how it can apply to service organizations.

2.   What are the advantages of the process layout facilities design?

3.   What are the advantages to having a small inventory?

4.   What is needed for a just-in-time inventory system to work?

Management Applications

Foxie Moves into California

Lynn Johnson had experienced tremendous success with her facial care products under the brand name Foxie. She had produced the products in her Phoenix facility and successfully penetrated the Arizona markets. Her products sold well and were liked by both consumers and retailers. In fact, many consumers and retailers had requested that she begin distributing her products in Southern California. She made a few visits to Los Angeles, called on wholesalers and retailers, showed her products at some trade shows, and determined that demand for her products there would be high.

1. What capacity planning considerations should Lynn take into consideration? Consider physical, personnel, and financial capacity in your answer.

2. Lynn did make the move into the Southern California market. Two years later she was out of business. She was not able to meet her expanded financial obligations nor produce the products in sufficient quantity to meet demand. What lessons can be learned from the experience for other small manufacturers?

MRP at Plectron

Plectron was a small manufacturer of electronic tonal devices including handheld pagers. Plectron employed workers to assemble these products manually. To compete more effectively, Plectron had recently installed a materials requirement planning system. However, the system had never been used. When asked why that was so, Jessie Bourne, the purchase agent and a major stockholder in the company, replied that she had determined that she could do just as good a job as any computerized system.

1.   Why did Plectron not use the MRP system in your judgment?

2.   Do you feel that Jessie could really do as good a job as the MRP system?

Mini Case

Beer for Short Stop

As the manager for Short Stop Market #1, Dan was wondering how he could sell more beer the next time a rock concert occurred. Short Stop Market #1 is the nearest convenience market to Tempe Stadium in Tempe, Arizona. This stadium is used for rock concerts from time to time. Many of the persons who go to the concerts pick up beer on the way home from the concert or before the concert for when they are waiting in line.

Since Short Stop #1 was a new store, Dan was not sure how to prepare for the first concert. He stocked the store up to its capacity on both the shelves and walk-in cooler space with cold beer in anticipation of the concert. When all the concert goers started stopping in on their way to the concert, Dan's supplies of everything except beer looked to be adequate. By the time the concert was over, Dan was almost out of beer, especially Miller, Budweiser, and Coors brands, which were the most popular. After the end of the concert, he sold out of these brands in about 10 minutes. This left him with unhappy customers and lost sales. Dan knows he could sell much more beer, probably twice as much of the popular brands, if he had it available. However, he does not have more space available to store it.

1. Based on the inventory concepts in the text, what would you advise Dan to do? Describe in detail your plan.

Experiential Exercise

Ordering the Lotion

As a buyer for a drugstore chain, Sheri was concerned about ordering suntan lotion for the coming year. She wonders how many cases she should order at a time, how many orders she will place during the year, and at what inventory level she should reorder.

Sheri has just learned about the EOQ and ROP formulas from reading the text. She has contacted various departments within her company and gathered the following information.

Annual demand = 10,000 cases
Annual holding costs = $200
Ordering cost = $20
Lead time for order to be received = 21 days

1. Based on the foregoing information, what is the economic order quantity?

2. The number of orders that will be placed in a year is computed by dividing the annual demand by the economic order quantity. How many orders will Sheri have to place?

3.   What is the reorder point for Sheri?

Study Guide Solutions

Chapter Review

Multiple-Choice Questions

1	2	3	4	5	6	7	8	9	10
c	e	c	c	d	a	b	e	e	c

11	12	13	14	15	16	17	18	19	20
e	e	d	b	d	a	b	d	b	b

21	22	23	24	25	26	27	28	29	30
E	b	b	c	d	a	a	b	a	A

True/False Questions

1	2	3	4	5	6	7	8	9	10
F	F	F	T	T	T	T	F	F	T

Short-Answer Questions

1. Operations management is the application of special tools and techniques to the production of goods and services. A service organization still must be concerned with scheduling, which is an operations management type of problem. The service organization must also obtain materials and supplies and be concerned with quality and productivity. The techniques of operations management will aid in these functions.

2. The process layout has the potential to reduce costs by achieving economies of scale. It is easier to control the production process in such a layout also.

3. A small inventory means that the funds of the firm are not tied up in inventory and can be invested in more profitable ways. It also means that the firm can have smaller storage facilities, fewer people, and less equipment to manage inventory.

4. For a just-in-time inventory system to work it must be kept simple and well coordinated. Coordination and management problems must be allowed to surface and be resolved. Scheduling must be precise, and employee motivation and cooperation must be high.

Management Applications
Foxie Moves into California

1. Lynn must make sure that she has a large enough plant to produce the product in sufficient quantity to meet expanded demand. She must also have enough personnel to produce and market the product, including managers. She will need the funds to finance this expansion also.

2. Other small manufacturers can learn that expansion into new markets too rapidly can lead to disaster. The capacity of the organization from the viewpoint of facilities, personnel, and financing must all be considered.

MRP at Plectron

1. There appear to be two major reasons for MRP not being used by Plectron. The first is company employees not really understanding what the system is or how it works. The second is that Jessie probably felt that her job was threatened by the MRP system. Since Jessie held a very powerful position in the company and was a major stockholder, her feelings toward the system dominated.

2. No, Jessie probably could not do as good a job as the MRP system. That is assuming that the business was complicated enough to warrant the MRP system to begin with. Plectron has since gone out of business.

Mini Case
Beer for Short Stop

1. In this case Dan could use just-in-time inventory management. In fact, that is exactly what Dan did in this real-life case. He stocked the store as fully as he could with the more popular brands of beer. He cut down on the less popular brands just prior to the next concert to make room for more of the popular brands. Since he knew the starting time for the concert, he arranged for the distributors of those brands to deliver a fresh supply of beer to his store during the concert. He had them come at different times so his employees could restock the sales. He found that he could tell about how much beer he would need after the concert based on the amount purchased before the concert. By the time the third concert rolled around, Dan had perfected this system and was able to maximize sales for the company. Now, he only had to worry about the shoplifting problem.

Experiential Exercise
Ordering the Lotion

1. EOQ = 44.72

2. 223.6

3. 575